Contents

Voluntary Social Action

Voluntary Social Action

Margaret Brasnett

A history of
The National Council of Social Service 1919-1969

 26 Bedford Square London WC1

© NCSS London 1969
SBN 7199 0777 2

Published by the National Council of Social Service
Design and typography by NCSS Publications Department
Printed in England by Latimer Trend and Co. Ltd, Whitstable

Foreword

FIFTY years ago the National Council of Social Service—colloquially 'NCSS' to so many here and overseas—was an untried idea favoured by a relatively small number of people deeply concerned about social conditions. Today, a body such as the Development Commission feels able to describe the Council as 'pre-eminent in the field of voluntary enterprise'.

In this book, Miss Margaret Brasnett traces, in an appraising spirit, the development of the Council and its work from inception to the present against the changing social background of the last half-century. The book is the product of much patient research and of an exceptionally wide knowledge of voluntary social work. The National Council is greatly indebted to Miss Brasnett; it is fortunate to have had such a student of its history.

Appropriately the history has been entitled *Voluntary Social Action*, because those words indicate the notion that has been at the heart of the Council's beliefs and purposes since its formation. The bridging of the gap between 'them' and 'us', by 'us' (because we want to) actively taking a hand in running social services, is what the Council has been concerned to encourage, to assist, and when needful, to safeguard.

The Council brings into communion a host of voluntary organisations and government agencies and is helping them to respect and relate their often very diverse aims and actions for the general good. But besides being an acceptable 'bringer-together', the Council may claim to have been a successful social innovator and launcher. A large number of voluntary organisations now flourishing and some present-day activities of public authorities were innovations when born of the Council and this is also true of a number of enterprises which constitute the inner membership of the Council. The Council has given proof that it is sensitive to changes in social conditions and attitudes and is admirably adaptable to new situations problems, needs and opportunities.

All the signs seem to indicate that voluntary social action is greater and more widespread than it has ever been and that more is wanted. Certainly the demands on the National Council for its help, support and, at times, leadership in the voluntary movement have never been more pressing. It is a trusted partner of public authorities. As it has always been, the Council is more concerned with the present and future than with the past. It is proud of its achievements; it holds in affectionate regard those who made those achievements possible. It hopes that Miss Brasnett's historical account will give pleasure and encouragement to all involved in social service, whether as professionals or amateurs. For itself, while accepting that the future cannot be planned from the past, it draws from its history the conviction that determination and goodwill can achieve the seemingly impossible. It celebrates its jubilee by an affirmation of its aims and priorities and a pledge of its determination to achieve them. They are to encourage and assist citizen involvement and voluntary action; to define social needs and then take steps to meet them; to continue and extend co-operation between voluntary organisations and between them and statutory authorities—a prosaic statement maybe, but of activities pregnant with dramatic consequences.

Recently a social administrator from abroad visiting the National Council told us how lucky we were to have so much support from government departments, from distinguished men and women in public life, from other voluntary organisations and from ordinary people. Lucky? I don't think so. This is what is to be expected in a society with the traditions and aims of the National Council. Long may it flourish.

Leslie Farrer-Brown
Chairman of the National Council
of Social Service

January 1969

Author's Note

IT is not possible to thank all those who have contributed, directly or indirectly, to the writing of this book; but there are five people to whom I should like to express my special gratitude.

To Mr L. E. White, now social development officer of Harlow, whose careful research and drafts for a history of the Council which he wrote seventeen years ago but which, owing to various circumstances, was never completed, I have freely used in the early chapters.

To Sir George Haynes who, as general secretary and then director, guided the Council's work for more than half of the fifty years recorded here, and whose advice and help, most generously given at every stage of the writing, have been invaluable—though I should add that the final responsibility for its plan and contents is entirely mine.

To Miss Margaret Stilliard, assistant administrative secretary, who put her knowledge and understanding of the National Council, to which she has given all her working life, at my disposal from the first page to the last.

To Miss Margaret Tims who has undertaken the heavy task of preparing the index, and to Miss Sarah Gowans who unerringly deciphered my handwriting and typed the script with impeccable skill and patience.

The National Council of Social Service wishes to express its appreciation to the Pilgrim Trust for a financial contribution towards the cost of this publication.

CHAPTER ONE

Pre-History

THE National Council of Social Service began to take shape on the day early in 1919 when six men—five leading social workers and reformers and one civil servant—met together to complete their plans for turning an idea which had long been in their minds into a new British institution. It assumed a definite form in March of the same year, not at a well-advertised public meeting but in a short memorandum issued from a back room in a government office, setting out the aims and objects of a national council of social service, the names of its members and officers, and of the bodies giving their support. These comprised a dozen national voluntary organisations and a corresponding number of members from central and local government bodies. The new Council had no premises of its own; no income or assets apart from one legacy of £1,000; and a programme with no direct appeal.

As the National Council approaches its golden jubilee year it has in membership 115 national voluntary organisations, and twenty-five government departments and local authority associations, as well as representatives of local councils of social service—area, rural, and urban—and of community associations and clubs from nearly every county and town in England, Scotland, Wales, and Northern Ireland. The budget exceeds £300,000. Its headquarters occupy several large houses in London, and it has regional offices in a number of provincial cities. The record and programme of work of the Council is so wide and varied that it touches some interest of every organisation and individual in this country, and far beyond.

These facts are a measure of the growth of fifty years; but the roots of the enterprise stretch at least as far back into the last century. For the conception of a national council of social service evolved gradually according to the fashion of most of our great institutions, public and private, over a long period of time from the minds, and also from the hearts, of a few concerned people.

The six men whose conference at the beginning of 1919, in the confused aftermath of the first world war, sketched the outlines of the new organisation, were its immediate sponsors. But they would not have claimed to be sole progenitors. The thought, labour, and devotion of these men and women and the work of many organisations over many decades had contributed to its creation.

The reasons for their concern are to be found in the growth of disease, poverty, ignorance, and crime, fostered by conditions in the great industrial cities of the latter part of the nineteenth century; and in the multiplicity of voluntary organisations formed all over the country in isolated endeavours to ameliorate some of these ills. A few of the bodies were concerned with the general condition of society and such problems as bad housing or crime. The aim of the large majority was the giving of relief to individuals. There was certainly great need for this work in the London of the mid-nineteenth century with its 100,000 abandoned children 'exposed for the most part to the training of beggars and thieves'; its ragged army of mendicants 'who march forth every morning not to work but to beg'; its silent legions of the poor 'bowing their heads for bread'. But for the most part there was little method, standard, or consistent purpose in the almsgiving. As described by J. R. Green there were 'hundreds of agencies at work over the same ground without concert or co-operation or the slightest information as to each other's exertions'. Alms were given at public houses; there were 'thieves' suppers', 'prostitutes' meetings', 'free dormitories', 'night refuges'.

There were several attempts to regulate the flow of misdirected charity, which could be degrading to those who gave as well as to those who received it. In 1868, G. H. Hicks, one of the founders of the Society for Relief of Distress, proposed in a letter in *The Pall Mall Gazette* the establishment of a Central Board of Charities supported by grants from the charities registered, based on a percentage of their income. At a stormy meeting the charities rejected the proposal. Later in the same year the Reverend Henry Solly, who had founded the Working Men's Club and Institute movement, outlined a proposal based on a careful statistical survey of crime and pauperism in London. He saw that both arose from the conditions of life in the metropolis and could not be cured merely by punishing crime more severely or by indiscriminate doles. He aimed at getting the support, not only of many existing organisations, but of all classes, creeds, and parties, for a central body, the Association for the Prevention of Pauperism and Crime. His proposals, requiring a high degree of co-operation between a multitude of agencies with different methods and aims, received little support. They led, however, through some vicissitudes, to the founding in the following year of the Charity Organisation Society (now the Family Welfare Association).

His first aim was to replace indiscriminate almsgiving by carefully planned help based on actual family or individual need, ascertained by the investigations of trained home visitors—help calculated to restore the recipient to independence. The other main aim was to ensure some kind of co-operation between the many competing and overlapping agencies dispensing relief. One of the methods proposed was the mutual registration in some central office of all assistance given either by the Boards of Guardians or by any of the charities or the churches. The campaign to secure such registration has continued to this day, with only partial and local success; but the movement was nevertheless an important factor in the eventual creation of the NCSS.

Another important nineteenth-century movement which, though it did not survive for long, pointed the way to a national council, was the National Association for the Promotion of Social Science. Founded in 1856, it arose from a suggestion made to Lord Brougham that there should be an association 'for affording to those engaged in all the various efforts, now happily begun for the improvement of the people, an opportunity of considering social economics as a great whole'. It was an association of social reformers rather than of reform societies; but its leaders were broad-minded enough to invite representatives from such working-class bodies as Mechanics' Institutes. Its membership covered all the social sciences and was divided into five departments: education, law amendment, prevention and repression of crime, public health, and social economy. It had a foreign secretary and foreign correspondents; and tried to ensure links with Parliament by ruling that any member of either House who was a member of the Association should automatically be a member of its council. Local branches were set up, one as far afield as Constantinople; and public bodies were encouraged to become corporate members. The main basis of the Association was enquiry, discussion, and the collection of statistics, and members were expected to report on social conditions as they found them and on any efforts at improvement.

This very active body met with immediate response because it epitomised the reforming spirit of the age. Affiliated organisations were formed to deal with specific reforms, including a Workhouse Visiting Association. In 1866 a conference of masters and matrons of reformatory schools was held; and four years later an annual conference for the chairmen of boards of poor law guardians was established. Weekly meetings were held at the Association's permanent headquarters in London; but the great annual conferences took place in a succession of different towns, where they often stimulated notable civic activity in matters of housing, drains, and water supplies. Among the speakers were many of the great reformers of the time: Lord Shaftesbury, Florence Nightingale, Ray Shuttleworth. Octavia Hill spoke on housing the poor; Dr Barnardo on 'the necessity for voluntary agencies in reclaiming the children of our streets'; and Robert Hunter campaigned for the preservation of commons and open spaces. Yet, in spite of the outstanding service which it gave in bringing together such a diversity of men and movements concerned with every aspect of social reform, the National Association for the Promotion of Social Science soon passed its zenith and began to decline. The reasons for this remain a mystery on which its reports throw no light.

Unlike this body with its wide, general aims and national influence most of the numerous societies which arose in this heyday of spontaneous voluntary activity were devoted to comparatively narrow and specific purposes and were centred in one particular town, although a few attempted to establish themselves on a nation-wide basis. Of these one of the earliest was the Young Men's Christian Association, founded in 1844, which sought to have affiliated branches in towns throughout the country.

In the long process of evolution towards the crystallisation of the NCSS idea another new type of society is important: the national association formed to foster and co-ordinate the work of locally established branches and aiming to cover the whole country with a network of services. One of the best and earliest examples is the National Association of Discharged Prisoners' Aid Societies which in due course had branches attached to every county gaol. Of special interest is the fact that these societies, though remaining completely independent voluntary bodies, were recognised by the state as early as 1862: one of the first examples of a pattern of development which was later to become a unique characteristic of social work in this country and not least of the work of the NCSS.

The mid-nineteenth century marked not only the zenith of uncoordinated voluntary activity but also the beginning of a great deal of new statutory intervention in the fields of sanitation, factory conditions, housing, and education, which was later to have a profound influence on voluntary social work. Meanwhile the developing relationship between statutory and voluntary bodies is best illustrated by the working of the Poor Law. During the Lancashire cotton famine of 1861—one of a series of similar crises in this period—when more than a quarter of the population of the county was on the verge of destitution, local 'Committees of Charity' were set up to work in close touch with the Guardians in order to avoid overlapping; and the success of this sort of venture in statutory and voluntary co-operation prompted Lord Goschen in his famous minute of the 20th November, 1869 (probably drafted in the office of the COS), to advocate its extension. 'The fundamental doctrine of the English Poor Law is *relief* given as a *legal* obligation not as a matter of charity, but to extend this legal obligation beyond the relief of destitution to a much larger class, i.e., those with insufficient wages, would be not only to increase expenditure enormously but to discourage independence'. The Poor Law Act of 1834 had made it clear that the *permanent* and *continuous* giving of relief to the destitute was not a suitable field of operation for the voluntary worker; and gradually the recognition was growing that the permanently and totally destitute should be left to the Poor Law whilst charity should be directed to giving supplementary aid, particularly such timely and constructive help as might save the recipient from falling into the hands of the Poor Law.

There can be no doubt of the success of the Charity Organisation Society's new scientific approach in the field of personal service. In a series of actions over nearly half a century they campaigned under the leadership of Charles Stewart Loch and greatly reduced the evil of indiscriminate and thoughtless almsgiving, and by their influence permeated the whole field of social work not only in this country but throughout the world, though their focus was in London, with a few societies in the provinces. Their co-ordinating work had mainly to be limited to organising a great body of charitable workers who could bring personal service to relieve the suffering and poverty of the victims of the social system; and, though they campaigned vigorously against many of the social evils of the day, they tended on the whole to be more concerned with the sufferings of the victims than with the condition of society, or with the relationship between voluntary bodies and the statutory authorities which were becoming of increasing importance in social work.

Meanwhile, in various parts of the country three small parallel movements were growing up which were to make an all-important contribution to the basic concept of the NCSS.

The first of these was the Guilds of Help movement, an adaptation of methods in use in German cities for nearly fifty years. The first guild was formed in Bradford in 1904 when, at a great public meeting presided over by the Bishop of Ripon, amid scenes of considerable enthusiasm 450 volunteers offered their services—enough to form forty-eight groups covering most of the town. Many of these were working-class people, for Bradford was the home of working-class movements and the cradle of the Labour Party. Indeed, this meeting must be regarded as a turning point in the history of social service, for it marked the end of the old order which rested on the implicit assumption that social service was good done by a favoured class to those less fortunate. Here was the first successful attempt on any large scale to enlist the support of every section and class of the community in a common endeavour to tackle the problem of poverty. The guilds sought to gather into a well-organised body 'all in the community who have the desire and more or less capacity for social service'. 'Not alms but a friend' was the motto of some of the guilds. The emphasis was still on personal service to the individual or family in need; but there was a new effort to form links with the civic authorities by stipulating that the mayor of the town should usually be the president of the guild. Under the leadership of pioneers such as A. B. Saint in Newcastle-on-Tyne, A. M. Daniel in Scarborough, S. P. Grundy in Manchester, F. G. D'Aeth in Liverpool, and Dorothy Keeling in Bradford, the new movement prospered. Through the devoted energy of its honorary travelling secretary, Eustace Charlton, it spread under a variety of names to about fifty towns and cities. In 1907 its first annual conference was held; and in 1911 a National Association of Guilds of Help was formed, largely through the inspiration of Edward Vivian Birchall who, still in his twenties, had already made his mark in social work in Birmingham as honorary secretary of the City Aid Society. He became the first secretary of the new National Association and helped to create and to direct its policy in the first difficult formative years.

Meanwhile, in Birmingham another parallel development of considerable significance had been taking place. Backed by some of the progressive manufacturers who were increasingly concerned about the health and homes of their workers, aid committees had been set up in various parts of the city to administer relief. These joined to make a Civic Aid Society, and in 1906 it amalgamated with the COS to form the influential City of Birmingham Aid Society. One outcome was the establishment on a firm basis of one of the few really successful schemes for the mutual registration of assistance covering over three hundred of the city's charities.

The third movement, even smaller but of great importance because it marked a significant stage in the evolutionary progress towards a council of social service, was gathering momentum in London where Thomas Hancock Nunn was slowly building up the first Council of Social *Welfare* in Hampstead. While still at Cambridge he had been influenced by the work of Canon Barnett and had helped him in the founding of Toynbee Hall. On his marriage in 1894 he moved to Hampstead where he was responsible for a remarkable series of social schemes, which included the first tuberculosis after-care committee in 1901, and the first school care committee in 1904. He campaigned for school nurses and founded the Hampstead Health Society and the Hampstead Infant Welfare Committee.

E. V. Birchall

As a Poor Law Guardian and a member of the borough council he saw the inter-relation of all these voluntary schemes with each other and with the municipal and statutory services.

So Hancock Nunn worked patiently to devise some machinery which would bring them together in fruitful co-operation. Although his friendship with old colleagues in the COS continued he was always trying to broaden the basis of the Hampstead Charity Organisation Society's work, and stimulated by him it branched out in many untrodden ways which did not find favour with the orthodox case-workers of the Society. In 1900 a survey of the borough was started, and the contacts and friendships among a wide variety of voluntary groups arising from this led to the foundation in 1902 of what were known as the Associated Agencies. Study circles of social workers were formed in churches, clubs, and institutions, and it became clear to them that something was needed to bring *all* the agencies serving the people of Hampstead together—a council of social welfare. Hancock Nunn, with his expert knowledge of local government (he was now serving on the famous Royal Commission on the Poor Law which had just been appointed), thought that co-ordination which left out the increasing contribution of statutory and municipal bodies was not worth having.

The Hampstead Council was therefore a slow, organic growth, beginning with groups of people interested in special projects such as TB care, maternity and child welfare, the prevention of overlapping in relief, and broadening out to cover wider aspects of the social scene, statutory and voluntary. The emphasis on the importance of including the civic side was, as had been shown, also characteristic of the guilds of help movement, and it drew the two movements closer together.

After a brief boom, poverty, unrest, and unemployment followed the end of the war in South Africa. Beneath the placid surface of rich, Edwardian England there were new stresses and problems which impelled Parliament towards more and more intervention in social life. They legislated for workmen's compensation, for unemployed workers, for school meals. There was pressure for old age pensions and national health insurance. The Poor Law was sharply criticised and sweeping changes were advocated; the idea of setting up labour exchanges was being discussed. Many people saw in all this statutory activity the end of voluntary action. Others, with a wider vision, saw that the new legislation created the need for a new partnership between statutory and voluntary bodies and could in fact lead to a new upgrowth and a new use of voluntary activity, enterprise, and devotion. How, for instance, could the new children's care committees work without an army of volunteers? The old age pensioner was certainly to receive five shillings a week, but that was little enough without the help of other forms of service. New societies and new volunteers would be invaluable in bringing the warmth of personal concern and friendship into the cold business of the new state welfare.

Between 1906 when the Royal Commission on the Poor Law was appointed and 1909 when its reports were published, the guilds of help movement spread, mainly in the north; while councils of social welfare after the Hampstead pattern gained a precarious foothold, mainly in some of the London boroughs. One of the earliest, established in Stepney by the Bishop of Stepney in 1906, worked in close and friendly co-operation with the cos there. Others were set up in Bethnal Green, Shoreditch, Marylebone, St. Pancras, and Westminster.

But it was the publication of the reports of the Royal Commission on the Poor Law which gave a real impetus to the movement. The Majority Report, though less outspoken than the Minority Report, was none the less highly critical. It found the whole system lacking in central control or policy, capricious in its operation and cut off from organic relationship with the rest of local government. In the administration of relief it had no adequate co-operation with the work of the charities, no proper investigation, and was devoid of discrimination, plan, or purpose. The Commission recommended that a new authority should be set up with a new name—Public Assistance Authority—which would be a statutory committee of the county or county borough council and work through public assistance committees. Considerably influenced by what had already been accomplished by guilds of help and councils of social welfare, but perhaps even more impressed by their possibilities, the Commission went to great length in elaborating a comprehensive scheme for linking the new form of state welfare and the voluntary societies. They recommended that a new body should be set up by each county or county borough—the Voluntary Aid Council. It would be distinct and separate from the Public Assistance Authority but would be associated with it by cross-representation. The voluntary aid councils would appoint voluntary aid committees for each locality to work parallel with the public assistance committee. The territory was to be divided as before, with Public Assistance looking after the completely destitute (or 'necessitous' as they were now to be called), while voluntary aid would care for other needs.

There were several other important recommendations. The schemes should be submitted to the Charity Commissioners for approval, and voluntary societies were to be encouraged to register on lines similar to the Friendly Societies. Help and relief given to applicants either by the public assistance committee or by a voluntary agency should be recorded in a mutual register of assistance. A system of voluntary visitors was recommended.

The Commission proposed that voluntary agencies should be entitled to nominate their own members for appointment to these two quasi-public bodies. It was moreover thought desirable that the voluntary aid committee should have its offices in the same building as the public assistance committee and that the new voluntary aid councils and local committees should both be eligible for grant aid. The report of the Commission summed up by saying: '. . . accepting the principle of Mr Goschen's minute we have recommended a general and intimate co-operation between the Poor Law and charity, so as to give to the latter not merely the opportunity to co-operate, if it may, but the *status* and encouragement that may enable it to become both in town and country the responsible and competent fellow-worker of the administrators of public assistance'.

It seems that these sweeping recommendations for co-operation between the statutory and vountary services went far beyond the ideas of most of the reformers who advocated some co-ordination of charity and wanted to relate it to state help. It certainly went far beyond the ideas of the charities themselves who, from 1869 onwards, had shown a marked resistance to co-ordination, a resistance which was to continue long after 1909. The proposal for grant-aid with its possible threat to their independence and the thought of sharing an office with the public assistance committee would be sufficient to scare many of the orthodox into the old lines of independent action.

Their alarm was, however, quite unnecessary. Like so many other recommendations of the Poor Law Commission, some of which had to wait twenty years for their fulfilment and others forty, the schemes for the regulation of charity did little more than stimulate the existing councils of social welfare and guilds of help, and inspire a number of other experiments in various towns. Prominent among these was the establishment of the Liverpool Council of Voluntary Aid in 1909, which owed its name to the new idea but its inspiration to Frederick D'Aeth who was to play so important a part in the next stage of development towards a national council of social service.

Although the idea of the voluntary aid councils and committees owed much to the powerful influence of Hancock Nunn on the Royal Commission, the findings of the Majority Report differed considerably from his wider ideal of the council of social welfare based on his pioneer experiment at Hampstead. He therefore insisted on adding a special memorandum on the function of his council. He feared that the projected voluntary aid committee would become a mere voluntary committee of *assistance* for individual cases of distress, dealing only with questions of relief. He was critical of the competition between the cos and the guilds of help and saw in his own conception of the council of social welfare a synthesis of the two. 'What each community needs is a co-operative civic body which will secure the organisation which makes all case-work effective. Concentrate on *social welfare*, raise the whole standard of life and character by the development of social responsibility'. Later developments were to show how essentially right was his insistence on building up a *representative* council comprising *all* the organisations at work in the locality.

Thus the council of social welfare came to stand for the co-ordination of *institutions*, and for the total and many-sided welfare of the community. Critics of Nunn and the Hampstead Council pointed out with some force and a certain amount of insight that what worked in Hampstead would not necessarily work in a poorer London borough where genuinely local leadership was often lacking and where local government was not always particularly enlightened. The cos, which did most of the work in such places, was most dubious; and clashes with Nunn and his followers were inevitable when three bodies with similar aims, not always clearly defined, were operating in the same field as co-ordinating agencies.

Nunn, immersed in ardent propaganda for councils of social welfare and for his ambitious scheme for co-ordinating voluntary work in the whole London area, was not in the best position to work for an effective synthesis of the three movements. It was left in the end to D'Aeth and Grundy, from their more detached position in the north, and unhampered by the complexities of London government, to steer them towards greater unity.

However, Nunn's London scheme went forward, and on the 4th March, 1910, the Social Welfare Association for London was established at a meeting described by the Lord Mayor, who presided, as 'one of the most widely representative ever held at the Mansion House'. The number of great and distinguished men on the platform was a tribute to Nunn's organising genius and a demonstration of the large measure of official support which the new idea of co-operation had produced. The Archbishop of Canterbury moved the resolution 'That it is desirable to form a Social Welfare Association for London'. Supporting speeches came from the Chairman of the London County Council, from the Rt Hon. Herbert Samuel, MP (soon to become President of the Local Government Board), from the Chief Rabbi, from Archbishop Bourne, Dr Scott Lidgett, and the Earl of Lichfield.

The Association was a vast elaboration of the Hampstead scheme, its central council designed to 'embrace in fair proportion all interests alike'. The basis of representation is interesting as marking yet another stage in the evolution of a national council of social service. The immense total of 420 seats (necessitated by the size and complexity of London organisation) were to be divided between: public departments and authorities; religious communities; endowed charities and City companies; friendly and trade societies; voluntary charities and agencies and local social welfare councils. Its aims, 'to secure co-operation between social, industrial and charitable undertakings . . . to bring into close relations public departments, local authorities, and societies and persons engaged in voluntary service, and to promote councils of welfare in every borough', bring it near to the pattern later evolved for the National Council of Social Service.

With all the blessings of the Church and the good wishes of the state the great ship was launched. For long it remained 'fitting out'; but it never put to sea. Had it done so it might well have foundered through being top-heavy and unwieldy. It had to be re-organised in the more favourable atmosphere after the first world war, and re-named the London Council of Social Service before it could attempt to put out again.

Another interesting Edwardian institution, later to link up with the NCSS, was the British Institute of Social Service, founded in 1907 'to promote civic, social and industrial betterment; to collect, register and disseminate information relating to all forms of social service in all parts of the world'. These were large aims and the BISS was a small body; but it ran an excellent journal, *Progress*, and began to build up a reference library and information centre for all those engaged or interested in social service. Since one of its aims was to facilitate co-operation between organisations with social aims, and to prevent overlapping, it is interesting to note that its council consisted of elected, nominated, and co-opted members. The representative members included those nominated by such bodies as the Sociological Society, Christian Social Union, Working Men's Club and Institution, Church Army, Salvation Army, Christian Social Service Union, National Union of Women Workers, Garden Cities Association, Fabian Society, National Temperance League, Ladies of Charity. It gave useful publicity to the guilds of help and councils of social welfare who were encouraged to use its library and information service.

From 1909 to 1914 the official records reveal only slow progress towards a closer link between the Charity Organisation Society, the councils of social welfare, and guilds of help. All three seem to be groping towards a new synthesis. Only the clear thinking, writing, and speaking of the two men whose close collaboration held guilds of help and councils of social welfare together in the north—Grundy in Manchester and D'Aeth in

Liverpool—saved all three from dissipating their energies in conflict and misunderstanding.

Grundy, in a remarkable analysis of the three movements in a paper prepared in collaboration with E. V. Birchall and presented to the Guilds of Help Conference in 1913, outlined the limitations and the incompleteness of each. He criticised the COS for testing all legislation by the measuring rod of casework experience; and the councils of social welfare for trying to influence policy and legislation without having the benefit of practical casework experience. 'To labour at casework which does not affect policy is to plough the sands, while to shape policy except in the light of casework experience is to build on them'. He therefore pleaded for a synthesis which would incorporate the best of each.

D'Aeth carried the idea a stage further forward in an article the following year in the *Economic Review*. He too saw the danger of confusion between the three more or less parallel bodies; but he saw also, quite as clearly, the great new opportunities for co-operation with the state in the administration of new legislation such as the National Insurance Act, the Mental Deficiency Act, and the Probation Act. Social work of this kind, though broader than the mere relief of distress, was not enough. He believed that each town needed a *civic* society concerned also with the *normal* life of the ordinary citizen who wanted music and playgrounds and athletics. This broadening out from the limited concept of relief work to a concern for the quality of life of the whole community was another important turning point. Only a few people understood its implications in 1914. Not very many years later it was to become the hall-mark of the National Council's work.

In other respects, too, D'Aeth's plea for a council of social service foreshadowed the pattern which was to emerge. He saw the need to relate together conflicting or overlapping voluntary societies and the new statutory services, and to provide links between local institutions and national voluntary bodies, and finally between the voluntary agencies and government departments. In addition he hoped that his ideal council would run a library and information centre and bureau for social workers and would issue bulletins explaining in simple language the latest social legislation; and would also keep a mutual register of assistance.

D'Aeth's own society, the Liverpool Council of Voluntary Aid, eventually did all these things, and he could claim that it was probably the most substantial and fully representative body in the city, not *one* of the town's institutions but *the* town's institution, 'able to undertake with dignity large and important affairs'. But he was not dazzled by grandiose schemes for large-scale co-ordination. He saw clearly that the root of the matter lay with the small local organisation, which was small enough for ordinary people to understand and gave opportunities for fellowship and citizenship to meet together in a way so often impossible in the huge, unplanned centres of population.

But the Charity Organisation Society with its clear, specific policy, was critical of the wider aims of the councils of social welfare. To D'Aeth's contention that the absence of a specific policy may be counted an advantage rather than a hindrance they replied: 'So we can imagine an apologist for the invertebrate maintaining the advantages of being without a spine, which is no doubt a stiff and awkward contrivance, greatly limiting its owner's powers of adapting himself or yielding to pressure. But in the long run it is the backbone that counts, and if social welfare councils are to become permanently useful institutions they will have to develop a policy and adhere to it, regardless of temporary advantages to be gained by its absence.'

Yet in spite of the tension which such minor skirmishes reveal, the societies were in fact drawing closer together; and in the summer of 1914, only a few weeks before the Great War broke out, they held a joint conference at Newcastle-on-Tyne. It was a considerable success, smoothing out many difficulties and misunderstandings, even though the official resolution did not go beyond 'expressing the hope that this may not be the last occasion on which charity organisation societies, guilds of help, and other kindred societies may meet in conference'. They decided, however, not to meet the following year. The problems and opportunities caused by the war were to reverse this decision.

The first months of the war brought disaster for many people in a country totally unprepared for mobilisation. The patriotic rush to join the colours and the dislocation of trade and industry left many families in distress. There was no standard system of dependents' allowances or disablement pensions; and the War Office did not always know which soldiers were married and where wives and children lived, so that in some cases remittances did not come through for months and large families had to exist on as little as ten shillings a week. 'It would have been "God help them" if there had been no Soldiers' and Sailors' Families Association', said Alderman Holt of Manchester, where 'women with babies at the breast queued all day at the pay offices', fainting from lack of food till kindly local people brought them help.

Nor was it possible, at a time when little state machinery existed, to do more than estimate the number of unemployed. A National Relief Fund was opened, and the first days of the war saw a remarkable outpouring of voluntary personal service, the Soldiers' and Sailors' Families Association alone recruiting nearly 4,000 helpers. The government decided to take action to prevent the confusion likely to arise from 'this outburst of spasmodic, unregulated energy'. The Local Government Board sent out an important circular (PRD (1)) on the Prevention and Relief of Distresses to every mayor and chairman of a local authority, suggesting the establishment of local representative committees (not unlike the earlier projected voluntary aid committees) to co-ordinate the distribution of relief. At the same time a Government Intelligence Committee was set up under the chairmanship of Seebohm Rowntree which 'enabled the government for the first time in history to get a bird's eye view of industry and the condition of the working classes'.

It was an unparalleled opportunity for the voluntary organisations; but the results varied widely. Some of the local representative committees failed. Others were very successful, particularly where a guild of help or council of social welfare already existed. In Birmingham, for instance, the City Aid Society was broadened into the Birmingham Citizens' Committee, an unusually democratic body enjoying the support of the trade unions, which drew some of its initiative from a distinguished Fabian group including John Drinkwater, Rutland Boughton, Professor Muirhead, and Sir Oliver Lodge.

There were, however, enough failures, misunderstandings and confusion to justify an urgent conference of all the great societies concerned with relief and personal service, which met at Caxton Hall, Westminster, from 10th to 12th June, 1915. Nearly 600 delegates attended and the bodies represented included the National Association of Guilds of Help, the Charity Organisation Society, Councils of Social Welfare, Local Representative Committees, the Soldiers' and Sailors' Help Society, the Soldiers' and Sailors' Families Association, and the National Association of Women Workers. Frederick D'Aeth, addressing the conference, spoke of the 'famous circular which may result in the foundation of voluntary social service on a civic basis which could be one of the greatest events of our day'. He hoped that the local representative committees would be no mere wartime phenomenon but a permanent feature, since the experience of war had shown so clearly the need for the co-ordination of voluntary work and its integration with government agencies. 'What is needed is a permanent Government Intelligence Department which could tell local voluntary organisations how the various new regulations . . . will affect case-work, its counterpart a permanent advisory body representing local voluntary organisations to assist such a Government Intelligence Department'—foreshadowing one of the functions of the citizens' advice bureau service which was to establish itself from the start of the second world war.

The conference took place against a background of confusion, perplexity, and distress: the long casualty lists; the multiplication of war charities, which were to reach a total of 10,000 by the following year; the seemingly endless vista of war, and ultimately at the end of it the problems of unemployment and disablement on an unprecedented scale. None the less, the pattern for the future of voluntary service was outlined at this conference in clear, unprejudiced and forward-looking debate and discussion. On the one hand the obvious dangers of 'nationalising' or regulating too strictly works of mercy and charity were set out, on the other the wastage, overlapping, and confusion of hundreds of unrelated societies. The question whether the new local representative committees should be merely a wartime expedient or develop into a permanent link was discussed; and the new voice of Labour spoke: 'Not charity, but the right to work and to social security'. Montagu Harris (later of the County Councils Association) urged the need for links with the local authorities if the wide ground was to be covered without undue centralisation. The COS warned of the dangers of mixing vote-catching with relief work. The independent northern towns, maintaining their view of the importance of the municipality, showed plainly that they would not be satisfied with any enlarged London society as the basis for co-ordination. Their aim was a truly national body.

With so much of the ground cleared, it is not surprising that an immediate result was the setting up of a Joint Committee on Social Service with representatives from the COS, Councils of Social Welfare, National Association of Guilds of Help, Local Representative Committees, Soldiers' and Sailors' Help Society, and Soldiers' and Sailors' Families Association. This committee met at intervals during the war years, and was soon strengthened by representatives in a consultative capacity from the Local Government Board, the new Ministry of Pensions, and the Charity Commissioners. Knowing that the future of voluntary service was at stake, and having in mind the delicate relations between the bodies involved and the lack of any precedents to guide them, the committee had no easy task in the work of constitution building. But the outstandingly friendly personal relationship existing between the members made the way much less difficult. They were a rare company. There was the small group who had campaigned together for the guilds of help movement, organising, writing, speaking, and travelling the country—D'Aeth, Daniel, Grundy, Heighton, and Saint; together with Dorothy Keeling who had been assistant secretary of the Bradford City Guild of Help for many years and recently acting general secretary of the National Association of Guilds of Help, and now became joint secretary of the new Committee on

Social Service with the Reverend John Pringle.

Pringle was secretary of the COS and his influence there was great. He had come to the COS by way of the Indian Civil Service and of the Church of England, of which he had been a missionary in Japan and then a curate in Poplar. He was a fine character but a strange one. He could write of the dreaded Poor Law as 'the wisdom of the ages set to the still sad music of humanity', tackling 'the hardest, the saddest, the most terrible problems presented by human life'. He was courteous and humble with a great gift for friendship; but he could be : gry and unbending over the havoc which short-sighted and thoughtless cu..rity could create in the lives of ordinary people, for whom he had a deep affection. He used his influence to defend the position of the voluntary societies which he felt were being assailed and undermined by the increasing incursions of the state into fields hitherto the preserve of voluntary action. He saw the part which a national body co-ordinating social service might have to play, but his deep distrust of state and municipal action prevented him from going the whole way and committing the COS unreservedly to the new movement. His policy was to offer friendly co-operation and await developments. In the fullness of time one of the most brilliant young men who had worked with him, Captain Lionel Ellis, was to become the first paid secretary of the National Council of Social Service. Meanwhile, while the war dragged to its end, it was Pringle's clear, incisive brain which helped to steer the Joint Committee on Social Service through many difficulties as its constitution was hammered out.

To Grundy, however, must go the credit for bringing in the representatives of government. Before long Aubrey (later Sir Aubrey) Vere Simmons, then First Secretary of the Local Government Board, who was a keen supporter of the new idea, was taking the chair at these meetings, some of which were held in the offices of the Board. And just round the corner, in the Cabinet Office in Downing Street where he was a Secretary to the Prime Minister from 1917 to 1918, Professor W. G. S. Adams was editing the War Cabinet Reports, quite unaware that he was the man who was to shape the destiny of the NCSS as its chairman for over thirty years.

One of the earliest tasks of the Joint Committee on Social Service had been the issue of a *Handbook of Information for Voluntary Workers*. Such was the need that over 11,000 copies were sold in the first year. This was but one example of the kind of work waiting to be done. Yet despite the clear evidence of the need to set up a new national organisation to bring the voluntary bodies together and into closer relationship with government departments, and the sympathy shown by the Government towards the scheme, the possibility of founding such a body at the end of a long, devastating war seemed remote. In the event it was one of the tragic losses of the war which helped to make it possible.

Edward Vivian Birchall, the young man who had played so large a part in founding the National Association of Guilds of Help and had been its first honorary secretary, died of wounds in France on his thirty-second birthday. Just a year before the action which was to win him the DSO and to cost him his life, he had scribbled a note to his friend S. P. Grundy which read: 'If I'm scuppered I'm leaving you £1,000 to do some of the things we talked about'. This scrap of paper, symbol of the idealism of a 'lost generation', is preserved in the Imperial War Museum in London. The legacy which he left sustained the National Council of Social Service in its first precarious year of existence, and thereby turned an idea into a reality. Vivian Birchall would have wished for no better memorial than the founding of this venture which was to carry on the ideals for which he had lived and died.

CHAPTER TWO

Beginning

THE first definitive step in turning the idea of a national council of social service into a fact was unspectacular but powerfully sponsored. The memorandum of March, 1919, setting out the aims, and the names of members and of bodies giving their support and commending the formation of local councils of social service was sent out from the offices of the Local Government Board with a covering letter signed by Aubrey Simmons, secretary to the Board and the first chairman of the Council, and was addressed to lord mayors, mayors, and chairmen of local authorities.

Even more important than this proof of official interest were the facts that the new venture was firmly founded on a fresh conception of social service proper to the age—'an idea whose time was come'—and that it was conceived and brought to maturity by a small company of men and women with foresight, skill, and long devotion. These were assets which could override the lack of money and premises; and the difficulties and misunderstanding which earlier attempts to co-ordinate the work of voluntary societies had shown could arise when the independence of voluntary agencies seemed to be threatened.

The idea was a simple one: the belief that the rich and varied pattern of voluntary societies which is the distinctive feature of English social life is worth preserving; that it could best be preserved if the diverse agencies were to come together into some form of overall federation or council to eliminate confusion and overlapping; and to work together as partners with the newly developing statutory services. It was not a totally new idea. It had begun to merge in some form in the administration of the Poor Law, the Charity Organisation Society, and the guilds of help. But it needed to be re-stated in new terms at a time of rapid social change when the new public social services were making an increasing impact on social life.

Some of the men and women to whom this idea had been a guiding principle of all their work were involved in the events leading up to the formation of the Council which have already been described. Some find a place in the list of those who comprised the Council at its inception. The first document produced contained the names of the following officers:

A. V. Simmons, CB (Local Government Board), Chairman;

W. G. S. Adams, Vice-Chairman;

Sir Charles Stewart, KBE, Honorary Treasurer;

S. P. Grundy, OBE, Honorary Secretary;

and the names of the following representatives of national voluntary organisations and statutory bodies: Mrs Barnes (National Association of Guilds of Help); C. W. Burnes (Friendly Societies); C. E. Clift (Juvenile Organisation Committees); Arthur Collins (Local Representative Committees); Major Sir A. Tudor Craig, KBE (Soldiers' and Sailors' Help Society); Sir James Curtis, KBE (Union and Rural District Council Clerks' Society); F. G. D'Aeth (Councils of Social Welfare); A. M. Daniel (Councils of Social Welfare); Miss Brodie Hall (Poor Law Unions' Association); C. Montagu Harris, OBE (County Councils); J. H. Heighton (National Association of Guilds of Help); C. F. Adair Hore, CB (Ministry of Pensions); Mrs Ogilvie Gordon (National Council of Women); A. C. Kay, OBE (Charity Commissioners); Miss D. C. Keeling, MBE (National Association of Guilds of Help); Captain Wickham Legg, MVO (Soldiers' and Sailors' Families Association); F. Morris (Charity Organisation Societies); Mrs Morris (Women's Local Government Society); T. Hancock Nunn (Councils of Social Welfare); F. H. Pelham (Board of Education); Reverend J. C. Pringle (Charity Organisation Societies); W. Pullinger (National Association of Local Government Officers); N. Schooling, CBE (National War Savings Committee); J. G. Small (Town Councils); Miss Thompson (Charity Organisation Societies); H. L. Woollcombe (Cavendish Association); Captain L. F. Ellis, DSO, MC, *Secretary*.

As soon as the new project was safely launched Aubrey Simmons, whose responsibilities were heavily increased when the Local Government Board became the newly-founded Ministry of Health, withdrew leaving the chairmanship of the Council to the man who, for the next thirty years, was to guide its fortunes—Professor W. G. S. Adams. Born in Scotland in 1874, William George Stewart Adams had a distinguished academic career as lecturer in economics at the Universities of Chicago and Manchester and as Gladstone Professor of Political Theory at Oxford. From 1905 to 1910 he served the Department of Agriculture for Ireland, where he came under the spell of Sir Horace Plunkett, the great pioneer of agricultural co-operation in Ireland, deriving from him a vision of rural renaissance which was never to leave him and which, through his associ-

Professor W. G. S. Adams

ation with the NCSS, was to exercise a deep and lasting influence on the social life of the countryside.

It was natural and proper that S. P. Grundy, who had perhaps done more than anyone else to bring the NCSS into being, should have become its first honorary secretary. But tremendous tasks lay ahead, calling in addition for a full-time, paid officer. The choice fell upon a young man, Captain Lionel Ellis, newly returned from France. He drew his knowledge of social work from his training with the COS in London where, before the war, he had been secretary of the Southwark committee. As a leader of men he had proved himself in France where his gallantry in charge of a machine-gun platoon of the Welsh Guards won him the DSO and the MC. It was thought that after demobilistaion he would return to the COS, but this new opportunity, precarious as it might have seemed with its wide-ranging ideas and inadequate resources, offered him the scope that he wanted. The experiences of the war had not dimmed an idealism which now saw a chance of harnessing to the tasks of peace and reconstruction the comradeship of war and that outpouring of activity in the service of the community which the threat to the life of the nation had evoked.

The difficulties were formidable. The new body had to evolve its own methods of organisation and work in the face of new social problems of unprecedented complexity which the war had left. Hasty and unplanned demobilisation was already causing widespread unemployment. Industrial trouble in the form of rail and coal strikes was just ahead. A serious housing shortage was soon to mock the 'Homes for Heroes' slogan. Mounting rents helped to inflate the already rising cost of living. The machinery of government, which had nearly proved unequal to the tasks of war, was equally unprepared for the tasks of peace; and the new social services which might have provided some cushion against widespread distress were emerging all too slowly. But more serious than the material distress was the deeper spiritual crisis. New freedoms had been gained; the old order was passing; with it went old stupidities and wrongs, but also standards, values and beliefs, the loss of which was to result in the cynicism and near despair of the twenties. Most serious of all was the loss of so many of the new generation—young men with the energy and the vision to lead the nation, exhausted and disillusioned by the war, in the campaign of reconstruction.

The first task of the new National Council was to make plain its purpose. This was done in the preliminary memorandum which, widely circulated, required reprinting by May 1919. It reviewed briefly the steps which led to the founding of the Council and set out three main objects: (a) To promote the systematic organisation of voluntary social work, both nationally and locally, with a view to securing (i) the co-ordination of the voluntary agencies, and (ii) their co-operation with the official agencies engaged in the same sphere of work;

(b) to assist in the formation for this purpose of organisations in each local government area representative of both voluntary effort and statutory administration;

(c) to provide information, particularly as to legislation and the regulations of government departments, for voluntary social workers.

Reference was made to the new problems created by the extension of the statutory social services and the simultaneous growth, forced on by the war, of a large number of new charities, some of unprecedented size. Attention was drawn to the very large number of voluntary workers and the need to bring the two sides into closer partnership, particularly as developments during the war years had given the voluntary agencies a more definite measure of professional recognition than ever before. The memorandum referred to the local representative committees, which were set up at the instigation of the government and were still in being, as 'a distinct advance upon any previous attempts to regularise the relation between public bodies and voluntary associations'. To the voluntary workers it suggested that their part in social reconstruction would be determined by their willingness to fit themselves into a recognised part of the social system.

Right at the start one principle was enunciated which was to be one of the hall-marks of the Council's many-sided activities in the years ahead. 'The Council believe that the general principles of co-ordination and co-operation are of universal application. But they have no desire to dictate and no wish to advocate a rigid uniformity. On the contrary they recognise the advantage, and indeed the necessity, of allowing full scope for special conditions and local needs. They have accordingly drawn up a model scheme which, while consistent with the common policy supported by the Council, is yet capable of such modifications as may be required by the variety of local circumstances.' A suggested scheme for local councils of social service was then outlined as follows:

1. *Area* Local councils should be formed to coincide generally with areas of local government, which might be the county, county borough, borough or, in sufficiently large urban districts, the urban district.

2. *Constitution* The local council for each area should include representatives both of voluntary and official bodies, the constitution of the council following, as closely as local circumstances will allow, the plan devised for representing various interests on the National Council. (NB—It is hoped

23

that each locality will promote such a council which will work in co-operation with the National Council. If local conditions require it, a large advisory council might be formed, on which could be represented such other local interests as may seem desirable.) The local council should be the recognised local organisation to consult with regard to voluntary social work.

3. *Objects* The objects of such a council should be the following, inter alia:

(a) to co-ordinate effort, voluntary and official, in social work, and to promote such new effort as may seem advisable

(b) to compile a list of local agencies engaged in social work, and of voluntary visitors

(c) to co-operate in promoting or developing a register of assistance

(d) to secure the provision in each locality of an organised body of workers, able to undertake on behalf of the locality, friendly visiting and other forms of personal service in social work, where such do not exist (Such a provision would probably involve the setting up of representative ward (or other district) committees)

(e) to promote the training of social workers

(f) to undertake enquiries into specific social questions, and to convene conferences thereon

(g) to spread information in the locality (local handbooks, journals, leaflets, etcetera), and to exchange information with local committees elsewhere

(h) to be a body capable of receiving and administering funds for the general well-being of the district, and for such special purposes as it may propose or be asked to undertake

(i) to act as correspondent with local committees elsewhere with regard to individual cases

(j) to act in co-operation with the National Council.

Here is set out the first great task to which the Council set its hand, 'to inspire the founding of local councils of social service in the major urban areas'. The campaign met with some success, for the first annual report (which was not published till December 1920 and therefore covered the first twenty-one months) records the existence of forty-five councils in various stages of development and others in course of formation. Inevitably the greatest success came where the ground had been carefully prepared by a guild of help, council of social welfare, or similar body, or a COS committee.

With its limited resources of money, and a staff consisting of one paid officer and an office secretary, the responsibility of fostering and servicing such complicated bodies as councils of social service spread all over the country would have proved impossible but for the generous decision of the National Association of Guilds of Help to support the National Council's programme to the fullest extent. Rather than have two central bodies which would work in approximately the same field, the National Association of Guilds of Help agreed to hand all its income to the National Council who in turn undertook its executive work. It was already clear that the two bodies were contemplating a complete merging of identities.

For a proper appreciation of the work of the National Council in its early days it is essential to take into account the activities of some of the early local councils of social service to see how the new ideas were working out in practice. Very properly the emphasis seems to have been on a varied programme of work to meet local conditions, and there is no uniform pattern except where it arose from the common social problems which the aftermath of war had left behind in most of the large towns. The work ranged far and wide: promoting after-care work in connection with tuberculosis; assisting in anti-VD campaigns; bringing together groups responsible for rescue and preventative work for young girls; also those concerned with infant and child welfare, or with the welfare of the blind or mentally deficient. In the field of education, councils were developing new juvenile organisation committees; promoting federations of boys' and girls' clubs; securing playing fields and open spaces; planning social centres, 'citizens' institutes' and, to a lesser extent, choral and dramatic societies.

Often more valuable than any executive action was the mere coming together of people and organisations who would not otherwise have met, to consider the common problems of their town or city, to discuss the new or impending legislation which affected their work, or to provide a common centre of information where social workers in various fields could meet, and where people with a diversity of problems could find the help they needed. Pledged to avoid overlapping in relief work many of the councils tried experimental schemes, with varying success, for the mutual registration of assistance; and one of the first and most obvious advantages of having a *national* council was that it enabled towns preparing to start registration schemes to benefit by the experience of cities such as Birmingham, Liverpool and Manchester where this mutual registration was already operating with some success.

Other advantages of having a national council with wide and varied contacts soon became evident. Through the co-operation of local councils of social service special reports were prepared on matters of current importance where the government was contemplating legislation. The first,

A Report on Some Effects of Widowhood on Wage-Earning Families—a small but thorough piece of research—was timely as the government was considering legislation on widows' pensions; whilst the second, a report on the registration of charities, reflected the great variety of experience represented on the NCSS in this field through local councils and national voluntary bodies. It recorded for the first time that, although 32,958 separate charities rendered accounts to the Charity Commissioners, not even an estimate existed of the total number of charities in England and Wales, nor of their income. It was a remarkable achievement to produce with such slender resources a report of such weight and of such a comprehensive character in less than two years, The subject was clearly complex for, as the NCSS report records, the Commission appointed in 1819 under Lord Brougham—the first attempt at a complete list of the endowed charities of the poor in England and Wales—had not completed its work by 1835, sixteen years later.

Local councils of social service co-operated loyally with the National Council and in their turn received great benefits from the central body. One of the most important of these benefits was the provision of accurate and up-to-date knowledge of changes in the administration of the public social services at a time when new legislation was continually altering their pattern and coverage; and of 'information as to voluntary movements new in form and method' in readily accessible form for all engaged in social service. The representative character of the National Council gave it unique advantages in this task; and with the co-operation of government departments it was able to publish a second edition of its handbook on the public social services, the sales of which had, at an early stage, reached the unexpected total of 13,000. A monthly bulletin was also issued which was so much welcomed by social workers that by 1923 its circulation had reached 1,250.

There were of course failures among the first local councils of social service. Some were formed hopefully and sometimes so quickly that the National Council, with no travelling officers and no development staff, could scarcely keep pace with their growth; they soon faded away for no obvious reason. Sometimes it was probably because they had started on the wrong lines for want of help and guidance. In other places the reason for failure might be rivalry between important local organisations, or between important local personalities. Indeed, the mortality rate among these early councils was high.

There was need to stimulate this varied activity in different parts of the country, but a clear need also to bring together in council and conference the pioneers in these new forms of co-operation. A large conference was planned, to be held in Oxford in October 1919, with the theme: 'Reconstruction and Social Service; the Relation of the Voluntary Worker to the Public Authorities'. As the NCSS still had no offices of its own in London, Barnett House, Oxford, generously offered hospitality; and the National Council established itself there temporarily to prepare for the conference. This period of preparation, and of partial separation from London, lasted much longer than had been anticipated, for a great railway strike prevented the holding of the conference in October and it had to be postponed till the following Easter.

Meanwhile it was possible to hold a very successful conference in Manchester to consider the use which could be made of the new opportunities for leisure arising from the general reduction in hours of labour. The work of this conference was continued by a provisional committtee which during the next year developed so as to include representatives of such bodies as the British Music Society, British Drama League, and others concerned with the use of leisure. This was a small but very important step because it marked the National Council's concern that the conception of social service should not be limited to relief work for the casualties of the social and economic system, and it opened the way to a lively partnership with many bodies whose aims were educational and cultural. Henceforward it was clear that the NCSS would be concerned with all aspects of the life of the community. The first annual report gives evidence of these broadening influences in the record of cultural and educational bodies which had already become members of the Council: British Drama League, British Music Society, Co-operative Holidays Association, English Folk Dance Society, League of Arts, YMCA.

The problem of London premises had now become serious as the greatly expanded Ministry of Health could no longer offer hospitality. The removal of the office to Oxford to prepare for the conference, and the temporary use of a room at No. 8a New Cavendish Street in the summer of 1919 provided no permanent answer. Many important visitors, including the great Lord Haldane, managed to find their way to this sparsely-furnished attic room, to offer advice and help, but it was a quite inadequate London office for a national organisation. While the search for premises went on the possibility of an amalgamation with a sister organisation which had ample accommodation of its own began to offer the hope of a solution. This was the British Institute of Social Service, whose activities have already been noted. Here Percy (later Sir Percy) Alden, MP for Tottenham until 1918, had become a leading figure, and he saw clearly the possibilities which lay in an amalgamation of the two bodies. The British Institute already had a certain amount of prestige, some useful international connections, a valuable reference library of books related to social service, and a journal called *Progress*. Most important of all, it had Percy Alden who had by now become bursar to the Educational Trust to which Sir Richard Stapley had bequeathed his fortune. The Trust acquired the lease of Sir Richard's London residence, Stapley House in Bloomsbury Square; and the plan was that it should become headquarters for the British Institute and National Council, as well as providing accommodation for the Educational Trust and the Library Association. The library of the British Institute was to be placed at the disposal of the joint organisations to become the nucleus of an information department headed by Percy Alden. It was expected that Stapley House would in time become an international centre for social service.

The arrangements for this fusion appear to have worked admirably at the outset. The first annual report, issued at the end of the following year, records that 'the two bodies now share the same headquarters and work as one under the presidency of the Right Honourable James W. Lowther, KC, MP, Speaker of the House of Commons'. As an additional link Percy Alden was made one of the vice-chairmen of the NCSS. No financial settlement was, however, made, and it was understood that the arrangement was to be tried out over an experimental period. It appears that even from the beginning there were some doubts on the part of the British Institute as to whether the National Council would survive; and the high hopes for this amalgamation were only partially fulfilled. After two years the NCSS had still attracted no large financial support, and the two organisations began to drift apart, although Stapley House remained the headquarters of the National Council until 1928 and Sir Percy Alden remained its firm friend and supporter until his death in 1944. When the promised amalgamation failed to materialise the British Institute reverted to the status of an ordinary national group in membership with the Council until it concluded its activities just before the war.

When the first major conference of the NCSS, postponed on account of the rail strike, was at last held in Oxford at Easter 1920, it proved to be a triumph for the organising genius of the secretary, Lionel Ellis. Over 400 delegates attended. The atmosphere was one of sober realism, for both the delegates and the guest speakers were men and women of considerable experience in the work they described and had been able to test their theories against hard facts; but there was also a basis of idealism and a readiness for bold thinking and the imaginative reconsideration of social problems.

The greater part of the conference was concerned with the relationship between statutory and voluntary workers, and contributions to the discussions were made by both these groups. Lieut.-Colonel Fremantle, consulting medical officer of health for Hertfordshire, spoke of the tremendous advance which the government had made in health matters during the war in connection with the welfare of the troops; but he recognised that, in applying this experience in peacetime to the civilian population, the co-operation of voluntary workers would certainly be needed. Britain, he said, had chosen to be a democracy and the elements of regimentation in the army health system could not be applied to the treatment of civilians. 'The individuality of the individual in civil life makes it necessary to employ every volunteer possible.' J. G. Legge, director of education for the county borough of Liverpool, dealt with education as well as health, and said that the work of statutory authorities could be quite inadequate unless there were volunteers prepared to carry over the ideals which prompted it into the out-of-school life of the children. This point was further developed by C. E. Clift, organising secretary of the Board of Education Juvenile Organisation Committee, who examined what was being done for children and young people during their leisure time and suggested lines of improvement. It was clear that the speakers had had personal experience of the difficulties which could arise when statutory authorities and volunteers worked together, but they obviously considered that efforts to resolve the problems were well worth while.

As if to provide chapter and verse for those who stressed that individuals could tackle pioneering work before the state moved in, addresses were given about their special spheres of activity by such people as Margaret MacMillan of the Nursery Schools Movement; Barbara Duncan Harris, honorary secretary of the Croydon Infant Welfare Association; and Arthur Greenwood who spoke as vice-president of the Workers' Educational Association. Arthur Collins of the Birmingham Citizens' Committee gave a resumé of movements and events which led to the creation of the National Council of Social Service, and an account of its present membership which proved beyond doubt that statutory and voluntary co-operation was not merely a good idea but a working reality. Countess Ferrers of the COS, summing up the theme of the conference, said that now more than ever, when there seemed to be an official for every crisis in human life, was there opportunity for imaginative voluntary service.

The conference ranged widely over other subjects also, and a particularly valuable contribution was made by Ronald Norman from his experience as chairman of the London County Council. Alderman Chaplin, Mayor of Leicester and general secretary of the Leicestershire Amalgamated Hosiery Union, while paying tribute to the work of many individual guardians, pleaded for a conception of social service which would remove it entirely from the old Poor Law notions of pauperising charity—a theme developed in much of the subsequent work of the National Council. Another sphere of NCSS activity was foreshadowed by the speech of Sir Henry Rew who was already chairman of the rural department and who spoke also as the chairman of the Village Clubs Association. The one unrealistic contribution to the discussions was made by a speaker who dealt with various plans for ensuring regular employment and concluded that 'there is hope that in the future the question of unemployment as we have known it may almost disappear'. Clement Attlee, who attended as Mayor of Stepney, was not much impressed by this conclusion, and urged that the first essential for the country was not only full employment but work so adequately paid that charity would no longer be needed and public assistance could be 'an effort made by the community as a whole'.

Already in 1920 the first major conference of the National Council gave a forecast of the characteristics which have distinguished it throughout half a century: an alert and imaginative reaction to new social conditions and new ideas; a catholicity of interests combined with an understanding of their relationships one with another; and an adaptability that does not belie principles nor ossify in maturity.

The long, enforced stay in Oxford, preparing for the postponed conference, was to have a profound influence on the future course of the National Council. It had been originally conceived as an urban movement; but its fundamental principle of co-operation was seen to be capable of wider application and soon after its inception some people began to give thought to ways of applying the principle in rural areas. In November 1919, a conference of organisations working for rural improvement submitted to the Council a report which drew attention to the inactivity of parish councils and suggested, among other things, that 'village social councils should be set up'. The immediate result was the establishment of a rural department of the National Council under the chairmanship of Sir Henry Rew of the Village Clubs Association. In this the Council was helped by the National Home and Land League which transferred its funds, assets, and goodwill to the new department of the NCSS.

The period immediately following the war was one of uncertainty and social change. Nowhere was this atmosphere felt more acutely than in the village where the old order, symbolised by the leadership of squire and parson, was passing away. Family ties had been weakened by the war. The internal combustion engine was bringing new mobility to the countryman. Villagers who before the war had never seen a train, the sea, or the streets of London, were now coming back from service in countries overseas. Having seen something of the world they would never again be entirely content with the slow, dull life of the old village where entertainment and recreation were mostly represented by the choir outing, the harvest supper, or the local flower show. After years of separation they certainly longed for the things of home, but they soon grew bored. Opportunities for social contacts with the other sex were limited in villages where there was no hall, institute, or club. So, for want of social life in the village the younger people continued to drift away, despite the schemes for settling ex-servicemen on the land which had only partial success. But a country which had almost starved because of its neglect of the land and its people could not afford to let the tide of young labour flow unchecked to the town simply because of the lack of rural amenities.

A number of organisations were trying to find solutions to these social problems of the countryside. Prominent among them were the women's institutes, now grouped in a newly formed National Federation and the Village Clubs Association. In Wales, particularly in Anglesey, attempts were being made to establish county associations of village halls and clubs. Other bodies were looking for opportunities to bring their services to enrich the life of the villages. The Carnegie United Kingdom Trust were ready with their public library scheme; the local education authorities had new powers for further education; the Workers' Educational Association were finding new possibilities in rural areas; the Agricultural Education Service was being established. What all these ventures needed, and few as yet had got, were active links with the villages—a representative village body through whom contact could be made, and a county body which could bring together in co-operation the providing and servicing agencies to meet the social and cultural needs of the villages.

One person who had given much thought to this problem was Arthur Griffiths who before the war had been a Free Church minister in an Oxfordshire village. His rooms had been the headquarters for the local scouts, the men's club, and a nigger minstrel troupe, and his motorcycle and sidecar provided the essential link to bring help from Oxford to all kinds of village groups. With it he transported books, lecturers, and the inevitable magic lantern, and so gave the small, outside stimulus needed in villages which could not from their own resources meet their own needs. While in hospital in Egypt after overseas service with the YMCA he outlined to their headquarters a plan for organising community life in the village. His offer of service was accepted, and in the spring of 1919, just as the NCSS was getting under way, he was appointed YMCA rural secretary for Oxfordshire and provided with an old Ford van which also had seen much war service with the YMCA.

Some village clubs and institutes started originally for the troops were still in existence, and these were formed into a county federation of Red Triangle clubs. A rapid survey showed the two things most needed. First the establishment of local clubs and institutes in the villages with management representative of all village interests but receptive of outside help to supplement local initiative. Secondly, a county basis to link up and bring together 'providing bodies'—organisations of various kinds which could help the village. A further essential need was transport between the county base and the outlying villages. This, the beginning of the YMCA's village work, paved the way for the larger ventures which were to come. An educational secretary, H. Warrilow, was appointed and village circulating libraries were set up in large centres. Such were the demands made by the villages for drama, music, cinema shows, lantern lectures, dance instructors—sometimes forty events a week—that a second Ford lorry had to be provided. The programme was certainly wide and varied, with lectures ranging from Plato to pig-keeping.

Meanwhile other people in various places had been thinking on somewhat similar lines. First, there was the NCSS rural department which, under the chairmanship of Sir Henry Rew, had many meetings to discuss the subject but had so far failed to resolve one fundamental difficulty. One member of the committee was Sam Bostock, a pioneer of the agricultural co-operative movement who, believing that the village was the essential unit, had set up in his village an admirable village social council representative of widely varied interests. Sir Henry supported this principle but naturally believed that his organisation, the Village Clubs Association, broadened by the inclusion of other village interests, was the best starting point and should be the one recognised co-ordinating body for the village. With this the women's institutes, now a strong national movement and represented on the committee, disagreed. There was apparently no way of solving the dilemma until the long, fortuitous stay of the National Council office in Oxford touched off a new train of events and transformed the whole situation.

It seemed as if something more than mere chance must have brought together in Oxford in the spring and summer of 1920 a small group of people, from widely varying backgrounds and different organisations yet with important ideals in common, at the one moment when their combined efforts were capable of achieving far-reaching results. The ideals which they shared were a deep concern for the welfare of the countryside and the renaissance of rural communities, and an interest in adult education in the broadest sense as a means to those ends.

It was a group of unusual distinction. First there was Professor Adams, now returned to Oxford from Downing Street. He brought the experience and the prestige of outstanding government service and high academic position. Above all, be brought his own clear-sighted vision and understanding. His report to the Carnegie Trustees on the library service had already aroused considerable public interest. He was fired by the enthusiasm of the great Irish pioneer of agricultural co-operation, Sir Horace Plunkett, whose ideals were very simply summed up in the slogan: 'Better farming, better business, better living'. With the Reverend G. K. Bell (later Bishop of Chichester) Professor Adams had been one of the chief inspirers of Barnett House as a memorial in Oxford to Canon Barnett. It was to take the form of a library and information centre on social and economic affairs, and to provide lectures and a training course for social service. Checked by the war but now about to go forward under the leadership of a remarkable woman, Grace Hadow, Barnett House was to provide both the link and the inspiration for the pioneer scheme to extend social and educational services into the hitherto neglected rural areas. 'A soul is needed there,' Professor Adams had said; and this need was truly fulfilled when Grace Hadow accepted the secretaryship in October 1919.

In the following March Barnett House adopted Dr Adams' scheme 'to place the facilities of the House at the disposal of the Oxford villages', and to meet the need for lectures there through co-operation with the WEA, YMCA, and women's institutes. Of Grace Hadow, with whom he was to be closely associated in the rural work of the NCSS, Lionel Ellis later wrote: 'She had in abundance the gifts of a true leader, conviction, energy, understanding. She was a beautiful speaker, easily the best we had, and combined a moving seriousness with great wit. She held her head high as she walked and faced difficulties undismayed.' Brought up in a village herself she saw clearly the true needs of the countryside, and her influence on the rural work of the NCSS was to be far-reaching.

It appears as though Griffiths of the YMCA was the first to see the possibilities of what was to develop the following year as the Oxford Rural Community Council, the pioneer of many such schemes; for he suggested a small informal conference at which Grace Hadow, Captain Ellis, E. S. Cartwright of the University Tutorial Classes, and Helen Denecke of the WEA met together with T. O. Wilson, Director of Education for Oxfordshire, who was most enthusiastic about this scheme to extend adult education to the villages. This informal meeting considered ways and means of taking to them books, lectures, music, and plays. It was clear that an organisation wider than the YMCA would be needed to bring in county groupings such as the women's institutes and the British Legion. Barnett

House obviously had the ideal machinery for co-operation, so it was Grace Hadow who was able to lay the foundation of the Oxfordshire Rural Community Council, which was set up on 8th October 1920. Before long this committee was to replace Griffiths' dilapidated old black Ford and its successor (the snub-nosed Morris car called 'Andrew', after Carnegie) by a specially constructed grey van bearing the letters ORCC.

The success of this Oxford experiment, achieved in the face of great difficulties, for the county council had earlier rejected the Carnegie library scheme, was not unremarked. The rural committee of the NCSS, back in London, still working on the intractable problem of village organisation, immediately saw the possibility of such a scheme. The result was a conference at St John's College, Oxford. This conference emphasised that the main difficulty lay in the fact that for generations British village life had been based on the remnants of the feudal system and that, although landowners and clergy often devoted their lives to the service of their people, the system tended to suppress initiative on the part of the great majority. 'The tendency has been on the one hand to give the village what was considered good for it and, on the other, to turn to someone else for help on all occasions. The essence of the country problem is to find means to enable country-men and women to help themselves, and to bring together all classes in co-operation for the common good.'*

Here then was the start of the national movement to form rural community councils in every county, and it was of great significance that representatives of the Ministry of Agriculture, the Development Commission, and the Carnegie Trustees were present, for the Development Commission and the Carnegie United Kingdom Trust were later to provide the important financial help which alone made possible the wide-scale development of the rural work of the National Council.

Since the Development Commission was to exercise such an important influence on this work, its origins and purpose should be made clear at this point. Created by Parliament in 1909 by Lloyd George's Development Fund Act, it was a permanent Royal Commission charged with the *economic* development of the United Kingdom. In this measure of 1909 may be seen the earliest beginning of state economic planning. The little-known Commission—'a constitutional curiosity, a Department with neither a Minister nor a Parliamentary Vote'—was empowered to recommend to the Treasury grants or loans to government departments, public authorities, schools, universities, or institutions not trading for profit, for the economic development of the countryside in certain defined ways.

---

* *Memorandum on Rural Development.* NCSS, 1922.

But there were added what have been called these 'releasing and invigorating words': 'and by the adoption of any other means which appear calculated to develop agriculture and rural industries'. By the wisdom of a great Commissioner, Vaughan Nash, these words were liberally interpreted to bring in those organisations concerned with social development, which alone could ensure the variety and depth of living that might arrest the alarming drift into the towns, characteristic of those post-war years. Thus in the truest sense the Development Commissioners became 'trustees of a fund for the countryside', and the three-fold partnership which was later to develop between the Commission, the Carnegie United Kingdom Trust, and the NCSS was to have a significant influence on the social life of rural Britain. Like the other bodies concerned with rural development whose activities have already been noted, the Development Commission required for some of its projects a link with both village and county organisations. At the very moment of time when they were seeking such a link, it appeared in the form of the first rural community council.

The Agriculture and Fisheries Act of 1919 empowered each county to set up an agricultural committee whose duties would include making preliminary enquiries with a view to formulating schemes for developing both rural industries and social life. Many of the counties had accordingly set up a rural industry or rural development sub-committee which sent out a postal questionnaire to the minor authorities, collated the replies, and reported to the Minister. Most of these committees then quietly ceased to function, having no funds to pursue the matter in any useful direction.

The Development Commission had in the meantime initiated another important agency, the Rural Industries Intelligence Bureau, to help all those concerned with the revival and extension of rural crafts, standards of workmanship, marketing, prices, and production. What it needed above all was the link with village and county which a rural community council could provide. It was not long, therefore, before a practical working partnership was also evolved in this section of the field.

Meanwhile the rural department of the National Council continued its active propaganda for the organisation of social councils in the villages and rural community councils in the counties, working closely with the rural department in London—a three-tier scheme for co-ordination at village, county, and national levels which was to be characteristic of the Council's future rural policy. It received most useful encouragement from the government when the Board of Education in its report on adult education in rural areas endorsed the principle and suggested that there should be an RCC in every county.

CHAPTER THREE

Growing

A LREADY the work has seriously outgrown the Council's financial resources and its development is being hindered by lack of funds', records the first annual report of the NCSS published in December 1920, at the end of twenty-one months of work. Apart from the Birchall Bequest and a little over £400 received from the National Association of Guilds of Help, income had amounted to only just over £1,000. The bank overdraft was £32. The rural department, however, brought in £235 and contrived to have a bank balance of £162. With the Birchall Bequest used up and little likelihood of increased income from the guilds of help the outlook was not encouraging; but the devoted treasurer, Sir Charles Stewart, never lost heart and at one of the worst moments he was able to announce a generous gift of £1,000 from Dame Janet Wills, to be spread over four years.

But the financial difficulties of the National Council were only a reflection of the condition of the country as a whole. By the winter of 1921 the unemployment crisis had sharpened, inflation was increasing, and financial disaster loomed. The King's Speech to Parliament called for 'the restriction of expenditure' in every department of life, both public and private.

The NCSS, representing the great and progressive voluntary social service societies, was deeply concerned by the threat of cuts in the newly developing health and education services, totalling £130 million. These were to affect particularly infant and child welfare, the school medical service, and the care of the blind, tuberculous, and mentally deficient. In a series of leaflets and pamphlets the Council urged that, while the need for economy was of paramount importance, it could not be achieved by cutting down essential public services which, far from being extravagant, brought a return in the increased health, productive power, and well-being of the nation. Such cuts would only involve increased expenditure on police, prisons, workhouses, hospitals, and asylums. Stressing the unique contribution which voluntary service had made during the war, the Council went on to suggest that, if it were mobilised now for the tasks of peace and reconstruction, essential services might be retained even if economies had to be made. But in spite of these reasoned arguments, finally submitted in a resolution to the Prime Minister, the axe fell heavily on many of the new services.

The National Council and the local councils of social service had to do the best they could in a worsening situation with the resources they had. One of these was the idea of mutual registration of assistance which, with growing unemployment and increasing sources of statutory help, was becoming more important than ever if wasteful overlapping and mal-administration of public funds were to be avoided and the maximum help made available in the most constructive forms for the most deserving cases.

In 1921 the National Council of Social Service drew attention to the possibility of serious overlapping likely to arise from the refusal of the employment exchange to disclose whether or not unemployment benefit was being paid. As it was clear that the same difficulty might arise with other government departments, and as this was a matter of principle likely to be of importance to many of the bodies represented on the National Council, they referred the question to the Chancellor of the Exchequer for a Treasury ruling. As a result the whole question of mutual registration of assistance came under review by the Cabinet Committee on Unemployment. It was known that the Minister of Health and some members of the Cabinet Committee were keen supporters of the idea of registration. At the same time it was obvious that nothing but a hard economic argument would convince the Treasury: that the saving in rates and taxes would exceed the considerable administrative costs of any scheme of compulsory registration of assistance, statutory and voluntary.

Both through the local councils of social service and through its central records the NCSS made available to the government a great deal of useful information on the subject. It was not easy to obtain evidence at this time as even the most efficient schemes were being overwhelmed by the un-precedented volume of long-term unemployment; and it was also difficult to assess the economies likely to be made, for the very presence of mutual registration tended to eliminate overlapping until it was impossible to ascertain what had been saved. The only sure guide would be test registrations in a new area where it had not hitherto been tried. To this the Cabinet Committee agreed. Halifax and Reading were selected for the purpose, and in Liverpool, where a scheme was already operating, additional special tests were applied; but the final results were not conclusive enough to convince the Treasury that the saving would exceed the cost of administration.

Nevertheless, the voluntary societies concerned with case-work still thought that registration had certain moral and social values which could not be assessed on a cash basis. So evident was it that there was a great deal wrong with the administration of the new public social services that the government came under heavy fire from all sides. In January 1923, Sidney Webb published his famous letter to the Prime Minister, Bonar Law, complaining that tens of thousands of men, including many ex-service-men, were failing to get provision for their needs by reason of the gaps between the various schemes and the imperfections of departmental co-ordination. Bonar Law replied sharply and publicly, refuting the charges but promising an inter-departmental committee of enquiry. It met imme-diately. The NCSS gave further evidence on mutual registration, and Captain Ellis, Hancock Nunn, Frederick D'Aeth, and S. P. Grundy were among the witnesses examined.

One result of the enquiry was a thorough overhaul of the machinery for co-ordination between the various statutory services. In addition the representatives of the Ministries of Health, Labour and Pensions who formed the committee made the following unanimous recommendation: 'That the central and local authorities concerned should promote the formation by voluntary effort, in areas for which such an organisation appears desirable, of local councils of social service constituted on the lines suggested in paragraph 147 of our Report. . . .' This stated: 'A number of such councils are already in existence, and we think that wider extension of their activities would be of value. While the actual constitution of such councils must be left to local initiative, their membership should, we think, be non-official and should include honorary workers upon the various statutory committees of the authorities administering statutory assistance in a given area e.g., boards of guardians, parish councils, local employment committees, local education committees, insurance committees, old age pensions' committees, together with representatives of any voluntary bodies who may care to co-operate. The initiative in the formation of such councils might be taken by the mayor or other head of the local government authority. The existence of such councils would, we believe, be of great value in promoting the smooth administration of the public service of the country by bringing into close and systematic association persons engaged locally in administering public and voluntary assistance.'

The report of the inter-departmental committee went on to suggest that such councils might appoint an information officer—thus once again foreshadowing the creation of the citizens' advice bureau service. 'We think, finally, that such councils might fulfil a further valuable function. In our view much avoidable dissatisfaction with the working of the public assistance services is due largely to the ignorance of the average citizen as to the forms of assistance available and as to the conditions under which they may be obtained. . . . We think it desirable that there should be in every large centre of population some officer conversant with the principles and methods of assistance authorities generally, not identified with any particular public service . . . who would be in a position to give reliable information and assistance both to individual applicants and to officers of the several services who might be in difficulty in dealing with cases falling apparently within the scope of a number of services. We think that such an officer might with advantage by appointed, and that his work should be supervised by the local council of social service.'

Here was yet another striking government commendation of the idea behind the council of social service; and support began to come also from many other official quarters. The Association of Municipal Corporations gave its approval to the views of the inter-departmental committee on the need for councils of social service. The County Councils Association paid warm tribute to their rural counterparts, the rural community councils. With official approval for both its urban and rural work, at national, county, town, and village levels, the NCSS could look with confidence to the future. An application for incorporation as a company limited by guarantee, and not for profit, had been accepted. After four years of preparation the National Council could claim to be soundly established and ready to move forward to meet the new and heavier responsibilities which recognition had brought.

This success was in no small measure due to the dynamic energy and foresight of Lionel Ellis, its general secretary. He had come to the NCSS believing in its essential purpose but with no clearly defined plan for what it might become. Now as he watched it growing, not so much in size as in influence, he could begin to see more clearly its great potentialities. But his work would have achieved little if it had not been supported by the loyalty of a small, devoted staff, and influenced by the vision and understanding of the men and women distinguished in many walks of life who met together in its councils and committees. Many more had by now joined those who had founded the Council and carried it through the first difficult years, in order to help in manning the growing number of special committees and in guiding its central work. It is not possible here to do justice to all the men and women who brought to the NCSS their wisdom as individuals or their experience in departments of state or in the great voluntary societies now in association with the Council. But some stand out for the unique character of their contribution. Among the notable civil servants, so important at this stage when the NCSS was beginning to help in shaping central administrative practice, mention must be made of C. F. Adair Hore of the Ministry of Pensions; A. T. A. Dobson of the Ministry of Agriculture; Vaughan Nash of the Development Commission; Montagu Harris of the Ministry of Health; and Sir Henry Pelham of the Board of Education. Some of these men were to give many years of devoted service to the Council. At this time also there came from the voluntary movement one of the greatest pioneers of the NCSS, Colonel (later Brigadier General) Sir Wyndham Deedes, first to represent the Federation of Residential Settlements, and later to lead the Council into new fields of thought and activity.

Sir Wyndham Deedes

In this period of expansion, as the Council's influence continued to spread, new names began to appear on the list of voluntary agencies represented on the NCSS in an advisory and consultative capacity; and the number of local councils of social service grew to forty. Their work was so varied that only a few examples can be given. Bradford, for instance, carried out a survey which revealed some of the very bad housing conditions in the city, and promoted a voluntary housing scheme under which several hundred houses were built. In Wakefield classes and lectures for prisoners were provided, on subjects ranging from 'efficient boiler-firing' to 'clean living'. Elsewhere councils organised health weeks, often in co-operation with their local authorities; assisted town planning and amenity campaigns; set up study groups; conducted local surveys; and published handbooks of information.

As local experiments multiplied it became more than ever desirable that details of local experience should be collected and shared. So the work of the National Council's standing conferences, such as that on personal service, grew in importance. In addition, the NCSS was able to develop its service to government departments and to the charitable and voluntary agencies by obtaining and collating evidence on important questions of social policy, such as the information provided to Mr Justice Finlay's Committee on free legal aid and advice to poor persons.

From the beginning the National Council, as well as the local councils, had regarded work with young people as of great importance. By this time the Boy Scouts, Girl Guides, YMCA, YWCA, and Church Lads' Brigade were all represented on the Council; but the boys' club movement though growing in strength throughout the country had no national association and no central headquarters. In June 1924, Captain Ellis, who had a keen personal interest in the movement, called a conference of leaders of boys' clubs; and as a result of this and subsequent discussions during the following year, the National Association of Boys' Clubs was founded. For its first year Captain Ellis acted as its honorary secretary and the NCSS provided accommodation at Stapley House; but within a year the new National Association was established in its own right with its own secretary and its own headquarters. This was the first example of a form of assistance to a new organisation which was to become familiar in the pattern of NCSS development, and several other well-known national institutions were later formed in this way. Some, like the National Association of Boys' Clubs, grew up, achieved independence, and moved out to their own homes so quickly that, save to the initiated, their origins are now unknown.

Despite the outstanding progress made in these early years not every project prospered. The collapse of the Leeds Council of Social Service was recorded in 1925. Other, smaller projects faded away almost unnoticed because of the lack of field officers to advise and support them. It was for this reason that, in the same year, a proposal was accepted from the Sheffield Council of Social Service that their energetic honorary secretary, W. E. Dixon, one of the pioneers of the movement, should devote himself to propaganda work for the ncss in the north-eastern region, particularly in the large towns of Yorkshire. One year of this activity convinced him that 'given time to devote to the work and funds to support it, efficient councils could be established in all the towns in the area'. But the problem of funds for the development of this type of work, which had so little popular appeal, was to remain beyond solution; and, as the first enthusiasm for the new idea waned, it became more and more difficult to maintain and consolidate even the existing work. An added difficulty was the obvious need in the larger towns, where the scope of the local council was continually increasing in size and responsibility, to employ a paid secretary with considerable experience and training who could give his whole time to the work.

As it was hopeless to find the extra funds to pay adequately a skilled officer, various expedients were tried. Some councils relied on the voluntary services of people of independent means who could, and often did, literally devote their lives to the cause in which they believed. In other places, by dint of much scraping, money was found to pay a small salary but nothing that was commensurate with the nature of the work and the calibre of the officer needed. In a few cases mutual arrangements with associated or kindred organisations enabled part of a secretary's salary to be met. Despite the amount of work carried out in co-operation with the local authorities and the consequent economies in public expenditure, no grant-in-aid was made to the council, except where, for instance, the board of guardians gave some help towards the keeping of a mutual register of assistance.

In an endeavour to face this problem of financing local councils of social service and improving the standard of work by attracting personnel of adequate training and experience, the ncss set up a strong Advisory Committee on Urban Work and started a school for secretaries. This school brought together for brief periods in the summer some of the most active workers, and helped not only to raise the standard of training but to create a greater unity of purpose and practice in a very diverse movement.

It had soon become clear, in the countryside as in the towns, that, if a community council was to do its work adequately, some permanent full-time staff would be needed and an office would be essential. While it was hoped that ultimately the statutory and voluntary bodies represented on the rural community council would supply the necessary funds, here again there was anxiety in the early years while the experiment was proving itself. But for the rural work the problem of finance was not insoluble. In October, 1922, the NCSS approached the Carnegie United Kingdom Trust for a grant to enable it to develop rural community councils experimentally in three counties; and the trustees generously promised £1,000 a year for a period of three years. The rural department was strengthened by the appointment of Grace Hadow as part-time organiser and it was largely her leadership and practical experience which helped to make possible the progress of the coming years.

Because it provided the answer to so many needs in the countryside, the rural community movement began to spread quickly. Inspired by the Oxford Conference, enthusiasts went back to their own villages ready to try to form village social councils and to their county organisations to try to pave the way for RCCs; and as many as ten councils were actually formed in 1923 and 1924. After Oxfordshire the first to get under way was Kent. The county was fortunate in the leadership at the county level of E. Salter Davies, director of education, and the assistant director, Arthur Richmond (later to become assistant secretary to the NCSS); and with the help of Leonard Shoeten Sack (who also, some fifteen years later, was to play a large part in the work of the National Council), they set up a pioneer village social council at Sparsholt and Lainston. Gloucestershire followed this lead soon after—the home county of Grace Hadow who had roused the enthusiasm of both Lady Cripps and Sir F. Hyett, chairman of the county council. Then came Leicestershire, Nottinghamshire, and Derbyshire, where the adult education committee of Nottingham University under Professor Peers set up a joint committee to sponsor a rural community council in each county. The first six were fortunate in receiving help from the Carnegie UK Trust. In Cambridgeshire the initiative of Henry Morris, chief education officer, resulted in the formation of an RCC by the autumn of 1924. The Hertfordshire Council, sponsored by James Dudley, warden of Letchworth Settlement, followed closely the Oxfordshire pattern. The next county to form an RCC was West Sussex. At the end of the year the plan to spread the movement to Scotland took shape with a council in Forfarshire. The following year saw councils at work in Somerset, Lindsey (Lincolnshire), Herefordshire, and Monmouthshire.

The work of these first rural community councils varied widely from one county to another, but some activities were common to almost all of them. They were all concerned with adult education in the broadest sense,

43

and they soon found themselves equally involved in youth work. Questions of public health linked up with their campaign for the provision of rural amenities. This in turn led them to enter the new field of town and country planning, and to an active interest in the problems of local government and the future of parish councils. But basic to all their work were the economic problems which would determine the future of the countryside. The development of rural industries therefore continued to occupy a position of paramount importance. Finally, but by no means least in significance for rural reconstruction, was the campaign for village halls.

To look first at the part which RCCs played in adult education, a wide and not easily defined term: they did not normally provide it directly but they had a dual function in the matter. In the villages they stimulated interest; at county level they brought together the various organisations which could meet the demand this created. Leadership was an outstanding problem now that the old order had passed away. So Oxfordshire RCC tried the experiment of a school for music conductors, and Kent a school for play producers; and local leaders soon began to show themselves. Gloucestershire held a great music festival for village choirs; and in other counties drama festivals were organised, or county drama societies formed. Tours of village concert parties were arranged. A few years later this movement to encourage rural music and drama was to be strengthened and extended through the co-operation of the women's institutes with the backing of funds provided by the Carnegie United Kingdom Trust.

Further-education lectures would have seemed likely to be less attractive to the inhabitants of remote country villages. Gloucestershire RCC, however, decided as a venture of faith to meet part of the salary of a full-time organising tutor from Bristol University. Somerset followed this lead and secured a grant from its local education authority. The response was astonishing. Soon reports came in that 'tiny villages tucked away on Exmoor, two of them nine miles from a railway station—hamlets hidden in the Mendips or almost lost in Sedgemoor—had all taken advantage of the scheme. . . . The audiences average thirty-five to forty . . . those in the professions, trade, industry, and agricultural workmen . . . A number of tenant farmers rode in on horseback, four, five, and six miles, to attend a lecture'. Nottinghamshire RCC reported that 1,709 adults and 183 children attended thirty-three lectures in twenty-four different villages, an average of fifty-seven people for each lecture. But for the cost and the shortage of competent lecturers the venture would undoubtedly have had even more success.

It was recognised that there would be no hopeful future for a countryside which could not keep its young people. Facilities for recreation were an urgent need, but not easily met when many villages were so remote and population so scattered. The first step was to find out what was already being done, and the young people's committees of rural community councils began a series of surveys. In Kent, for example, a committee was formed which brought together representatives from local branches of some of the principal national youth organisations to explore the field; and, though the results were not encouraging, the report on them at least indicated a possible line of policy, which the NCSS set out in a circular advocating the establishment of permanent county youth committees. Where rural community councils existed, the youth committees would be attached to them; elsewhere they would be set up independently. Here was yet another strong argument in favour of rural community councils. The youth committees would compile a list of the organisations already existing in the villages, and go on to stimulate the formation of new youth groups of all kinds with the help of experienced workers from the national youth organisations who would visit and advise the villages. Finally the committees were invited to study the difficult problem of the recruitment and training of club leaders. The soundness of this plan was definitively proved in 1939 when, at the beginning of the war, the government embodied it in the national Service of Youth scheme. Critics of the voluntary system argue that, by means of one Circular,* the government accomplished in about thirteen months much more than a non-statutory organisation had achieved in as many years. But it was largely due to the pioneering work of the National Council that the government became aware of the nature of the problems in rural areas and of possible ways to solve them; and even so it needed the emergency of war to goad the government into action.

One of the most significant developments in rural youth work in the twenties had been the emergence of a new youth organisation, the young farmers' clubs. Prominent among those who inspired the movement was Lord Northcliffe, and the idea was taken up by the Ministry of Agriculture working through the county agricultural organisers and backed by that 'trustee of the countryside', the Development Commission. It was soon realised that, if the project were to develop, the many new clubs would need some form of county federation and the sense of being part of a national movement. Here again the value of the rural community councils, with their roots in the villages and their links with the National Council in London, was obvious and not least to the Ministry of Agriculture which, in the autumn of 1928, asked the NCSS to join them as partners

---

* Board of Education Circular No. 1486, 1939.

in developing these clubs. First, county federations were formed through the RCCs. Then, with assistance from the Carnegie United Kingdom Trust and the Ministry, the NCSS undertook the work of general organisation. A strong, representative committee was set up, and the secretary of the Somerset RCC was appointed to the staff of the NCSS as organiser.

It soon became clear that this was going to be a strong movement which could do much for the future of the countryside, but that it could fulfil its potentialities only if the clubs were linked in an independent national association of their own. By the following year this was formed, the NCSS assisting by providing office accommodation and staff. The young organisation grew and prospered. By 1931 it had achieved full independence as the National Federation of Young Farmers' Clubs. Another member of the NCSS family had grown up and was ready to move to a home of its own.

This principle of growth and development was obviously right, and none recognised it more clearly than those responsible for NCSS policy. But its application was to create some difficult problems in the years ahead. Were all the strong groups, capable of supporting themselves and 'earning their own living', to move out from the family circle, leaving those which needed more careful nurture and which by their very nature were never likely to become independent or 'bread-winners' for the family? The family tradition that children help their parents according to their means could not be easily applied to the complex relationships within the NCSS.

The rural community councils in their concern for young people of the countryside were dealing not only with leisure but with basic economic needs. In Kent, for instance, the RCC brought together farmers, farm workers, and the education and agricultural committees of the county to discuss the apprenticeship, training and education which might encourage the young to enter agriculture; and both Gloucestershire and Kent undertook an enquiry into the existence of charitable trusts which might finance such apprenticeships.

Nor was this concern limited to young people. Ever since the war the position of older craftsmen and of their ancient crafts had been causing anxiety. The government, through the Development Commission and the Rural Industries Bureau, had been giving thought to the problem. Although there was a continuing need for men who could shoe horses, repair farm machinery, thatch ricks, and lay hedges, their numbers had fallen because bigger money could be earned in the towns. In addition, the old blacksmith whose services were needed to keep the new farm machinery in repair found himself being ousted by less competent but progressive young men. The older men had not moved with the times and they

Rural craftsmen
skintling (*top*)
making a fishing creel (*bottom*)

had no organisation to look after their interests, to help them to obtain tools and materials wholesale, or to find new alternative markets for their produce. Here was an obvious need and an opportunity for the rural community councils to help these country craftsmen to adjust to the new conditions. But this was not a mere romantic revival. As the secretary of the Cambridgeshire RCC explained in an address to a conference of rural community councils: '. . . if rural industries cannot conform to new conditions they will perish. You cannot fight an economic fact. If the village blacksmith will not adopt modern methods, will not make the best use of machinery, will not meet a changing market, he will disappear; and no amount of sitting under chestnut trees and singing in the choir will save him. And we should not want to save him. The rural industries movement we favour today is not based, as some people seem to imagine, on a desire to bolster up the romantic, though decrepit, in its losing fight against the unromantic and efficient. The decrepit must not be bolstered up; it must be changed or abandoned. We do not stand as champions of an economic defeatism.'

As with so much of the National Council's work, its efforts in this field were a unique piece of team-work: in this instance between the rural community councils, the Rural Industries Bureau, and the Development Commission. Many of the RCCs began by encouraging the formation of guilds of craftsmen or co-operative societies, to buy tools, plant, and simple machinery; to arrange courses of technical instruction and to organise exhibitions of the craftsmen's work. The Development Commission, through the rural community councils, helped with finance.

The general results exceeded all expectations. There were also some interesting by-products of the experiment. For example, West Sussex RCC when enquiring into the prospects of willow-growing found that, although lobster fishermen required lobster pots, practically no willow was being grown in the county; but discovered that it grew profusely in Somerset. The willow growers there, however, complained to the RCC of the crippling cost of rail transport. Representations made by the RCC to the Railway Clearing House saved at least £1,000 a year on transport charges and helped the basket industry considerably.

The task of organising the village craftsmen to help themselves was not easy, as this report from Cambridge illustrates: 'Last Saturday we had a meeting of fifty rural craftsmen in this town. It needed the most heroic efforts of our rural industries organiser to get them in, but get them he did: smiths, carpenters, cabinet-makers, and saddlers. The chairman harangued them. I harangued them myself without result. We called for questions. But there were no questions asked. We asked for objections, but none were made. We asked them to propose names for a committee, but no names were proposed. Then one of them got up from the back bench and said: "No one of us knows another." Everybody laughed. Everybody started talking at once, and the upshot was that thirty-four of them signed their names to come to another meeting to form a co-operative society. They left the room talking to each other, although they had come in silent. It was the first meeting of rural craftsmen in Cambridge since the Middle Ages.'

The rural community councils showed the same sort of initiative in the field of public health. At a moment when the government was proposing to re-organise the rural health services, the Oxfordshire RCC completed a careful survey of existing facilities. Most of the councils set up health committees which organised health weeks, lectures, and demonstrations, campaigned actively in such matters as rubbish disposal, set up information bureaux, organised transport to hospitals and clinics, and played a notable part in the promotion of TB after-care services.

Their interest in health services led on to campaigns for better rural amenities and brought the RCCs into the new field of town and country planning. The Cambridgeshire RCC, for example, planned a regional survey and sent six-inch scale maps to every village so that they could mark up new houses, commons, wells, drains, and rubbish dumps. By July 1927, rural planning had become the chief topic for the annual conference of rural community councils.

In all these different ways rural community councils were proving their worth. But as the report of 1924 stressed: 'County organisation is of value only in so far as it proves useful to the villages; it is for the enrichment of village life that the rural community councils are formed;' and it seems clear that up to this time the movement to bring together the various interests in the villages was making only slow headway, although a number of village social councils or village community councils were being formed in different parts of the country. Villages set in traditional ways can be highly resistant to what they feel to be new-fangled ideas, particularly if they come from outside; and rightly suspicious of neat patterns of organisation which do not take into account the varieties of village life. Against the forces of inertia, suspicion, and indifference the new ideas would have made little progress if they had not become directly linked to the greatest of all social needs in many villages—the need for a village hall. In some places they had been provided by wealthy benefactors, or with the help of the Village Clubs Association, Women's Institute, YMCA, or British Legion. But the obvious need in very many villages was a hall available for use by everyone, and therefore under some form of village

49

ownership and management and not the property of any particular organisation. The strenuous venture of building and maintaining such a hall provided the very type of community project required to bring the varied interests in the village together; and their coming together in council provided just the sort of management needed for the hall, or so it seemed to the NCSS rural committee. Two other points stood out. The provision of such a hall was beyond the resources of most villages unless they could get some form of temporary outside assistance. Secondly, the provision of village halls was vital to the social well-being of the countryside.

In July, 1924, the NCSS approached both the Development Commission and the Carnegie United Kingdom Trust to enquire tentatively whether they would be prepared to consider giving financial aid to villages in need of a hall; and offering to administer an experimental scheme through the rural community councils in a few selected villages. The Carnegie UK Trustees were unable to add to their existing commitments; but in December of that year a favourable reply came from the Lords Commissioners of HM Treasury. They were prepared to advance up to £5,000 from the Development Fund for an experiment designed to ascertain the minimum state contribution required to enable village communities to erect or extend village halls.

The conditions were that the village must prove the need for the hall and have acquired a suitable site. The applications were to be approved by the NCSS, and interest-free loans up to one-third of the cost of the building were to be made through the rural community councils to fully representative village bodies. It was further laid down that, as the loans were repaid, the money must be used solely to extend the same facilities to other villages, and that no part of the grant could be used for administering the scheme.

In commending this project the Ministry of Agriculture had stated: 'In the Ministry's opinion no central body can properly administer a grant made by the State for this purpose unless it has an effective county organisation to assist it in the matter, as a connecting link between headquarters and the village. In this respect the position of the National Council of Social Service is a strong one. As the Development Commissioners are aware, the Council is now concerned with the setting up of Rural Community Councils in various counties and in this they have the support of the Carnegie Trustees. It is felt, therefore, that if the principle of State assistance in the direction indicated is to be accepted, the Development Commissioners would be well advised to select this body as the most suitable one for an experimental grant.'

A fully representative committee was set up to consider policy, consisting of Z. F. Willis (later Sir Frank), the educational secretary of YMCA; Sam Bostock, an ex-chairman of the Agricultural Organisation Society; Miss I. Ferguson, secretary of the National Federation of Women's Institutes; Grace Hadow; and S. P. Grundy.

At first the claims on the fund were not heavy, but by 1928 twenty new village halls had been built with loans from this source. There were many enquiries to be made and much preliminary work to be done. A *Model Trust Deed* had to be drawn up and a *Handbook on Construction and Management* issued. The Royal Institute of British Architects gave valuable assistance in the preparation of suggested plans, with the result that the risk of disfiguring villages by corrugated iron structures or unsightly huts was avoided, and some beautiful halls were built, even in quite small villages.

The results of this village policy in its early years were just as the promoters might have hoped. The loan fund was 'stimulating the villages to put their hands into their own pockets to provide themselves with a village hall. . . . It is not supplanting local effort but galvanising local people into making fresh efforts to help themselves.' There were no defaulters. All loans were repaid as they became due or even before.

An early village hall

So far the work of the National Council in the rural and the urban areas had developed on parallel but different lines, and this was logical because there was a fundamental difference at the root of many of the problems in the two areas: urban problems were in the main due to congestion in the towns and rural problems to the wide scattering of the population. Local government also had tended to develop in the same way as the voluntary work. But by 1924 it was becoming clear that there were many areas where these problems met and intermingled and where the distinction between urban and rural was blurred. The need to think of regions rather than counties had been partly recognised in some of the joint town planning committees of the time. Should the provision of social services be considered in a similar way and what, indeed, was the whole relationship between town and country to be in the future? In an endeavour to find an answer to these questions the National Council, with the help of a grant from the Carnegie UK Trust, began in 1924 a survey of social services in two areas where there was no clear division between urban and rural interests: the Cheshire and Fifeshire regions. This survey committee brought together men of great administrative skill. R. C. Norman of the London County Council was its chairman and other members were Sir Percy Jackson of the County Councils Association and C. Montagu Harris of the Ministry of Health. It could also draw upon the unique town and country planning experience of Professor Patrick Abercrombie and the sociological knowledge of Alexander Farquharson who carried out the local enquiries.

Meanwhile the rural and urban sides of the National Council's work developed in their separate ways. The rural work was full of promise. By 1926 rural community councils had been established in seventeen counties. The village halls loan scheme was in operation. Relations with the Ministry of Agriculture, the Development Commission and the Carnegie UK Trustees could not have been better. The Trustees had increased their grant to the NCSS from £1,000 to £2,000 a year, had renewed their grant to the original pioneer rural community councils, and had undertaken to consider grant applications from not more than five additional rural community councils in the quinquennium from 1926 to 1931. Somerset, Lindsey (Lincolnshire), and Hertfordshire were already formed but had not received financial aid. Now these three, together with the two new councils set up during the year, Herefordshire and Dorset, had their applications for grant approved by the Trustees. Others went ahead without the promise of financial help; but it is significant that in one of them, Shropshire, although a constitution was approved in 1927, the council did not survive its early difficulties and closed the following year.

By contrast with this hopeful record of rural progress, the work of the urban councils of social service continued to meet with much less favourable fortune. It is not easy at first sight to account for this difference since the reasons for it are complex. One of them has already been discussed: the fact that the urban councils had no funds comparable with the Carnegie grants which would have enabled them to employ full-time secretaries, and had consequently to depend on a variety of unsatisfactory expedients.

More important, perhaps, were the political trends of the time. The Labour Party, which had just had its first brief term of office, was also a rising power in most of the great cities in which councils of social service had been formed. To this new element in municipal life it seemed that the councils of social service were content to treat symptoms rather than the underlying economic causes of bad social conditions. Consequently they were not always sympathetic to the voluntary movement. In the countryside, work for village halls, library services, music, and drama, showed the rural community councils reaching for new opportunities. But in the towns, where so much time had to be spent in personal service for the relief of distress and in helping the casualties of the social system, the councils of social service often had no resources left for the development of a wider programme. 'This will come in time', said the annual report of 1926 optimistically, 'as councils grow stronger and the idea that all social life is their province gains wider recognition and support. It is largely a question of finance, for without sufficient income no council can obtain the staff for a comprehensive programme of constructive work.'

To the growing body of Labour supporters and the young intellectuals of the Left, talk of the mutual registration of assistance was not exactly the clarion call to action which could rally them. Moreover, the rift was likely to widen, for the long bitter coal strike of 1925, the rising unemployment figures, and the threat of even worse labour disturbances to come, meant that the councils of social service were more than ever preoccupied with the problems of relieving distress. Applications for assistance increased in every town, with appeals for boots and clothing, especially for children. School clothing guilds and loans to provide outfits for girls entering domestic service were typical of the times. In one town there was a Christmas appeal to every employer and to private individuals to provide one week's work for an unemployed man. In Birmingham there were 135,000 new notifications on the mutual register of assistance in which seventy-seven organisations were now co-operating.

Nevertheless, relief did not use all the resources of the urban councils. Following in some small measure a recommendation of the Inter-departmental Committee on Public Assistance, already mentioned, many of the councils of social service became advice centres, often setting up some form of 'citizens' friend' service, the forerunner of the citizens' advice bureau. The provision of legal aid and advice was closely allied with this service. So much experience was gained in this field that the National Council was able to give valuable evidence to the committee presided over by Mr Justice Finlay which was investigating the subject. Advice and help on the possibility of emigration was another service which some councils gave to families which saw no future for themselves in the straitened conditions of the home country.

A wide variety of other tasks were undertaken. Sheffield Council organised blood donors; Stafford a car rota for hospitals; Belfast a survey of blind babies for whom help was needed; London a great housing conference to consider the neglected needs of the poorest; Edinburgh a club for mentally deficient girls; Scarborough a clinic for crippled children. In some forty towns and cities the councils provided the means by which the sympathy, generosity, and personal service of numberless ordinary people were brought to bear on the many-sided problems that the work of the councils brought to light.

Nor was the work only for the suffering and the delinquent. Useful things were done for the ordinary young people: running camps, finding additional playgrounds and sports fields, keeping play centres open even when the authorities had decided that they would have to be closed.

The old too had their share of attention. As far back as 1926 the Liverpool Council of Voluntary Aid which, with the associated Liverpool Personal Service Society, was one of the oldest established and strongest of the local councils, had concerned itself with the needs of the old for auxiliary pensions and social facilities. Because of the work of its notable leaders, including Frederick D'Aeth and Dorothy Keeling, Liverpool had been able to enrich the work of other councils all over the country through its own unique contribution to the NCSS.

One of its most useful contributions had been in connection with the scheme for recovering income tax on charitable subscriptions. The origins of the scheme were as follows: The Finance Act of 1922 provided that, if a person contracted or covenanted to pay away a portion of his income annually for a period exceeding six years, these annual payments could be treated for tax purposes as income of the beneficiary. If these payments were made out of taxed income, it was logical that the amount of tax paid could be recovered from the Inland Revenue by the beneficiary if his own income was below taxable limits. By another provision of the law charities were placed in the same position as private beneficiaries where income was below taxable level. They also, being exempt from tax on income solely devoted to charitable purposes, had been allowed to recover tax already paid in respect of the services received by them under such contracts. This had represented an important addition to the funds of many charities.

The Liverpool Council of Voluntary Aid, which had done much work in organising the distribution of charitable funds in their city, were the first to conceive the idea that a council of social service or similar body might be constituted as a general purpose charity to which subscribers could covenant to pay subscriptions; the council would then distribute these funds to the charities named by the subscriber, recovering on their behalf the amount due from the income tax authorities, and paying it over as a substantial additional contribution to the charities. Liverpool passed on this sound and practical idea to the NCSS who organised it on a nationwide basis for a wide range of recognised charities.

There had been some initial difficulties to overcome but, the principle once established, the charities department of the NCSS grew rapidly and by 1925 was distributing over £40,000 to the charities and recovering over £6,000 in tax on their behalf. However, the Treasury began to have doubts about this provision; and the Chancellor of the Exchequer put forward proposals to amend it. The National Council took immediate action. They brought the voluntary societies together for consultation; and R. C. Norman, vice-chairman of the NCSS led a representative deputation to the Treasury to plead for the deletion of the clause. A letter signed by all the members of the deputation was sent to every Member of Parliament. As a result, an amendment was moved in the House of Commons and supported by members of all parties; this was accepted by the government. Here was a signal demonstration of the value to the voluntary movement of the kind of corporate action for which the National Council stands, and one of the earliest examples of the manner in which the NCSS has been able, over the years, to ensure that such action is prompt and effective.

Its own budget remained commendably small in comparison with the volume of work undertaken and the growing influence of the Council in many departments of national life. Total expenditure in 1927 was only £4,430, of which salaries accounted for nearly £2,500. To meet these costs the main source of income was the £2,000 grant from the Carnegie UK Trust. As donations, subscriptions and affiliation fees reached only £750, the special importance of the Carnegie grant in these early years is obvious.

Another service of the National Council which was continuing to increase in importance and influence was the production of publications on the social services. About this time the old *Social Service Bulletin*, which for four years had reported new and changing legislation and had kept its 2,000 readers informed of the latest developments in social work, was improved in content and appearance. The new edition of the handbook on *Public Social Services*, with its concise summary of all the existing statutory services, quickly sold 4,000 copies. Leaflets and pamphlets on the urban and rural work of the NCSS continued to be issued as they were needed.

The record of these years is one of steady growth and progress. There were no spectacular developments. The National Council worked rather by trial and error; by experiment to meet new needs and a gradual consolidation of ground gained. As it grew in prestige and its influence spread in village, county, and town, it was increasingly consulted when new bodies were being formed which required wide contacts. When, for instance, the Council for the Preservation of Rural England was created in 1926 the NCSS rural committee was represented on it; and in order to help the new organisation the National Council initially gave it free office accommodation.

In the same year the BBC consulted the National Council on a subject of growing importance: the broadcasting of charitable appeals. At the suggestion of the Council an expert committee was set up under the chairmanship of R. C. Norman to advise on this new development.

After the quiet period of preparation 1927 was to prove a memorable year. It began with an outstanding event which in time brought a chain of consequences destined to influence the course of the Council's work, and to lead temporarily to some diversion from its original broad aims and purposes through concentration on one specific type of activity. Towards the end of the year, His Royal Highness the Prince of Wales (later Edward VIII) expressed his willingness to become patron of the NCSS. In the event, this was to be no mere formal title to grace the headed notepaper in the traditional manner, but was to symbolise a close and active personal relationship to the Council's work, founded on a genuine interest in what was being done.

At about the same time the Council learned that Stapley House, which had been its headquarters since 1921, was to be demolished, and a move became inevitable. More suitable premises, which the NCSS would be able to call its own, were available nearby at 26/27 Bedford Square; but some £12,000 was needed to cover the cost of the lease and the necessary adaptations. A fund was set up for this purpose; and prominent among those concerned with raising this large sum was the Rt Hon. J. H. Whitley, MP, Speaker of the House of Commons, who had been President of the NCSS since 1921. This long association with the man who represented the whole House and all the political parties had been a particularly happy one

The Bedford Square offices

and of great value to the National Council. Although in June 1928, he was compelled by ill-health to resign as Speaker, he was able first to see the fulfilment of his work for the NCSS. At the end of May 1928, he opened the new headquarters in Bedford Square. A distinguished company gathered for the occasion; and amongst many messages of goodwill, Mr Speaker Whitley read this letter from the Prince of Wales:

St. James's Palace
sw1.
May 28th 1928

Dear Mr Speaker,

I am keenly interested in the work of the National Council of Social Service, and sincerely hope that the new headquarters which you are opening will help that work forward. We in this country have good reason to be proud of the spirit of service which leads so many men and women to join in the work of voluntary societies or public authorities, and I am sure that they can help each other in many ways by working in close co-operation. Councils of social service in towns and rural community councils in counties and villages are already proving the value of such team-work in social service. It is work in which all can help and it needs to be very greatly extended; in promoting health, education and recreation and in the personal service of those who are in trouble there are endless possibilities for every man and woman who will lend a hand.

The fact that there are already community councils in some parts of India leads me to hope that the movement to develop team work in social service may spread to other parts of the Empire. For I believe that the team spirit is just as important in social service as it is in games or business—in national, Empire or International affairs. Above everything else just now we want to learn to pull together and I sincerely hope that in the new home the National Council will be given widespread support in the work that it is doing.

Yours sincerely
Edward P.

Later, in continuation of the tradition set by the two previous Speakers of the House of Commons, the new Speaker, Captain the Rt Hon. E. A. Fitzroy, MP, was elected President of the NCSS.

With new headquarters of its own and its financial house in order; with the goodwill of an increasing number of individuals in all walks of life; and with the support of public authorities and of government departments, the National Council could indeed look with confidence to the future. A new chapter in its history was ready to begin; but there were few present on that June day who could have foreseen the turn which events were to take.

CHAPTER FOUR

'Out of Adversity'

IT was well for the NCSS that its foundations had been soundly laid, for the second decade of its life was to bring unprecedented problems and strains. In the winter of 1928 distress in the coalfields became acute, and distress funds began to multiply. The Mansion House Fund was re-opened with promise of government assistance. Towns and villages in the still comparatively prosperous home counties sought to adopt the worst affected towns in the North and in the mining valleys of Wales.

But all this good work was handicapped by the lack of a central body to co-ordinate the new spate of generosity; and to circumvent overlapping and confusion the National Council called the principal agencies together. Seventeen of them in conference recommended to the Lord Mayor that local representational committees should be set up in the coalfields to co-ordinate the distribution of relief, with similar committees in the adopting areas to stimulate the collection of money and goods, and a central committee to plan and advise, particularly about adoption schemes.

This machinery was quickly set up and worked surprisingly well. Some 5,000 volunteers manned 500 local committees and nearly £1,000,000 was distributed. But those who really understood what was happening in the coalfields recognised that the best-run charitable funds could not solve the basic economic problem, or do more than alleviate the material distress of the men thrown out of work.

In the belief that many men would never find work again in the pits, plans were put on foot to transfer some miners and their families to new work in other areas and even overseas. Other students of the situation tried to discover the root economic causes of the disaster in the coalfields and elsewhere. At Brynmawr, under the leadership of a settlement established by the Society of Friends, an industrial survey was being carried out. In Tyneside, where industry was at a standstill, a council of social service was formed as the result of the remarkable social survey carried out by Dr Henry Mess, which showed that the best hope for the area lay in creative co-operative action of all its towns together.

For those who must stay in the derelict villages and depressed towns something at least could be done to relieve the monotony of their days. Standards of living were vital; standards of life were not less so. The chance to hear and to make music; to read and study; to attend lecture courses, would provide some outlet. With a grant of £5,000 from the Carnegie UK Trustees concerts were arranged in the Miners' Institutes of the Welsh valleys and in the halls of bleak northern towns, and thousands of people attended them. In one month 19,000 came to hear the Cymric Oriana Choir, the Mountain Ash Girls' Choir, the Cardiff and Bangor Trios, and other choral and orchestral societies. In the Rhondda Valley where no public library service existed, the miners' institutes' libraries were stocked with new books. In districts where no university extension course had ever been held before, twelve courses ranging from the study of the Hebrew prophets to international relations were arranged and qualified for Board of Education grant. In South Wales these schemes were not to be a mere emergency measure, but through the continuing work of the University College, the Workers' Educational Association, the National Council of Music, and the YMCA, were to lead to permanent achievement.

Another movement, which was to enhance the health and happiness of young people from that time until today, and obviously far beyond, was helped forward by the NCSS early in 1930. Throughout the winter of 1929/30 vigorous groups had been meeting in various parts of the country to discuss their plans for establishing holiday hostels for young walkers and cyclists. As it was clear that a national body would be needed, they asked the National Council to convene a conference of all the interested organisations. They met under the chairmanship of R. C. Norman, and made such good progress that Captain Ellis was afterwards able to send to the bodies concerned a draft constitution and enquiries about setting up an establishment fund to enable the new movement to start work at once. The interest was so great and the contributions so generous, coming from the Co-operative Holiday Association, the Holiday Fellowship, the Cyclists' Touring Club, and the Workers' Travel Association that, at a further meeting in the offices of the NCSS, a unanimous decision was taken to form a national association to promote youth hostels in Great Britain. In this way the Youth Hostels Association* was born, and began work immediately as a fully independent national organisation.

---

* The full history of the YHA has been told in *Youth Hostel Story* by Oliver Coburn. NCSS.

In this period of industrial and social crisis, with new problems and opportunities for the National Council, it was more than ever necessary to know what the local councils of social service were doing and could do, and more difficult than ever, with no possibility of providing field officers and advisory staff. For some time the advisory committee on urban work had been concerned about this lack of knowledge; and in December 1929, it was decided that Sir Wyndham Deedes, now an assistant secretary to the NCSS, whose distinguished leadership in this work was well recognised, should tour the country, visiting as many as possible of the councils at work in nearly sixty cities and towns. In the next six months Sir Wyndham carried out an impressive survey of the field, visiting twenty-five of these councils. He spoke at their meetings, watched them at work, and discussed their problems and programmes not only with their secretaries and leading personalities but with local government officials and town councillors.

This was the first attempt to obtain a comprehensive picture of the work of urban councils and to assess the progress made. Sir Wyndham's report, informed with his wide experience and keen insight, gave a shrewd though kindly judgment, and not such as to induce complacency. He recorded his admiration for the devotion and industry of those engaged, often with very slender resources, in this public service; but regretted that their work was so often based on inadequate information about the social and economic life of their towns. Moreover he found that they failed to generalise from such information as they had, and concentrated too exclusively on personal service for individuals whilst ignoring the conditions which had caused their difficulties. To counteract this tendency he recommended that locally, and centrally at the NCSS, research or intelligence departments should be set up. The local councils had the opportunity of continually discovering facts about the everyday lives of the people which were much more significant than statistics or general theories. An intelligence office could use this evidence and become a laboratory for training the young social workers who were urgently needed. Sir Wyndham had noted with concern that at one meeting he addressed on 'The City of Tomorrow' there was not one person in the audience under forty-five.

The survey found that co-operation between voluntary and statutory bodies was occasionally excellent but not nearly so general as had been hoped. It was particularly poor in towns with a Labour council. Their members were strongly opposed to home visiting by voluntary workers on the grounds that they were untrained and that, for every voluntary worker, one paid worker the less was needed—a view easily to be understood when unemployment was widespread. Only in a very few places had public assistance committees co-opted voluntary workers, in spite of the earnest official recommendation of the Inter-departmental Committee of 1923. Nor was the co-operation with the churches as close as Sir Wyndham had hoped. He found that the churches tended to do their own parish work in isolation, and the establishment of Christian Social Councils was rare and difficult. Of charitable and relief societies he records: 'Their number is great, is getting greater, and should surely be diminished. The amount of time, money, and energy which is expended by each separate society must be quite out of proportion to the results achieved.'

The opinions on local councils expressed by the many people of all classes whom he met on this tour varied widely. Some saw in the councils of social service a 'bulwark against the Reds'. Others regarded their charity as demoralising, or as 'quenching the flame of divine discontent in the workers which it is the task of their leaders to fan . . . bridging the gulf between rich and poor, it weakens the solidarity of class consciousness'. In Sir Wyndham's judgment it was clear that, until social service 'proved itself to be a constructive force in society, it is not likely to enlist the sympathy of the leaders of the masses'. This was to become a crucial argument in the new work for the unemployed which the National Council was soon to develop—a task so large and urgent that for some years it ruled out the possibility of taking up the many issues raised by Sir Wyndham's report.

Sir Wyndham did not limit his visits to the offices of councils of social service. He went also to the new housing estates growing up on the outskirts of towns, where some significant developments were happening. For the past six years, while these new estates had been developing fast on the suburban fringe, the NCSS had been observing them and their growing problems. Some of the estates were of immense size. Slums were being cleared and whole populations transferred to the new places; 100,000 people were moved to Becontree and Dagenham alone. The houses were good and the conditions open and healthy; but they were huge, one-class dormitory areas, not new towns, and they lacked all the essential features of a town—industry, shops, transport, schools, places of entertainment and worship. Lying beyond the city boundaries they had lost their sense of 'belonging' and yet were incapable of building up any significant civic or social life of their own, as they had neither places in which to meet nor natural leaders to help them. The new settlers felt themselves to be isolated in a foreign land, far from friends and neighbours and the familiar life of streets and markets in their old homes. Wives were lonely; children ran wild; men came back in the evenings exhausted from long journeys to work.

As far back as 1925 the National Council, with its concern for the quality of life in towns and country, had begun to see that there were even more problems to be considered on new housing estates with no provision for normal social life or leisure time. An attempt was made in that year to convene a conference on the subject but the needs were not then widely recognised and nothing came of it. But as the years went by and the great estates were completed, evidence of the problems piled up in the NCSS offices; and evidence also of the efforts which people were making here and there on the new estates to help themselves. Small groups were coming together, meeting in each others' homes or in dilapidated builders' huts, trying to make some sort of social life for themselves and their neighbours. They planned socials and whist drives and flower shows, for entertainment or to help in getting friends together to build for themselves a community hall or centre. Some groups called themselves 'tenants' associations' and campaigned for buses, shops, post offices, and other essentials which the estates often lacked.

The NCSS, watching these developments, realised their potentialities and their need for help and encouragement. In 1928 a conference between the National Council, the Educational Settlements Association, and the British Association of Residential Settlements resulted in the setting up of a joint New Estates Community Committee. As for so many similar ventures, the NCSS provided the secretariat. Prominent among those who advised and helped were Professor J. L. Stocks who had himself gone to live on one of the new Manchester estates, and Professor Ernest Barker (later Sir Ernest) who became chairman of the new committee.

In this new enterprise of creating living communities where community life seemed almost extinct the NCSS played its traditional role as co-ordinator of other movements; and out of this synthesis of movements something greater than the sum total of the constituent parts was destined to emerge. The educational settlements brought their conception of broad, popular education; the residential settlements their tradition of neighbourhood service; the National Council its own unique experience of village halls and social councils. The problem was in some ways the same as in the village: the need to provide a common hall or centre for both social and educational purposes for young and old, and to devise some form of council to run it, representative of the neighbourhood. The term 'community centre' appears to have been borrowed from the educational settlements who were the first to use it. The idea that it should be run and managed by a combined council drawn from both the individual members who used the centre as a club and the various neighbourhood groups without accommodation of their own, which shared the premises, was an entirely new idea. The tenants' associations then beginning to form brought their own special contribution in the shape of a close knowledge of particular needs of the estates and their direct experience of meeting those needs. Out of this synthesis the community *association* was born: 'a democratic fellowship of individuals and organisations bound together by one common purpose, the common good'.

The new estates were not rural and there was no Development Commission to provide funds for community centres as the urban equivalent of village halls. So the Carnegie UK Trustees were asked for help and they, in accordance with their established policy of aiding the initial stages of a social experiment, made a grant of £10,000 in 1930 to provide salaries for seven or eight field workers for two or three years of pioneering. Later they agreed to make a further grant of £3,500 to encourage the erection of five community centres; but it is important to emphasise that the first grant was made for workers to foster community *associations* rather than for buildings—an order of priorities which the National Council has advocated consistently from that time onwards.

Here again, in this new field of community enterprise, the value of the NCSS as a 'clearing house of ideas' was demonstrated. In 1930 residents from nine different estates, not yet calling themselves community associations, were brought together in conference; and the interchange between them, allied to the experience of the National Council in parallel fields, proved extremely useful and led to the emergence of similar groups on other estates and a much clearer conception of what their purpose and function could be. But it led to no stereotyped pattern. Each association grew in its own way to meet the needs of its neighbourhood. At Watling, one of the LCC estates, the tenants managed to raise £500; and with the aid of a £2,700 grant and loan from the Pilgrim Trust, the first community centre was erected. The Watling Association, inspired by its secretary, Edward Sewell Harris, played a notable part in a campaign to improve the estate, thus demonstrating the value of a community association in reviving an active democracy in these new urban settlements.

Housing authorities had statutory powers to assist these experiments, but they were only permissive and rarely used, a notable exception being the founding of the Manor Settlements by the Sheffield Corporation in 1932. Although there were signs of life and activity on some of the new municipal estates, many efforts were frustrated by the lack of premises or leadership, or the means of financing them; and throughout the early years of the new movement progress continued to be slow. The pioneer field workers appointed by the NCSS with the help of the Carnegie UK Trust travelled the country visiting the new estates and sometimes living on them, advising and encouraging the often despondent tenant groups still meeting in houses or tin shacks; but with the industrial depression deepening month by month the outlook for a new movement was not very hopeful, despite the good beginnings.

The rural work of the NCSS was suffering no less than the urban from the economic conditions of the time. By 1931 twenty-three rural community councils had been formed; but the period of subsidies from the Carnegie UK Trust was near its end, and as the grant diminished the crisis increased. All the RCCs were in difficulties, but in four of them—Dorset, Hampshire, West Sussex, and Hertfordshire—which had no grants from their local authorities, the position soon became desperate. The NCSS spent much time and effort in trying to interest these local authorities and to secure sufficient voluntary income to enable the RCCs to survive. The Carnegie Trustees were persuaded to continue help for a time; but when it became clear that nothing could be done to save them permanently it was decided to let them go.

The effect on the rest of the movement was depressing. At the Rural Life Conference in Oxford in 1933 gloomy views were expressed, with considerable criticism of the National Council. There was even a move to establish a separate organisation for rural community councils at the national level. This proposal was not accepted as it was obvious that there was no possibility of financing another national headquarters and no means of securing experienced staff. In any event the more thoughtful delegates saw that the affinity of interest between the community councils and the National Council made separation most unwise.

The conference broke up in a mood of disappointment; and at headquarters it was felt that everything possible must be done to build up morale. The Development Commissioners were asked to make general administrative grants to replace the terminated grants from the Carnegie Trustees; and while an answer was awaited, a campaign was started to broaden the financial and constitutional basis of the rural community councils. Since many village hall committees had been greatly helped by services which the NCSS had provided, efforts were made to bring them into active partnership with the RCCs, but these efforts met with only partial success. Attempts were made to broaden the basis of RCC work in the hope that they might win increased financial support by having a more varied programme of activities. Three groups were started in London— public health, local history, and parish councils—to encourage rural community councils to take up these subjects. The Kent CSS had done useful pioneer work in public health, particularly in TB aftercare; and it was hoped that other counties, stimulated by the new central group, might follow this example and so increase their chances of winning the interest and support of their local authorities by including services for which the county council rather than the education committee was responsible. Here again the response was not very encouraging. But the local history group under the chairmanship of Sir Allen Mawer met with some success and several counties took up the idea.

The parish council work, later to prove one of the most outstanding ventures undertaken by the NCSS, started under grave difficulties. An earlier attempt to form a parish councils' association had already failed. The National Council was told that it was wasting its time in trying to prop up a form of local government which was already doomed and which in Scotland had been finally abandoned. But Donald Hall, then field officer of the rural department, believed in the idea and was not to be discouraged. He produced the first Parish Councils booklet and a series of pamphlets. A committee under the chairmanship of Sir Lawrence Chubb was formed and an advisory service of parish councils was started. It may well be that this decision was a vital turning point in the long history of this ancient English institution of local government and that, but for the intervention of the NCSS, the parish council might have disappeared in England as it had done in Scotland with far-reaching consequences for the cause of democracy.

With the withdrawal of substantial Carnegie UK Trust support and the collapse of RCCs in four counties, consolidation rather than expansion was the order of the day. Nevertheless, experiments were made in a few selected counties to find out whether councils could be established with limited programmes concerned only with village halls, rural industries, and music and drama, and requiring only a small staff. The experiments only proved the impracticability of trying to start a rural community council on a part-time voluntary basis, and demonstrated the fact that a county co-ordinating body must be at least as efficient as the bodies whose activities it seeks to co-ordinate.

Faced with the difficulty of forming new RCCs, the National Council had to devise ways of bringing its services by other means to non-RCC counties. Among these plans was an affiliation scheme to give every village hall a contact with national headquarters and an advisory service. But this and other services threw heavy additional burdens on the central department and the travelling staff of the NCSS at a time when they were increasingly preoccupied with problems of finance. All sort of means were sought for raising money. Among the more popular were county fairs; and, though the financial results were rarely commensurate with the work and worry involved, these fairs at least had considerable value of another kind.

By bringing together in one place all the societies at work in the county they could help people to begin to see and understand just what the RCCs were trying to do.

From the difficulties of the early 1930s many valuable lessons were learned. First, that financial stability could only come from a wise 'spreading of the risk', with approximately one-third of the income from central government sources, one-third from local government, and the remainder from voluntary sources including subscriptions, money-raising events, and payment for services rendered. Secondly, that a rural community council could not survive long without local authority backing; for the recognition of the county council was essential to give the community council status, even more than some financial security. Moreover, it was obviously easier to ask a local authority to make an increased grant for an RCC it was already aiding than to beg a grant for the first time to save an organisation in danger of collapse.

Perhaps the most surprising thing is that despite these grave financial problems, the rural work continued not only to hold its own but in some respects even to gain ground. In villages, as elsewhere, it seems as if one result of the crisis was to quicken the spirit of self-help, and the raising of local funds for building halls was in many cases pushed forward in spite of greater difficulties. During the severe crisis of 1931 the National Council decided to forego its grant from the Development Commission, but the loss was made good by the generosity of the Carnegie UK Trustees who agreed to allocate £20,000 as a reserve to the Loan Fund provided by the Treasury and to increase the allocation to their Fund for grants.

One of the main hindrances to the development of the rural work was the amount of time and resources that the National Council was devoting to work with the unemployed, which by this time was growing to immense proportions. The beginning of this work lay in the educational experiments carried out in South Wales, Durham, and Northumberland in 1929, and in the work of the Coalfields Distress Fund. Even before that time two interesting developments had taken place which had a great influence on the work of the National Council in this field. In 1927 a small group of the Society of Friends under the chairmanship of Dr A. D. Lindsay, Master of Balliol (later Lord Lindsay) founded an educational settlement at Maes-yr-haf in the Rhondda where unemployment was already severe. In the same year the Workers' Educational Association set up the People's Service Club and Workshop in Lincoln.

At first the influence of these projects did not reach far beyond their own locality; and in other parts of the country little was being done to help the unemployed because it was thought that the crisis would soon be over. But by September 1931, the number of insured persons on the unemployment register had reached a total of 2,804,000. One in every six families had lost their livelihood; and numberless others lived under the same threat. The situation seemed beyond control; and the whole country was bewildered by the spectacle of 'able-bodied men and women standing like dumb, driven cattle in the market place, willing to work but forced by circumstances beyond their control to remain idle'. In the still prosperous areas most people did not fully realise what was happening elsewhere. Those who knew the facts and wished to help did not know what to do, for nothing like this had happened before. There was much misunderstanding of the true nature of the problem and much misplaced enthusiasm. Some people thought only in terms of soup kitchens and the relief of material distress, not realising that the depressing monotony of empty, workless days could be more damaging to the mind and spirit than to the body. Others saw in the situation the complete breakdown of the capitalist economy and thought that voluntary help for the unemployed would only prop up a decaying system when what was really required was a change in the whole social and economic structure.

Here was a challenge and an opportunity which the National Council felt bound to take up. For some time already they had been giving earnest thought to the huge and complex problem. If the NCSS were to be responsible for evolving a policy to help in meeting it, evidently a cautious middle course must be set between soup kitchen and revolution. They themselves were convinced that the only radical cure for unemployment was employment. But that was a matter for the government and industry and could not be divorced from political action in which the National Council as a broadly representative body could not join. In any event, such action could only be effective over a long period. In the meantime it was essential to do something for the unemployed.

Equally the NCSS were convinced that, in this meantime, the unemployed needed and deserved something more than the bare minimum of material necessities which the dole provided. They needed friendship, a place in the community, the sense of being wanted—things which money could not buy. Moreover, whatever was done should be designed also to prevent the unemployed from becoming unemployable. The Council had not yet been able to work our the practical measures that should be taken, but here were useful principles by which any projects might be tested.

It was seen that the first essential was to bring home to the whole country the real nature of the catastrophe. So the National Council convened a great meeting for the 27th January, 1932, in the Albert Hall. The Prince of Wales, Patron of the Council, who shared a deep personal concern for the plight of the workless, agreed to address the meeting. Simultaneously other meetings were arranged in towns and cities throughout the country.

THE CLARION CALL
'When duty whispers low "Thou must",
The Youth replies "I can"—Emerson's 'Voluntaries'
Punch, February 3rd 1932

In a simple but moving speech the Prince spoke about some of the hopeful schemes emerging in various towns, and called upon the whole country to accept the challenge of unemployment as a national opportunity for voluntary social service; to undertake such service in the spirit of the good neighbour and, refusing to be paralysed by the size of the problem, to 'break it up into little pieces'.

The response to the Prince's appeal was immediate and overwhelming. Offers of help began to pour in and a special department had to be set up to deal with them. From all parts of the country came reports of initiative by individuals, voluntary service organisations, councils of social service, and special committees. By the autumn the National Council was in touch with seven hundred schemes. They were of great variety, and not all were well-conceived or managed. Many were hampered by having to function in derelict buildings or premises which they could use for only a few hours each week. Some were mismanaged through sheer inexperience. In other places it was thought that the crisis would soon be over and that meanwhile the unemployed only needed to be entertained with games, lectures, and concerts. There were fears too on the part of some of the established case-work agencies that this new movement might lead to a return to the discredited tradition of soup kitchens and indiscriminate charity. Even more serious for National Council policy was an undercurrent of criticism which could be detected among some of the agencies represented on the Council that this action was a grave departure from the original concept of the NCSS as a purely co-ordinating body not itself engaging in executive work. There was a real risk that some of the organisations associated with the National Council would now regard it as a rival concern competing with them for support and finance from the public. There could, however, be no turning back now. The work would go forward, with or without the critics; but the doubts and questioning remained.

In spite of these, and of occasional failures, the movement spread quickly because it was touching an urgent need. The sound and promising enterprises—clubs like those founded in South Wales by the Maes-yr-haf Settlement—grew and prospered. From many parts of the country came reports of interesting experiments, some helped by the Pilgrim Trust and others relying solely on local funds. It was now becoming clear that some central agency was needed to pool all this experience, to guide and advise those who were starting schemes, and to co-ordinate what promised to be a profusion of voluntary activity.

In November 1932, the Ministry of Labour invited the NCSS to act as a central advisory body for the movement throughout the country. It was understood that Ministry of Labour grants would be available but that the National Council would preserve its freedom of action as a voluntary body. The announcement of this grant provoked a storm of criticism from left-wing opinion which saw in it a sinister attempt to buy off the unemployed cheaply; and on the other hand from those who saw in it the end of the Council's independence. The situation called for statesmanlike action; and the NCSS rose to it by setting up a special unemployment committee representing a balance of interests, under the chairmanship of the Master of Balliol, with Sir Edward Peacock as vice-chairman.

By the following year some 2,300 centres had been opened, catering at the peak for about a quarter of a million men and women. No brief survey can do justice to the lively variety of pattern and activity which they displayed, but there were certain characteristic trends. All owed their existence to local initiative. This was never a movement dominated and run from the centre. Some wealthy people had started from the understandable desire 'to do something for the unemployed'; but before long the best of them found themselves doing things 'with the unemployed'. The centres were a partnership between the unemployed and the men and women of goodwill who are to be found in every community; and in some places the greater part of the initiative came from the unemployed themselves.

A good example of this kind was the club at Garth, Glamorganshire, where in the winter of 1934 a group of unemployed men in the reading room of a local hall heard a broadcast talk about clubs by an NCSS speaker. This, they felt, was exactly what they wanted. They had no experience of running a club, so they listened regularly to a series of broadcasts on the subject. Guided by these unseen helpers, the Garth Club began in a local mission hall. As each new suggestion came over the air, the men put it into practice. They cobbled shoes for their children; they made furniture for their homes; they drew up their own educational programme and organised their own activities, with some additional help and advice from the South Wales Council of Social Service. The club was entirely self-governing. Their choir became famous. They broadcast a feature programme on the club's many-sided activities. Soon they outgrew their premises; and the National Council made a grant to enable them to build a new hut. Bricks from the dismantled colliery on which Garth had once depended were used for the foundations so that out of the ruins of the past they built something towards the future, in more senses than one.

At Nantynoel unemployed men and boys were so enthusiastic that they worked on by lamplight and by moonlight to level a part of a mountainside to make a playing field for their community. On Tyneside the Hexham

Social Service Club began when a football team of unemployed lads took up Scouting and built themselves a Rover Den. Their friends joined them in a wider scheme. A derelict site was rented from the urban district council and with grants from the NCSS other huts were erected to form a community centre for both the unemployed and men in work, with workshops, kitchen, gymnasium, and showers. Further ground was rented for poultry and allotment schemes which were run co-operatively; gardens were laid out and a bowling green turfed. Again on Tyneside, a group converted an old ship's lifeboat into a fishing boat to augment their food supplies.

In the best of these schemes self-help broadened out into service to the whole community, following the remarkable lead of the People's Service Club at Lincoln which over a period of years helped to furnish nine children's homes and nurseries with toys and equipment, mended clothes, repaired boots, and supplied equipment for the local infirmary. At Brynmawr, typical of a number of schemes in South Wales, the unemployed gave their labour in a co-operative job of converting a rubbish heap into a recreation ground, children's paddling pool, and swimming bath. No scheme of help for men, who had been thrown on the scrap heap of industry as no longer wanted, could be as satisfying to them as this kind of chance and encouragement to use their unhired skill to bring some relief and happiness to others.

There were of course few clubs which reached these standards, and some distressing failures, particularly in some of the large cities where the lack of community tradition prevented the clubs from growing beyond the 'occupational centre' stage. These tended to have a large floating membership, the men leaving whenever they got work. As those with the most initiative were the first to find employment the problem of leadership was serious. Despite the active co-operation of local education authorities, YMCA, WEA, the settlements, the women's institutes, and the Rural Industries Bureau there were never enough instructors and teachers to go round. In order to help to provide leadership and to encourage the clubs to develop on democratic lines the NCSS set up in 1933, at King's Standing in Staffordshire, a residential demonstration centre for men who were playing a leading part in running their clubs. The house was the property of the Duchy of Lancaster, and was placed freely at the disposal of the Council 'at the King's pleasure'. To it came groups of unemployed men, fifty at a time, for courses ranging from three to six weeks, to receive expert advice and instruction in club management and the conduct of activities. The warden, W. H. Durst, was a distinguished artist and craftsman, and his staff of qualified instructors were able to train the men in woodwork, cobbling, weaving, metal work, upholstery, music and drama, so that they could in turn teach others in their own clubs. In the first two years nearly 1,000 men and women passed through King's Standing. Their contribution to the leadership of the movement was incalculable. Similar centres at Wincham Hall and Hardwick Hall were set up by bodies working in association with the NCSS and with the help of grants made to them by the Council. At Coleg Harlech unemployed men attending courses in craftwork and physical training also took some part in the normal educational courses, including economics, literature, philosophy, and music.

The plight of the women in the workless areas was in many ways as distressing as the men's, whether they were themselves unemployed workers or the wives of unemployed men. Their lives were a struggle to hold home and family together on the meagre allowance of the dole: a ceaseless routine of contriving cheap meals, patching clothes, counting the pennies, and watching their men come back day after day from the hopeless quest for work. After the coal strike in 1926 the Society of Friends had started sewing groups among the wives of miners in the Rhondda

King's Standing Demonstration Centre

Valley; and similar groups were formed in Lancashire where unemployment among women workers was high. These groups had grown and spread into a women's club movement which by the early thirties had established itself in many other parts of the country. Like the men's centres, these clubs gave their members not only material benefits—the opportunity to make things needed for the home, expert advice on budgeting and cooking, cheap materials and the use of sewing machines for making clothes—but above all the warmth of companionship for women whose poverty segregated them in loneliness; the bliss of doing nothing for a little while; or, for some, the chance to find new worlds through music and singing, drama and play-reading.. Some of the men's clubs too had recognised how heavily the burdens of unemployment fell on the wives and offered them membership, usually in special women's sections; and a training centre for leaders in women's clubs and women's sections was set up at 'The Beeches', just outside Birmingham, to give them much the same kind of help and encouragement as the men found at King's Standing. Here hundreds of women attended short courses in cookery, hygiene, child welfare, and nursing, in addition to a wide range of crafts and recreational activities including play-reading, community singing, and country dancing. But all this work for the women's side of the problem was hampered and stunted by lack of funds, because the Ministry of Labour maintained that unemployed men's wives were not unemployed and could not benefit by Ministry grant.

At a time when the whole national economy seemed to be grinding to a halt, with one in six of the insured population out of work, with long queues at the labour exchanges and the factory gates but none at the shops, it was essential to try to convince the trade unions and the Labour movemen that all this voluntary enterprise would not endanger the cause of the workers. In Scotland the unemployment committee with such stalwart trade unionists to back it as the chairman, Baillie Elgar, and Eleanor Stewart, had the full co-operation of the Scottish TUC. Elsewhere there were some difficulties. The NCSS therefore emphasised that no attempt was being made to train unskilled workers for skilled jobs and that jobs of community service, whether concerned with repairing children's shoes or creating playgrounds or club rooms, would not have been done at all but for the self-help of the unemployed. Despite these explanations, however, misunderstandings did occur. The National Council, with Royal patronage, the help of a company of distinguished men, increasing subscriptions from some of the big industrialists, and now grants from the Ministry of Labour, was an obvious target for a sustained barrage of criticism from the extreme Left, the Communist Party, and the National

Unemployed Workers' Movement. 'Work and wages, not lectures, classes, and camp holidays from charity', was the burden of their complaint. This criticism* of a local scheme from a left-wing writer illustrates the point: 'Comment is superfluous. Here is "fellowship and sacrifice" run riot. Every organisation, whether religious or civic, is offering its quota of service to the pool of economic bankruptcy. Here in the middle of a prosperous tourist seaside resort—a complex mechanism—we have a twentieth century "Swiss Community Robinson"—a negationary economics, a revel of romanticism (for pewter and handicrafts flourish here), a paradise of philanthropy. In January 1934 there were over two thousand of this type of centre all over England, and since then they have increased considerably. Beginning in many cases as emergency measures to meet the local problem of unemployment, they have lately become in many people's minds the substitute for any genuine political attempt to abolish unemployment.'

This tension of ideas ran right through the work. It made the unemployed often suspicious and wary of new schemes. It worried the trade unions, guarding the rights of their members still in work, yet anxious to help their comrades who had fallen on hard times. It was present in the National Council itself with its wide range of member organisations, and of individuals as varied in their opinions as social reformers and very Conservative peers. Between these extremes a careful middle course had to be steered; and it says much for the wisdom and tolerance of the unemployment committee of the National Council that the course, though uncharted, was fairly consistently and safely followed.

Despite misunderstandings and opposition the work increased in strength and stability as the occupational centres gradually tended to become social service or community service clubs. Beginning in old houses, stables, a disused railway station, many of them managed to build their own huts with grants and help from the NCSS and other bodies; and they devised wide-ranging programmes: craftwork, physical training, music, drama, debating, radio listening, general education, gardening.

The actual running of the clubs was always left to local initiative. But the unemployed, without money, without resources, and at first without premises could never have helped themselves in the way they did without the assistance which the NCSS was able to bring to them; and it was the National Council that carried the immense burden of creating the nationwide system of co-operation by which the combined resources of government, local authorities, voluntary organisations, educational bodies, and

* *Totem* by Harold Stovin. Methuen.

the creative goodwill of countless citizens were focussed on this cruel problem. Government grants had to be obtained and supplemented by the raising of voluntary funds, then apportioned to the areas of greatest need. Leaders must be found and a training centre established. Building schemes had to be visited and approved; and a national network of services set up to advise on the wide-ranging activities of the clubs. There were contacts to be maintained with a hundred different organisations which could help the work forward. Broadcasts were arranged through the BBC to aid the clubs. A series of twelve broadcasts, 'Question Time for the Unemployed', by Richard Clements, then chief advisory officer for the Midland area of the NCSS, brought in 7,000 problems which were all answered by personal letters. Thousands of pamphlets and leaflets on many aspects of the work were produced, both to help the clubs and to inform the public.

The business of informing the public was made very much easier by the unstinting help of the Prince of Wales, who followed up his Albert Hall speech by two anniversary broadcasts and by tours of Tyneside, the Midlands, Lancashire, Yorkshire, Scotland, and Wales. During these tours he visited several hundred of the clubs and schemes for the unemployed, refusing to be deterred from going to the most sordid surroundings and the poorest homes. It would seem that at this time the Prince knew more than some of his Ministers about the problems of the derelict valleys and the silent mills. Nor were the endless ceremonies, openings, and presentations accomplished without personal cost in nervous strain and sheer fatigue. One one occasion, worn out with day-long travelling in Wales and the pain of helpless sympathy, the Prince slept exhausted on the shoulder of Sir Percy Watkins, chief NCSS officer for Wales, waking dutifully each time Sir Percy warned him that the car was approaching groups of children waiting to see their Prince.

As the complex network of services spread it became obvious that the work could not be efficiently administered solely from London. So nineteen regional organisations were set up with help and support from the NCSS to cover all the major industrial areas. Area offices in Leeds for the North and Birmingham for the Midlands were established, and a Welsh department set up in Cardiff. Meanwhile in London important changes had also been taking place. Captain Fitzroy, Speaker of the House of Commons, had no alternative but to resign as President of the National Council now that it was in receipt of government grants which might have been the subject of debate in the House. This resignation broke the long tradition that the Speaker of the House of Commons should be President of the NCSS, and it was deeply regretted. His place was taken by

Prince of Wales with unemployed men (*top*)
A Lancashire women's club (*bottom*)

the Rt Hon. J. H. Whitley, who returned from retirement to continue the work he had laid down in 1928. A further loss to the Council at this time was the death of Sir Charles Stewart who had worked hard and faithfully as treasurer from the founding of the NCSS till the day he died.

Now also it became clear that the old machinery of the National Council could no longer cope with the strain of the great new burdens placed upon it. So a new and larger executive committee of thirty members was elected, charged with the duty of advising on the constitutional changes which were likely to become necessary. One of the heaviest responsibilities of the NCSS was that of administering grant-aid on a large scale to other organisations. The Ministry of Labour unemployment grant amounted to nearly £80,000 in two years. The Development Commission and the Carnegie UK Trust made substantial grants for village halls; and from the Carnegie UK Trustees there came also grants to rural community councils and community associations, as well as funds for promoting music and drama in the countryside. From the Pilgrim Trust there were grants for camps for boys and girls, and for training in voluntary social service. Another large grant was made by the Trustees of the London Parochial Charities towards the unemployment work. The Charities Account of the NCSS, established in 1924, showed nine years later that the sum of £218,000 had been distributed to other organisations in 1933. An adoption scheme through which comparatively prosperous towns in the South were linked up with hard hit towns involved the handling of other considerable funds. Civil Service staffs alone contributed nearly £10,000 in one year to adopted towns and villages in the distressed areas.

Because of the large sums made available to the NCSS by the Ministry of Labour, it was sometimes questioned whether this was indeed a purely voluntary movement. In reply the National Council pointed out that, although the Ministry grants between January 1933 and March 1935 amounted to £79,415, the total voluntary income raised direct by the clubs, by regional and national bodies, and by the NCSS, exceeded £100,000. Within this total would be found such diverse items as the £15,000 collected in pence from the members' subscriptions to the unemployed clubs; the £2,533 raised by the 'Cathedral Pilgrimage', and the wedding gift of £1,532 presented by the Rotary Clubs to their patron, the Duke of Kent.

The task of the National Council was to administer these very considerable and disparate sums, grant-aiding local schemes and regional and national bodies who were contributing to the welfare of the unemployed. It was a revolutionary idea that a voluntary body should act in this way; but despite the obvious difficulties it was done with such integrity and efficiency* that when the Government decided in 1934 to use unorthodox methods to assist the social development of distressed areas (the Special Areas as they were designated) in which long-term unemployment had brought a catastrophic decline in prosperity, it asked the National Council to accept still heavier responsibilities. The weight of these responsibilities can be partly judged from the extent of the grants to be administered. In the year 1936-37 the grant from the Special Areas Fund amounted to £227,575; while the Ministry of Labour grant had by this time risen to £105,000.

The grants from the Commissioner for the Special Areas made many valuable social experiments possible, and re-invigorated many existing projects which had been hampered by lack of funds. In the first year, for instance, £87,000 of the Special Areas grant was spent on equipping and maintaining seventeen camps for schoolchildren, which gave nearly 20,000 boys and girls from homes overshadowed by unemployment and poverty an unforgettable break in their dreary lives. It was a fair example of the kind of team-work characteristic of the National Council's enterprises, for the Commissioners, the NCSS, the YMCA, and other voluntary organisations, together with the education authorities and the teachers, joined forces to make it a success; and by the time the war came and interrupted the service some 150,000 children had benefitted by these camps. Not only did the children gain in health and happiness but the authorities learnt most useful lessons from the project, later to be incorporated in the Camps Act of 1939 and to influence the post-war development of open-air schools.

Grants from the Special Areas Fund were of particular significance for the work of the voluntary youth organisations, so greatly needed in the distressed areas. The poverty of these regions and the drain on leadership as the younger and more resourceful members of the community made their way south in search of work had brought much of the youth work to the verge of collapse. In the three years before the war the NCSS was able to allocate grants totalling well over £100,000 from the Special Areas Fund to the principal national youth organisations, which helped their work not only to survive in these regions but to make striking progress. They were able to provide new and improved premises, gymnasia and playing fields, to arrange training courses for leaders, and to promote camping projects. In 1937, 125 new youth units were formed; existing groups which had nearly faded out through lack of funds doubled their

---

* The costs of administration, in spite of the very complicated nature of unemployment work, were kept below 6 per cent.

membership in one year; others reported that by 1938 they had four times as many members as in 1935. It was a remarkable resurgence, no doubt accelerated also by the emphasis which the nation was at this period giving to the welfare of youth, through the National Fitness Campaign, the Physical Training and Recreation Act of 1937, and the establishment of the King George V Jubilee Trust.

Another effect of the Special Areas grant was to extend considerably the work of the women's clubs. Though this had made good progress because the clubs were so ardently desired and worked for by the women themselves, the movement had always been short of money since none of the Ministry of Labour grant could be used for the wives in the distressed areas. There was no such ban on the allocation of the new fund, and grants from it proved invaluable in giving the stimulus and skilled leadership needed, and made it possible for over 400 women to attend the courses run at 'The Beeches' in one year.

Although by 1937 some measure of prosperity seemed to be returning, there were still one and a half million unemployed on the register and a far greater number who were out of work at some time during the year. There was still much work for the NCSS to do in this field, but its nature was changing. After nearly six years of continually expanding work it was necessary to pause and take stock of the situation. An impressive administrative machine had been created capable of handling great sums of money from both statutory and voluntary sources and allocating it with integrity, efficiency, and a sympathetic understanding of the problem as a whole. It is true that the machinery creaked badly at times and mistakes and errors of judgment had been made. But it was evident that it had more flexibility than any purely statutory machinery could have had and this allowed for improvisation and experimentation of all kinds in meeting new or changing needs. Unique experience had been gained. But what was to be the future of the movement? How were the clubs themselves meeting the changing situation? To answer such questions a survey was set on foot. It began in 1937 and the results, *Out of Adversity*, were published two years later.

The main conclusion of the survey, so far as the future was concerned, appeared to be that despite the decline in unemployment the occupational club had come to stay. By this time there were some 700 clubs for men and 450 for women with a membership of 120,000 and 40,000 respectively. They had ceased to be merely places where unemployed men and women could go to fill in their time when out of work and had made for themselves a place in the community as a permanent social institution, serving primarily those whose lives were shadowed by low wages and insecure employment. The value of the clubs lay in their ability to provide a reasonably full social life at a cost within the reach of the poorest members of the community, whether at work or not; and it was clear that the movement could not hope to develop sound leadership or stable finances unless it could keep the support of its own leading members after they had regained employment. But the diminution of unemployment without its complete disappearance brought new problems, for now the clubs were dealing with the occasionally employed as well as the young men who had never known a day's work and the old men who were never likely to find work again. For the young men it was of course recognised that the only hope lay in work, or in training leading to work, and that was far beyond the scope of the clubs.

One the whole the clubs in the smaller towns, where a sense of community already existed, had made the better progress. The difficulties in the cities were great. In order to play a significant part in the life of a big city, where it was hoped that the clubs might become 'workers' clubs' or 'community clubs', they would no doubt need good premises and full-time paid staff; but it would not be easy to secure the stable income necessary to pay for them. Already there were signs that some of those who supported occupational clubs for the unemployed would not give their help to community clubs for those in work.

Other points brought out by the survey were the importance of gaining trade union support wherever possible; the extent to which the religious bodies had been the backbone of the movement; and the very great value which clubs of this kind had for women, though there was evidently need to provide more adequately for their requirements.

In the early days of unemployment, when every day brought new and complex social problems which the NCSS must try to find ways of meeting, this work tended to absorb a great deal of the Council's resources. But by 1937 the stress had somewhat lessened and other departments of the National Council were once more claiming their full share of attention. This was particularly true of the work of the urban councils of social service. Although some, like Liverpool, Tyneside, and Lancashire, kept in close touch with the NCSS because they had been in the forefront of unemployment work and had made an outstanding contribution to this task, others had faded into the background. Some indeed had the impression that they had been abandoned by national headquarters which, they felt, had become out of touch with their local needs and had left them to struggle with their own problems as best they could.

An urban policy committee had been formed in 1933 to take up some of the questions dealt with in Sir Wyndham Deedes' report of 1930 and to help in discharging the obligations of the National Council to the local bodies. This committee met several times and made certain recommendations, but its meetings ceased owing to the urgency of other work. In 1937 the matter was taken up again, and an assistant for urban work was appointed to undertake a programme of work over a period of three years. He made contact with the organisations in over 100 towns and was responsible for organising national conferences in 1938 and 1939 and a series of experimental regional meetings. Though family case-work, which had dominated the work of some of the older bodies, remained an important part of the activity of many of the local councils, it was emphasised that the National Council did not itself undertake to act as a centre of guidance on this aspect of social work, recognising the London Charity Organisation Society as the expert body in this field. The significant part of the councils of social service here was seen to be the promotion of the right relationship between this service of help and advice to families—a service which, in the face of the complexities of modern social legislation and conditions, must become evermore skilled and broader in scope—and the services for the community or for groups of citizens that formed part of the wider responsibilities of local councils of social service. There were many new experiments in such services in different parts of the country at this period; but before developments in the css field had time to mature fully, the war came.

Another effect of the Council's concentration for so long on unemployment work was to divert attention from its wider conception of social service as something contributed by the whole community to the whole community; and to narrow its encouragement of culture to those organisations which were attempting to restore self-respect to men and women of whom apparently society had no need. Nevertheless, the wider purposes were not completely forgotten and were realised especially in the work of the local history and drama and music groups. These groups also had a specific contribution to make in helping to bring back a sense of neighbourliness in a period when organic communities were being replaced by mere agglomerations of people; and it is significant in this connection that the idea was a spontaneous growth in several different localities, and not a suggestion coming from the National Council. As early as 1929 the Lindsey (Lincolnshire) RCC had held a conference to interest local villages in the study of local history and this had led to the founding of the Lindsey Local History Association. Kent followed in 1930 with local history exhibitions and lectures, first in the towns and later in the villages as well, and eight local village history groups were formed. In Cheshire thirty villages co-operated in work on a new history of the county. In 1934 the National Council called three conferences to consider what part it could take in this development. It decided to form a central committee 'to provide guidance and inspiration to local effort' through rural community councils wherever possible; and money was provided for this purpose. The project developed very slowly, however, and it was not till 1936 that the committee met again. Then the Carnegie UK Trustees agreed to make a grant, and six counties were chosen to receive grant-aid for an experimental period. During the next three years policy began to take shape; but here again the outbreak of war brought the work to a temporary halt.

A new development of the mid-thirties which was not to be thwarted in the same way by the exigencies of war was the bringing together in 1936 of the principal national youth organisations to form the Standing Conference of National Juvenile Organisations. This move had been fore-shadowed ten years earlier on a regional scale when the National Council had recommended that rural community councils should, wherever possible, set up county youth committees, with representatives from local branches of national voluntary youth organisations, and was stimulated now by the co-operation of these bodies in Special Area work. But the creation of the national Standing Conference was an important new departure in NCSS policy, for the conference was to be a full autonomous body responsible only to its constituent organisations and not answerable to the executive committee of the NCSS. Some of the youth organisations had behind them a century of experience; others had come lately into the field to meet new needs. All were fully independent voluntary bodies responsible for their own policy and management. Several were highly organised on an international scale; most of them had close links with the churches. Their combined membership was approximately a million. The aim of the National Council was merely to provide a forum where the problems common to all these organisations could be discussed, and to offer such administrative services as the conference required. The full importance of this enterprise was only proved in 1939 when, on the verge of war, the government set up its Service of Youth scheme and was able to make good use of the voluntary organisations' three years' experience of working together.

In the same year that the Standing Conference of National Juvenile Organisations was established the government started a new policy, mainly concerned with young people, which was to have a far-reaching effect on much of the Council's work. For some time past there had been increasing concern about the poor standard of physical fitness of the youth of Britain, and in 1937 the government decided to launch the National Fitness Campaign. A National Advisory Council for Physical Training and Recreation was set up, and the Physical Training and Recreation Act passed, giving powers to the Board of Education to make grants to local authorities or to local voluntary organisations for providing gymnasia, playing fields, camps, swimming baths, and centres and clubs for physical recreation and training.

It seems clear that those who devised this revolutionary machinery had been considerably influenced by the National Council's principle of co-operation between statutory and voluntary bodies. No doubt the remarkable partnership built up between the NCSS and the local authorities in connection with the unemployment work had also impressed them. It was hoped that the statutory authorities might work in a similar way with the voluntary organisations in the new and large task of improving the nation's physical fitness. In spite of its faults, which showed themselves as the machinery came into operation, the Act certainly helped many of the projects in which the National Council was interested, including community centres, village halls, and youth work.

One of its first effects, however, was to cause something of a crisis in the domestic affairs of the National Council. In 1936 Captain Ellis, who for eighteen years had been general secretary of the NCSS, resigned to become the first secretary of the new National Advisory Council for Physical Training and Recreation. This was a very great loss as Captain Ellis had been one of the chief architects of the Council's fortunes. It was his dynamic energy which had brought it through many crises; it was his vision that had inspired much of the work which was the Council's title to distinction; and it was his great administrative skill which had helped to fabricate and to run the complex machinery of committees and departments which showed the way to put visions and theories into practice. He had a great gift for winning the interest and enthusiasm of many people to help in the work; but so forceful a personality did not always find it easy to tolerate his colleagues' opinions when he disagreed with them; nor did he suffer fools gladly. But whatever friction and misunderstanding there may have been now and then, his work stands as an abiding memorial to his skill, courage, and devotion. He came to the Council when its work lay uncharted before it and no one knew the way ahead. He did not even know whether his salary could be met after the first year. His first office was a borrowed room. Co-operation in social service was still an unrealised idea. When he left, the Council stood at the height of achievement; its patron the King, its committees drawing on the wisdom of some

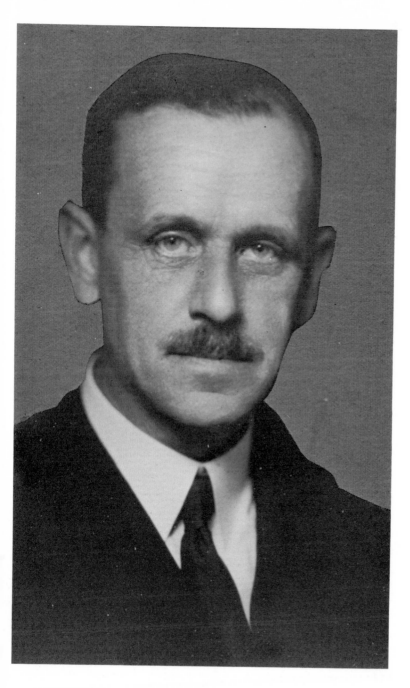

Lionel Ellis

of the most distinguished men and women of the day. It was the trustee of great sums of money from government and voluntary sources, enjoying the confidence of departments of state and of more than forty of the principal voluntary societies. All the branches of its work appeared to flourish. There were now rural community councils in twenty-three counties and links with nearly a thousand village halls and with community associations on eighty municipal housing estates, while 1,450 clubs for the unemployed had nearly 150,000 members.

Impressive as the figures were, there were no illusions as to what still remained to be done, even in the territories so far mapped. The unemployed clubs were catering for only one in ten of those without work. Only half the country was covered by rural community councils. For every village with a hall there were more than two without. The community associations on the new estates were in touch with only about 2 per cent of the population. Less than a third of the boys and girls from city or town belonged to any youth organisation. But whatever remained to be done, the means to do it had been created. Beyond the value of any statistical assessment lay the triumph of an idea: the principle of co-operation and team work in social service had been tried and found valid.

At the time of Captain Ellis' resignation the Council suffered another great loss in the resignation on the grounds of ill-health of Arthur Richmond, the deputy secretary whose wise leadership of the rural department over many years had made so important a contribution to the soundness of its policy; for his had been the task of working out in practical detail the aims and ideals of Professor Adams who, throughout his continuing chairmanship of the NCSS since 1919, had been the great inspirer of its rural policy.

Dr Adams was now Warden of All Souls, Oxford; and since 1924 he had been a member of the Development Commission. In that time he had seen the idea of a rural renaissance, which he had brought with him from his work in Ireland with Sir Horace Plunkett, develop under his inspiration into a major part of the National Council's achievement. Through all the changes of fortune and personnel, the rugged figure of the Warden stood like a rock; and it was his wise and kindly judgment and his genius for friendship which had enabled the Council to weather many a crisis in those difficult years.

The choice of Leonard Shoeten Sack to succeed Captain Ellis was a happy one. In addition to his early experience at the Ministry of Health he had been one of the pioneers of the voluntary movement in Kent where he had been secretary of the council of social service from 1925 to 1936, at a time when the county was in the forefront with many notable experimental schemes. It had been largely owing to his vision of what could be achieved with real co-operation between the voluntary organisations, the Carnegie UK Trust, the Development Commission, and the local authorities, and with funds from these sources to support an adequately paid staff, that a rural community council had been converted into a full county council of social service, combining urban and rural work on a broad scale and establishing its role as a vigorous and respected leader in the area. To strengthen the headquarters staff at this critical time George Haynes, formerly warden of Liverpool University Settlement and for four years chief advisory officer in the north for the NCSS, was moved to London, soon to become deputy secretary.

The effects of the new National Fitness Campaign on the NCSS soon made themselves felt, most particularly in the embryonic movement for community associations and centres on the new housing estates. When the Act of 1937 was passed the National Council was in touch with 171 schemes. In less than a year this number had risen to 304, of which fifty-three were established community associations with some buildings though these were usually quite inadequate. A further forty-two schemes were in progress and ninety-nine more under consideration. This was experimental work, with few precedents to guide those responsible for shaping it; but the New Estates Committee was fortunate in having such men as Professor Ernest Barker and Sir Wyndham Deedes to advise it; and the daily interchange of ideas, the annual conferences, the publications from Bedford Square, and the contacts which the newly-appointed travelling officers made with local residents and local authorities, soon built up a useful reserve of experience and knowledge. The work indeed grew so rapidly that the number of regional officers had to be increased from two to six, with help from the Carnegie UK Trust and the Board of Education. That this was a movement of real significance in the community life of places where it seemed to have died, or never to have been born, was recognised by both local and national authorities. Sociologists, educationists, religious leaders, housing and planning experts, watched its development with attention.

But there were many delays and disappointments. Some of these were due to the fact that the new machinery of the National Fitness Council was not popular with certain of the local authorities. Some considered that it relied too much on direction from the centre; others disliked the by-passing of the local authority which could occur when grant-aid was made direct to a local voluntary organisation. There is no doubt that it was both complicated and unpopular and would have required considerable revision if the war had not come to put an end to all further progress in this direction. But the lessons learnt from it were not overlooked when the 1944 Education Act came to be drafted.

In the countryside also the National Fitness Campaign, despite weaknesses, had its effect. Its area committees found the experience of the rural community councils of great value, and the number of village hall and playing field schemes, helped to develop, increased considerably. From 1937 to 1939, ninety-two grants totalling £13,119 were approved, compared with thirty-seven totalling £5,974 in the three previous years. By 1939 there were 245 schemes under consideration by the NCSS compared with 139 the previous year. This increased help from government sources was very welcome; but it should not obscure the value of the pioneer work accomplished with the help of the Development Commission and the Carnegie UK Trustees. From the beginning of the scheme in 1925 up to 1937 over 400 villages had been helped, the total expenditure in grants amounting to nearly £60,000 and in loans to £75,000. Even more significant was the fact that the villagers themselves had contributed some £340,000, representing about £1.12.0 per head of the population of the villages concerned.

Perhaps most hopeful of all was the attempt to revive the parish councils. A central Parish Councils Committee under Sir Lawrence Chubb had been set up to administer the scheme in counties where there was no RCC, and to issue leaflets and advice explaining to the parish councillors and theirs clerks in simple language the powers and opportunities of parish councils as they were affected by changing legislation. Many people at that time thought that the parish council was too small to have any real function in modern conditions. Others saw it as the parliament of the village, helping to preserve some of the best traditions of village life and worth retaining as a vital unit of democracy. This view was indicated by the fact that by 1938 nearly 700 parish councils had availed themselves of the new service, an increase of 250 in that year. Despite misgivings that some councillors might have difficulty in travelling so far, it was decided to hold a conference in London. The response exceeded all expectations, with 273 delegates from 151 parish councils in twenty-five counties. One resolution called for the abandonment of the traditional method of election by show of hands in favour of the secret ballot. The campaign for this important electoral reform was supported by 1,200 parish councils and over 2,000 women's institutes (which made a most important contribution to the whole movement); but here again the war postponed developments by preventing presentation of the case to the Home Secretary.

In 1937, when the greatest pressure of the unemployment work had abated, there came at last the opportunity for fresh thinking about the nature and purpose of the National Council and the trends of its work. The annual report for 1937/38, in attempting to assess the progress of the Council in its first eighteen years, is full of searching self-criticism.

Two fundamental questions were at the basis of this self-examination. First: was the large-scale and seemingly successful work for the unemployed to be regarded as a major deflection from the Council's original aim and purpose? The original purpose had been consultation and planning, certainly not direct executive action which was to remain the function of the constituent groups that made up the Council. But executive action on the largest scale had in fact outstripped and indeed obscured the planning and consultative function. There was little doubt too that this action had alienated the support of some of the influential voluntary agencies who saw in the NCSS a competitor rather than a co-ordinator. And yet, faced with the tragedy of unemployment and the need for exactly the kind of team work which the Council was able to build up, could the responsibility have been evaded?

Secondly: with the increasing activity of the state, what was the true function of social service within the changing framework of society? Was the only aim of voluntary work to pioneer new services which the state would eventually recognise as essential and take over as its own responsibility?

In considering these questions of social policy the report of 1938 suggested that the evolution of a new and better social order could not be left merely to the play of blind, conflicting forces but needed deliberate planning and experiment which the state alone could not and should not do. It defined social service as: '. . . the name, perhaps inadequate, for that thinking and acting which the community has got to do for itself outside, but often in partnership with, the State . . . not merely the work for the relief of poverty and the evils with which its name has come to be peculiarly connected, but all work for the enrichment and better ordering of better social life. It is not service rendered by one class of the community to another; it is the self-government of the community in all that part of its social life which cannot be left to the regulation of Act of Parliament, administrative order, or local by-law.'

Needless to say, the breadth of this definition was later to come under some criticism but it certainly inspired fresh thinking. Within such a broad framework the need for a National Council as a focus was clear. Towards this large aim the NCSS had made only limited progress in eighteen years. 'With few exceptions,' said the report, 'the urban Councils of Social Service have not yet made their full mark as bodies representative of local interests and usefully engaged in constructive planning for future needs.' Rural community councils were established in less than half the counties; the work on the new estates, though full of promise, was touching only the fringe of the problem; the total membership of the unemployed clubs was only one-tenth of those unemployed at any given time.

The report was critical too of the Council's failure to act as an adequate centre of information and research, making available to everyone interested the great resources of knowledge and experience which could have been drawn from the diversity of its membership. There was criticism also of the Council's failure to reach a common mind on some of the major issues of the day, where the common voice of the voluntary bodies might have carried great weight and authority. It was recognised that this was sometimes inevitable when these had become issues of party politics on which a body representative of a wide cross-section of political opinions could not be expected to commit its constituent groups. Nevertheless, the point was made that a truly 'National' Council should be more than the sum total of its constituent members.

Despite its searching criticism the report was stimulating. Even amidst what might at times appear 'a wasteful and bewildering confusion of committees, standing conferences, surveys and reports, paid organisers and administrators', the Council saw its essential purposes shining clearly: 'Men will organise themselves as they have always done into social groups. The choice which confronts them is between groups which are diverse, flexible, self-governing and self-confident, and groups which are uniform, rigid, governed from above and docile. Social service means, then, building groups; helping men and women, boys and girls, to build their own groups, and helping to remove those obstacles of poverty and lack of knowledge which blind their vision and tie their hands. . . . Social service rightly interpreted is a business not of doing what the State or the churches, or the political organisations leave undone, but of using the strength and influence of each and all of these forces in a more effective partnership. The task of the National Council of Social Service is one of liberating the will and fashioning the means to make this partnership a reality.'

As an earnest of its own intention to make these hopes a reality, the Council embarked on major changes in its own structures, so that both the Council and its main committees should be more representative of the constituent organisations and the new interests which were emerging. Although its necessarily complicated structure did not lend itself to simple forms of direct representation, efforts were made to ensure that the representation of new interests should be on a democratic basis. Thus the new

Consultative Council of Community Associations, built up of delegates from approved associations, would elect seventeen members to the National Council's Community Associations and Centres Committee, and four of the number to the Executive Committee of the NCSS. Similar arrangements were made for the councils of social service, and the regional councils for unemployment work. The National Council would therefore now comprise the following membership groups:

1. Representatives appointed by:
   (a) national voluntary organisations;
   (b) government departments;
   (c) associations of local government authorities and local government officers;
   (d) rural community councils and regional councils of social service.
   (e) regional unemployment organisations.

2. Representatives elected by:
   (a) National Conference of Town Councils of Social Service;
   (b) Consultative Council of Community Associations.

3. Individual members.

Each of the groups was to be represented on the Executive Committee responsible for general policy.

This reorganisation was scarcely completed before the war clouds began to gather, and during 1938/39 they overshadowed much of the Council's work. The Munich crisis of September, 1938, demonstrated the urgent need for joint planning and consultation amongst the voluntary societies if they were to be ready to play their important part in the national emergency. In order to provide the necessary link between them and the government on matters likely to affect them all—finance in wartime, requisitioning of buildings, reservation of workers—a Standing Conference of Voluntary Organisations in Wartime was set up in December 1938. Of itself this was an indication that, even after nearly twenty years of patient work, the NCSS could still not speak for the whole voluntary social service movement. The new conference widened the consultative basis of the Council but at the expense of constitutional clarity, for to some extent the Conference duplicated the consultative functions of the NCSS itself. But there was an important link between the two bodies in that the Council provided the secretariat. At first the conference comprised seventy members but additional groups came in during the first few months.

Though it was conceived solely as a wartime necessity, it was in fact to have an important influence on the future structure of the National Council.

The government made it clear from the outset that they attached importance to the contribution which the voluntary bodies could make in time of emergency; and in spite of their pre-occupation with urgent matters of civil defence, government departments gave every assistance in formulating joint plans.

Throughout the intervening months before war came preparations for the emergency which all hoped might yet be avoided went quietly forward. Thought was given to the difficulties which the widespread dislocation caused by the planned evacuation from cities would bring. The problems of maintaining morale, caring for the old and the handicapped, and providing for the welfare of young people, were all discussed. Most vital of all, in collaboration with ministries, local authorities, and voluntary organisations, the foundations were being laid for a network of centres of information and advice to which citizens, bewildered by the dislocation, the emergency regulations, and the alarms of war, might bring their problems. The recognition of the need for such a service and the plan for its creation was one of the first results of the constructive thinking of a special group set up by the Standing Conference—the Personal Service Group. Another of these special groups, the Women's Group on Public Welfare, gave much thought to the problems likely to arise from evacuation; and the outcome of this study was eventually to make a notable contribution to social history.

CHAPTER FIVE

War

I T was inevitable that the war which produced such revolutionary changes in the life of the nation should have an influence equally profound on the character and work of the NCSS. Its effects were fourfold. In the first place, it changed the structure of the Council itself; secondly, it slowed down or stopped, at least temporarily, much of the existing work and transformed the work in other important sectors; thirdly, it drove the Council into quite new fields of activity; finally, it provided an opportunity to assess the achievements and failures of the past and to plan for the new world which it was hoped would rise from the ruins of the old. That the Council was able to undergo such changes in a time of emergency while still retaining its essential character suggests an inherent flexibility which would enable it to adapt to the even more fundamentally altered pattern of society in the post-war years.

The fear that the reduction of voluntary subscriptions and other wartime difficulties would face many of the voluntary organisations with the threat of collapse had drawn them closer together in the Standing Conference of Voluntary Organisations in Time of War, and had brought in a number of important bodies which had hitherto remained outside the orbit of the NCSS. Thus for the first time they were able to speak with one voice to the government. The first outcome of this new unity was an agreement with the government that it would be prepared to give some financial aid for the work which it wished the voluntary organisations to undertake; and for other work of vital national importance which was in real danger of being stopped or seriously curtailed if help was not given. An important corollary to this arrangement was the setting up of an inter-departmental committee to co-ordinate the actions of government departments in respect of grant-aid not falling clearly within the scope of any one department; and the establishment of an advisory committee under Lord Rushcliffe to advise the government on the contribution which the voluntary organisations could make to the wellbeing of the civilian population and the best means of using their services.

The existence of the new Standing Conference of Voluntary Organisations improved the consultative capacity of the NCSS, but it tended to duplicate the functions of the Council itself and to put the officers of the NCSS in the difficult position of having to consult both these bodies at a time when war conditions made meetings with either of them singularly difficult to arrange. As a temporary solution an emergency committee of thirty members, nominated by the executive and acting in their personal capacity, was set up for the duration of the war. A number of members were co-opted from the Standing Conference to ensure better representation of national and regional interests. The Standing Conference was to remain in being, meeting two or three times a year.

Prior to this another important decision had been taken. The government, anticipating the dislocation of central government machinery under heavy aerial attack, set up a number of regional committees responsible for civil defence and for certain functions of government in the event of a breakdown of communications. In each of these twelve Civil Defence Regions the National Council appointed, with the approval of the Minister of Home Security, a regional officer from among its own senior staff or the staff of associated bodies to act as a liaison officer between the Civil Defence Commissioners and the voluntary organisations in these regions. The importance of this decision was that it not only brought the National Council into close, official touch with this new regional machinery of the state but it contributed to building up a decentralised provincial organisation, thus helping to close some of the gaps in the pre-war distribution of its services.

In keeping with this trend, and indeed accelerated by it, were the moves to set up an independent Scottish Council of Social Service in association with the National Council. As long ago as 1931 the NCSS annual report had recorded the appointment of an officer to study in Scotland the possibility of enlisting support for developing a distinctively national movement to stimulate local enterprise on co-operative lines. Now early wartime conditions temporarily postponed the scheme and instead a special committee of the NCSS was set up to assist the Council's regional officer for Scotland, A. M. Struthers. But the ideal of a Scottish Council of Social Service, rooted in the life of the Scottish nation, remained; and in spite of difficulties, plans went quietly ahead in the first years of the war, inspired by a small group of distinguished Scots, including Baillie Elgar and Sir Hector Hetherington. By 1942 the work was completed and the Scottish Council of Social Service was founded, with its headquarters in Edinburgh under the presidency of Lord Elgin and with Lord Wark as chairman. Its first secretary was the National Council's regional officer for

Scotland, A. M. Struthers, who with his deputy regional officer, Grace Drysdale, played a vital part in building up the Scottish Council during the difficult years of the war.

It was not easy in the grim days of 1940 to hold together so complex an organisation as the National Council. Air-raids, black-out, breakdown of communications, and the loss of staff added to the confusion and uncertainty of the time. At this difficult moment the general secretary, Leonard Shoeten Sack, was unhappily forced to retire owing to ill-health, though he was able to retain the post of general adviser to the Council. The leader-

Leonard Shoeten Sack

ship of the NCSS at so critical a period thus fell to the deputy secretary, George Haynes. No appointment could have been more fitting. For the heavy task of guiding the Council, not merely through the problems thrown up by the war but out beyond to the opportunities which peace would bring, he was equipped with the unusual and priceless gift of being able to see both the wood and the trees. Behind the work of committees, standing conferences, and group relationships, all so necessary but so complicated and time-consuming, he could always see in perspective the essential purpose of the NCSS. His logical mind understood how to adjust this complex machine to meet changing conditions; modest, yet steadfast in his sense of right purpose, he brought to his important work a temperament and personality admirably fitted to the tasks ahead. Above all else he believed that, since the Council was in essence an experiment in team work, its whole future depended on creating the right relationships between its many groups and often conflicting interests. Moreover he saw that, while these relationships had to be defined within a constitutional framework, they depended far more on warm, friendly, personal relationships between the leading members of the committees and groups than upon paper constitutions. To the building up of these good relationships the new secretary brought all his skill and devotion as a patient, sympathetic negotiator.

The war caused frequent losses and changes in the staff at headquarters, already short-handed and working at great strain. But it brought some powerful compensations. Chief among these was Dorothy Keeling, one of the few survivors of the small group which had paved the way for the NCSS in 1919 and who, for the next twenty years, had served the Liverpool Personal Service Society as its secretary. She came down from Liverpool at the beginning of the war to share the assistant secretaryship with Major Eyre Carter until his secondment to war duties, and thereafter to carry on till the end of it, contriving to do with great courage, imagination and persistence what in normal times would have been considered work enough for several people.

One of the sad losses to the Council in the early war days was the death of its well-loved rural officer, Laurence Ramsbottom, after an accident in the black-out. Not long before this the Council had learnt of the passing of two of its greatest pioneers: Grace Hadow who played a vital part in the founding of the Oxfordshire Rural Community Council and the rural department of the NCSS; and Frederick D'Aeth of Liverpool who, with his colleague S. P. Grundy, did so much to lay the foundations of the Council during the first world war. Percy Grundy, who was perhaps the prime initiator of the NCSS and its honorary secretary for ten years was

soon to follow them; and, as both the Reverend John Pringle and Hancock
Nunn had died some time before the war, there was now only one sur-
vivor of the little group which had met on a day early in 1919 to lay their
plans for the first national council of social service.

A third important development, under pressure of war, in the structure
and relationships of the NCSS, in addition to the creation of the Standing
Conference of Voluntary Organisations and the trend towards decentralisation under the regional officer system, was the extension of the principle
of autonomous groups representing specialised interests working in
association with the Council but not answerable to its Executive. The first
experiment, the grouping of youth interests in the Standing Conference of
National Juvenile Organisations, had started as far back as 1936. During
the war years its usefulness was fully demonstrated in providing a link
between the government and the voluntary youth organisations at a
critical time when the whole future of the youth service and its integration
with the educational system was coming under review. Moreover, there
were special problems concerning the welfare of young people in wartime,
both in their leisure time and at work. Enquiries undertaken by the Standing Conference during this period included a study of the problems of
young people in industry, juvenile delinquency, mixed youth clubs, and
international youth work; but perhaps their most important contribution
to the future of youth work was their suggestion, accepted by the government, that the new Education Bill should include a recommendation that
local education authorities in drafting their plans should have regard to the
part which the voluntary organisations could play.
    Two other specialist groups which had begun before the war now had
useful achievements to record. The Churches Group brought together
in common council representatives of not only the main Protestant denominations but also of the Roman Catholic Church and the Jewish
community to consider, with representatives of the National Council, the
unique contribution which the churches could make to the problems of
social welfare and the common life of the community. This group was
particularly significant in representing the broadest grouping of religious
forces so far achieved. Its pursuit of this ideal of joint consultation through
which the work of the churches could be more fully integrated with the
life of the people owed much of its inspiration to the first chairman,
Dr Fisher then Bishop of London, and to his successor for many years,
Dr F. V. D. Narborough (later Bishop of Colchester), and to the devoted

work of its secretary, the Reverend Malcolm Spencer. Already it was issuing a bulletin of information to ministers of religion; and it was soon to publish important statements of policy, accepted by all its constituent members, setting out briefly the principles governing co-operation between the churches and the voluntary organisations in social activities.

The second group of specialist interests, the Women's Group on Public Welfare, which had come into existence just before the war under the leadership of Margaret Bondfield, had found itself faced almost at once by an array of problems, of deep concern to women's organisations, arising from war stresses and restrictions and the disruption of home life by evacuation, by the father's absence on active service, and the mother's war work. At once the Group set itself to investigate the nature of these problems and to devise means by which the varied resources of their member organisations could be mobilised to help. Their enquiries ranged over a wide field, from problems of the Women's Auxiliary Services to the difficulties of clothes rationing, from nurseries to fruit preserving. They played a considerable part in urging the government to initiate the invaluable 'Make do and Mend' campaign. But the work which had the

Margaret Bondfield (on right)

greatest and most far-reaching social importance was their study of the conditions of life for the mass of people in our great cities, in the light thrown on it by evacuation. This report was published in 1942 as *Our Towns: a Close-up.** The idea had originally been suggested by the National Federation of Women's Institutes, whose members had first-hand experience of the difficulties which many of the evacuated families brought to their refuges in the countryside. The report's sober, factual documentation revealed to many people for the first time the direct connection between the squalor and meanness of life in the cities and these problems in the reception areas to which thousands of children and mothers from the cities were being sent for safety from the expected air-raids; and it was to have a remarkably far-reaching influence on family social policy in the future.

The increase in the consultative activities of the National Council through the operation of these standing conferences and autonomous special groups was important, but an even more significant effect of the war on the Council's work was to call into being two new services of far-reaching consequence: citizens' advice bureaux and the old people's welfare movement.

The citizen's advice bureaux† had been planned as part of the emergency preparations made before the war, but their roots went much deeper into the past. At several points in the history of the NCSS their emergence had been foreseen. Frederick D'Aeth had realised the need for such a service in 1915 in the first world war. The 'Citizens' Friend' department of the councils of social service had been set up following the recommendations of the Inter-departmental Committee on the Administration of Public Assistance in 1924. Further evidence of the need came in the 1930s when, arising from their broadcast series 'Question Time for the Unemployed', the Council was almost overwhelmed by enquiries not only from the unemployed but from many other sections of the community. Such was the need that it is probable that this national service would have developed even without the impetus provided by the war, but it was certainly accelerated by the emergency; for it seemed clear, from the time of the 1938 crisis, that if war came civilians would be as much involved as members of the armed forces and would urgently need guidance through a labyrinth of restrictions, provisions, and personal problems which no one authority would be responsible for giving them.

---

* Oxford University Press. [Out of print.]

† The history of the first twenty-five years of the bureaux has been told in *The Story of the Citizens' Advice Bureaux.* NCSS 1964.

In the winter of 1938–39 the NCSS had initiated discussions, under the chairmanship of Sir Wyndham Deedes, between some national and local organisations with a special interest and experience in advisory work for individuals; and out of these consultations a national plan took shape for the establishment all over the country of local centres of advice and information, free and unbiased, to which any citizen could go with his questions and problems, certain of getting reliable answers or being guided to places where he would find them. The centres would be linked together by national advisory services so that accurate and up-to-date information could be supplied from the centre, help and guidance in their management, and the co-operation of government departments and local authorities assured; but the bureaux would be autonomous bodies conducted by local organisations or committees.

The plan was welcomed by the Lord Privy Seal, Sir John Anderson, and other Ministers concerned; and, largely through the co-operation and initiative of many societies experienced in social service, 200 citizens' advice bureaux were able to begin work at once on the outbreak of the war. These were mainly off-shoots of established bodies in London and the large cities (the Charity Organisation Society and the London Council of Social Service, Liverpool Personal Service Society, Birmingham Citizens' Society, and many others); but in smaller places where there was no experienced casework organisation or council of social service, a variety of societies and individuals—a Toc H branch, a local Rotary Club, a Soroptimist Club, a schoolmaster and a few friends—seized the opportunity to start what they saw as an essential service.

Premises were as varied as sponsors. In some places the local authorities provided a room in the town hall or the public library; or an estate agent might lend an empty house or office. Established organisations in large cities might house a central bureau in their own premises and set up branches in a youth centre, a hall lent by a church, a YWCA club. Some of the bureaux were open every day; some several times a week; others only on market day.

The first bureaux, being off-shoots of social service organisations, were staffed or at least organised by trained social workers; but it was not possible, nor ever intended, that this should be the pattern of the whole service. Of the 10,000 men and women who worked in citizens' advice bureaux at the height of the war, ninety per cent were part-time volunteers from the most varied occupations and none—people coming from every walk of life with, between them, a remarkably wide range of knowledge and experience.

The fact that the whole service was an experiment, growing at an extraordinary rate (by the end of September, 1939, there were 381 bureaux at work, 670 a month later, and 926 at the end of the year), and that it was so widespread and various, meant that a very heavy responsibility for sound central organisation and direction fell upon the NCSS.

From the beginning the Council was ready through its regional officers to guide the setting up of bureaux in places where a new organisation was needed and to provide from headquarters a prompt and accurate service of information to brief bureau workers. An information department was set up which, in addition to answering often with the co-operation of government departments particularly difficult questions for which the bureaux could not find the solution, supplied a digest and explanation in plain language of all the constantly proliferating and changing legislation and regulations of the day, in the form of stencilled, then printed, *Citizens' Advice Notes*. So prompt, reliable, and comprehensible was this service that it was used throughout the war as the 'bible' not only of every voluntary CAB but of many local authority information centres and other statutory offices; and it had, and continues to have, nearly thirty years later, a list of subscribers that includes professional and business men, universities, government departments, local authorities, libraries, and many private individuals.

But the remarkable development of the CAB movement was above all the work of Dorothy Keeling who, with the long experience of the not dissimilar service she had devised at the Liverpool Personal Service Society, came to London early in 1940 to take charge of the CAB department. Special CAB travelling officers were attached to the various regions, and working with the regional officers they kept in touch with existing bureaux, advised on administration and recruitment and training of workers, and encouraged the formation of new bureaux.

A study of the categories of problems brought to the bureaux gives a picture of civilian life during the war years. At first, questions about postponement of military service, maintenance allowance for the wives of servicemen, difficulties caused by the disruption of business, and problems of the first wave of evacuated children from the big cities, headed the list. Then, with the battles of France and Flanders, there were thousands of enquiries about missing or wounded soldiers, widows' pensions, allowances for the wives of prisoners of war. With the threat of invasion and the air-raids in cities came evacuation problems again; war injury and damage compensation claims; and real emergencies when bureaux, at an hour's notice, improvised a point of information and advice in rest centres, shelters or, as after the great 1940 raid on Coventry, on a pavement outside the ruined town hall. Not that the workers were unprepared for such crises. Throughout the quiet early months of the war the NCSS had advised on training courses held in each locality to prepare CAB workers for supplementing the Civil Defence services with a personal service of advice and guidance to people too bomb-shocked even to make full use of those official services. In addition, officers of the National Council from its London and regional headquarters were ready to go at once to the help of local workers in the bombed cities; and soon a mobile force of trained personnel was formed and mobile citizens' advice bureaux were provided, first in a horse-box converted with the aid of the British War Relief Society of America and manned by volunteers from the Friends Ambulance Unit, and later in buses, caravans, or box-body cars.

But though problems arising from the devastation caused by air-raids in home and family, business and public services, continued throughout the war to provide a main part of CAB work, it was only a part. There seemed to be no aspect of life, and death, with which the bureau workers were not called upon to cope. They helped refugees from occupied countries; tried to solve landlord and tenant problems complicated by war conditions; advised on clothes rationing; co-operated with the Red Cross in

The mobile citizens' advice bureau at Bath

running the Postal Message Scheme which was the only, much restricted method of communicating with relatives and friends in enemy-occupied territories (they handled well over 900,000 messages in all); arranged free legal advice and Poor Man's Valuer services; told people of the special arrangements for sending parcels to prisoners of war or for getting married at short notice; or explained income tax demands to wage-earners required for the first time to pay tax; and more and more often they found that, as the CAB became better known and accepted, the background to a call might be a domestic difficulty or serious family problem which they must try to find some way of solving when there might be no one else to do it.

The contribution of the bureaux to the maintenance of civilian morale throughout the war was incalculable. The late John Hilton, who had a unique understanding of the anxieties of ordinary people, said of them in a broadcast not long before he died: 'I've worked in close touch with the citizens' advice bureaux from the first day of the war. I know what we owe to them. In years to come, when the secrets of our strength emerge, it will be clear, I think, that outstanding among the agencies which kept us up was the citizens' advice bureau.' He was in the best position to know this for, among its many other duties, the information department had advised and assisted him at the BBC in the weekly series of broadcasts 'Can I Help You?'

Nor was it only in this way that the experience of the bureaux could be used on a national scale. They were one of the most important channels by which official information reached the public, but the kind of questions asked at the bureaux also provided the government with a reliable index of the problems and anxieties uppermost in people's minds and of their reactions to new legislation. A two-way traffic was started between the government and the CAB service from the very beginning of the war, and it has continued and developed to this day.

In spite of these close relations with the government, it was not until 1940 that state aid was forthcoming and the National Council had at first to finance the rapidly developing new service entirely from its its voluntary funds. In that year, however, the Ministry of Health made a retrospective grant of £9,459, and by 1944 the annual grant had reached the peak figure of £33,406. This grant had the dual purpose of helping in the establishment and maintenance of local bureaux, and of meeting a major part of the costs of the central and regional services which the NCSS provided It enabled the Council to increase the value of the service both by providing better central guidance and help, and by insisting, when making grants to bureaux, on certain standards of efficiency. Many bureaux were able to obtain help also from their local authority, in the form of grant or of free premises, and sometimes both. Indeed, the CAB movement was following the traditional NCSS pattern: autonomous local committees with the widest possible representation, linked through regional machinery with the National Council in London; and finance provided by a grant from central government sources, by help from local authorities, and from local voluntary sources in the form of volunteers to staff and often to run the bureaux.

In May 1945, just before the war with Germany ended, the first national CAB conference was held at Westminster. It was addressed by the Minister of Health; and it is indicative of the widespread interest in the movement that, among the 500 people present, there were representatives of fourteen government departments, four foreign governments (USA, France, Netherlands, Poland), together with UNRRA and numerous other national and international bodies.

This conference was convinced that the service would be even more needed in the period of resettlement and reconstruction; and, guided by this opinion, the National Council set to work to plan the future of the bureaux in the changed conditions ahead. The difficulties were formidable, finance not the least. The Ministry of Health had made it clear that they considered a local information service in normal times should be supported by local funds, and that grant-aid from the state for the assistance of local bureaux would cease in 1946. In line with its general policy, the National Council had always held the view that a proportion of money from voluntary sources was essential to the independence of the movement; but some of the autonomous CAB committees did not share this view, regarding it as impracticable or maintaining that voluntary unpaid service should be reckoned as a contribution of equal importance with statutory finance. Staffing and premises were likely to be other serious problems for the service, as there was certain to be a decline in the number of voluntary workers once the war was over, and many bureaux might also find themselves homeless.

The National Council had consultations with the Ministry of Health and with the associations of local authorities; and towards the end of 1945 the Ministry issued a circular to local authorities which, while urging them to provide information centres, gave them at the same time provisional powers to do so through a voluntary agency, such as a citizens' advice bureau, which they could grant-aid for the purpose.

Renewed efforts were made to recruit and train new workers; to encourage them to develop wide consultant services (on legal matters, tax and business questions, domestic and matrimonial problems, moral welfare, factory legislation, and so on) to help with the more complicated problems likely to come their way; and to assist in finding new accommodation where necessary. At the same time headquarters machinery was re-designed to meet new conditions. Further representation of bureau workers on the central committee and the setting up of a representative Standing Conference were steps in this plan.

Dorothy Keeling, who played the leading part in the wartime history of the citizens' advice bureaux, was also in large measure responsible for the second of the new services begun in this period: the old people's welfare movement.

In August 1940, when the great air-raids on London were beginning, the officers of the National Assistance Board, now charged with the payment of supplementary pensions to old people, were disturbed to find many of them living in shocking conditions in shelters and basements. Some were in physical distress; many were lonely. The state, which was showing so much concern for the mothers and children, almost seemed to have abandoned the old to their fate.

The Assistance Board turned for help to the voluntary bodies, and suggested that the ncss might bring together the appropriate organisations. Miss Keeling had long been interested in the problems of old people through her work for the Personal Service Society in Liverpool, and with her initiative, the energetic leadership of Eleanor Rathbone, and the interest of Miss B. Ibberson of the Assistance Board, a small group came together on 13th September, 1940, in the basement kitchen of 26 Bedford Square, in the middle of an air-raid, to make tentative plans for an Old People's Welfare Committee. Three weeks later a preliminary conference was held at Bedford Square at which eleven voluntary organisations interested in some aspect of the welfare of old people were represented; and it was agreed to ask the ncss to consider how the extension of work for the aged could be achieved. A committee was established representative of eighteen voluntary organisations and the state departments concerned with the welfare of old people. It was agreed that the new committee should be recognised as a committee of the ncss, and it began work on the 22nd November, 1940, under the chairmanship of Eleanor Rathbone, who agreed to act temporarily. In fact, she continued to be the great source of wisdom and inspiration for this committee until her death in 1946.

At first, the Committee was inevitably preoccupied with immediate problems due to air-raids, evacuation, and food shortages, rather than with long-term questions; and with the need to ensure that old people had some simple explanation of state provisions, which was made in *Notes for Old Age Pensioners*, the committee's first publication. But, even so, it was ready, less than eighteen months after its formation, to submit evidence to the Beveridge Committee on Social Insurance on the long-term problems of old people; and a year later to present to the Central Housing Advisory Committee of the Ministry of Health a memorandum on the special housing needs of the elderly.

From the outset the Committee had encouraged the formation of regional and local committees, formed on the same basis as the main committee, with representatives of voluntary organisations, religious bodies, local authorities, and local officers of the Assistance Board; and by 1942 there were seven regional committees and forty-four local committees, which grew to 116 by the end of the war with many more in process of formation. These local committees undertook a wide variety of tasks and experimental projects to help the old, many of whom were lonely, isolated by evacuation from their familiar environment or by the wartime break-up of their families; and some too bewildered or infirm to look after themselves properly. The committees provided clubs and activities for the able-bodied; visited those who were lonely or in hospital; organised canteens or a mobile meals service; supplied home helps; found and equipped houses that could be made into homes or hostels. And, above all, they were able to give the National Committee first-hand information about the real needs and problems of the old, as an invaluable basis for the studies of fundamental questions of policy with which the committee was concerned.

The provision of emergency accommodation for old people from the target areas of air-raids was one of the first cares of the National Committee; and they were able, by 1941, to make available grants and loans to local groups to help in providing additional homes and hostels. From there they went on to consider the future, and in 1945 a deputation discussed with the Minister of Health the need for carefully prepared plans for the resettlement of old people evacuated from London. As a result the Minister agreed to help voluntary organisations in this task by releasing requisitioned premises, facilitating applications for licences for repair and adaptation, and so on. Even more significant for the future development of standards in services for old people was the Committee's interest in the organisation and management of homes caring for the aged; and their representations to the Ministry on the need for all such homes to be registered. As early as 1943 two conferences had been organised for matrons and organisers of voluntary homes, to give them the opportunity of sharing their knowledge and experience and of receiving guidance on ways of handling their difficult task.

By 1944 the Old People's Welfare Committee was able to note a far-reaching change both in the recognition of the place of old people in the community and also in the financial and social provisions which should be made for them—a change in which the voluntary organisations, as well as the Assistance Board and many local authorities, had played a large part. Though the welfare of its older members would become more and more an important responsibility of the state, the opportunities for the voluntary bodies to help in the provision of services beyond mere material aid would grow with the immense increase in the proportion of the aged in the population during the next few years, and with the changing attitudes to their place in modern society. Need they be regarded as a social liability, the Committee was asking? Might not old age in a progressive and healthier community be an asset—a positive element in life? 'Better diet, healthier occupations during the hard working-days will mean a sturdier old age which will not be content to withdraw from active life at sixty.' These and other questions were reviewed by the secretary of the Committee, Miss E. D. Samson, in *Old Age in the New World*,* which provided a guide to the Committee's approach to national policy in this field.

In the same year, 1944, the Committee was established as an autonomous group of the NCSS to be known as the National Old People's Welfare Committee, thus following the developing pattern of the NCSS organisation.

It was not only old people who were suffering from the effects of the heavy bombing of large cities in the earlier stages of the war. The whole population was at risk. In London, which endured for weeks on end the first intensive air-raids, the London Council of Social Service whose secretary, William Hogarth, was regional officer for the NCSS, quickly saw the need to divert much of its energies to the task of mobilising the assistance of London's social workers to meet the manifold problems which were arising in the over-crowded air-raid shelters and the rest centres for the homeless. When the Rest Centre Service was almost breaking down under the unexpected strain, one of the most valuable contributions of the LCSS was a suggestion, welcomed by the Minister of Health, that the knowledge of experienced social workers whose help to the local authorities had already been outstanding, might profitably be used to advise the

---

* Pilot Press. [Out of print.]

Ministry. Accordingly, eleven social workers of the highest standing were seconded to the Ministry of Health for special survey work in the rest centres. Their report was of such value that the newly appointed Special Commissioner for the Homeless, H. U. Willink, decided to set up a permanent advisory group of four or five voluntary social workers with special knowledge of London conditions, who would meet regularly with him to discuss welfare problems and to advise on the appointment of welfare inspectors for each of the London boroughs.

Though it was the cities which were affected most directly by the war, the countryside was suffering in less obvious ways, and at first it looked as if the emergency would put an end to much of the work being done in the villages and through the rural community councils. The blackout covered the country; transport, so necessary in scattered areas, was becoming more and more restricted; village halls were commandeered by the authorities and no new ones could be built; leaders were being called up. At the same time, hundreds of mothers and children were evacuated from the threatened cities to the villages and small towns, bringing with them new and perplexing problems. It was a situation of great difficulty for both sides: for the hosts, invaded by a horde of town-dwellers with quite different habits and ways of life, and for the guests, often bored by the quiet countryside, frustrated and lonely. Here co-operation on the NCSS pattern came into its own in many an awkward corner, making it easy for the country people to come together to help each other, to give a welcome to the strangers, and to bring them the services they needed, though by no means always with complete success.

The following extract from a letter to the chief rural officer of the NCSS after one of his wartime broadcasts on the work of parish councils gives a lively illustration of the way in which the rural work was being adapted to the needs of the day:

'*We all listened to your broadcast and are grateful. Use of village hall: you know our scheme for accommodation for schooling evacuees. Our hall has two schools Wall Steet, Poplar, and Brixton Senior Girls, in daily session.*

It is also the ARP first aid post, the LDV HQ; and the recreation ground on which it stands is rifle range and drill ground for the LDV (Local Defence Volunteers). It is literally open day and night and on Sundays the RCs have mass in the morning and Brixton's have Sunday School in the afternoon.

The shower bath is the "arsenal" for the four rifles and twenty rounds of ammunition for the LDV. This is hush-hush!

We are going to start an infant welfare centre. We have had to postpone our
flower and vegetable show which we held for the first time last August, but the
horticultural society is the "goods".

Do make this clear that no government can do anything. Some individual has
to do it. Both the CC and the RDC in the end have got to use human beings and
the parish council is the organ to get them.

Shall listen in again next Monday.'

Even if the flower show might temporarily give way to sterner things,
the horticultural societies were never more active and it was here again
that a network of services, in this case to help food production societies
of every kind, demonstrated its value. Here too the old partnership with
the women's institutes was to prove particularly important.

It was naturally assumed that cultural activities would be among the
first casualties, for music and drama were not likely to be nourished by
black-out and the exigencies of total war. In the event, exactly the
opposite happened. While many people certainly looked for relaxation
from the grim pre-occupations of wartime in the lightest kinds of escapist
entertainment, at the same time from all over the country came reports of
a new interest in serious arts and particularly in music. Out of this new
interest came such significant wartime experiments as the Council for the
Encouragement of Music and the Arts.

Even before the war the Carnegie UK Trustees had been considering
the encouragement of music as the major object of their policy for the
quinquennium 1941–45, and had appointed the Hichens Committee to
advise them on it. Reporting just before war broke out, this committee
recommended the establishment of three new music committees to further
the policy of the Trust: Music Executive, Music Societies, and Musical
Education; the last, under the chairmanship of Arthur Richmond, to take
over the functions of the music section of the existing NCSS Joint Music and
Drama Committee. The Trustees were in this way freed to assist music in
its own right and through its own machinery. So successful was this new
committee—'the nursery garden' of amateur musical activity—that by the
end of the war music-making was firmly established on a county basis
with committees in more than thirty-five of the sixty-two administrative
counties, and twenty-four music advisers had been appointed under the
direction of Dr Sidney Northcote.

Although the most spectacular results were in the sphere of music,
drama also shared in this wartime renaissance of popular culture. With
the help of the Pilgrim Trust and CEMA, productions of a high standard
were taken even to the remote countryside and helped to inspire village
drama societies to carry on. In order to assist them the old Joint Music and

Drama Committee of the NCSS, now relieved of its music commitments, was re-constituted on a broader basis to include representatives of the British Drama League, County Councils Association, CEMA, National Federation of Women's Institutes, National Association of Townswomen's Guilds, and the Carnegie UK Trustees. By 1942 expenditure from the Trust on encouraging drama had reached £1,888; forty county drama committees were flourishing and eleven organisers had been appointed. Summer schools were well attended; and the local education authorities were showing increasing interest in the work. A Travelling School for Variety Entertainment, to help those village societies which were finding it difficult to produce dramatic programmes under war conditions, was another useful experiment; and in 1940 nearly 4,000 students attended some forty schools.

With the imaginative and generous help of the Carnegie UK Trust both music and drama activities were not merely surviving the impact of war but were growing in size and strength.

As far back as the early nineteen twenties the National Council had shown its concern for the economic prosperity of the countryside, and through rural community councils, with the co-operation of the Rural Industries Bureau and aid from the Development Commission, had done a great deal to keep some ancient crafts from dying and to help country craftsmen to adjust to new conditions. Now in 1940 the desperate need for home-grown food produced a new opportunity for the village craftsman. If the new mechanised agricultural implements were to be kept running they would need prompt and efficient servicing, and here was the village blacksmith and wheelwright to do it, if only he had modern equipment and the knowledge to use it. Discussions with government departments took place; a thousand key blacksmiths were listed; and the Rural Industries Equipment Loan Fund was set up, with interest-free loans from HM Treasury through the Development Commission, to equip country workshops with modern machinery. The NCSS was to be responsible for administration, through the rural community councils and with the assistance of the Rural Industries Bureau. By the end of 1946 applications had been received from 3,200 rural craftsmen; £118,500 worth of equipment had been installed; and many hundreds of craftsmen had received instruction in the use of their new tools. Later, the original scheme was broadened to cover a larger number of trades, including brickyards and potteries.

Meanwhile the Parish Councils Advisory Service was growing steadily. Even in the critical days of 1940–41 conferences attended by more than 3,000 people had been held. By this time, 60,000 parish council leaflets had been distributed, to help in making the parish council a more efficient instrument of local government and thus to relieve the larger authorities of a great amount of detailed administrative work and to bring more local people into the running of their own affairs.

Those in the National Council responsible for guiding the movement were convinced that the parish councils, after fifty years of work (they were established by the Local Government Act of 1894) were now at a turning point in their history. Far from being an outmoded form of local government they had a larger part to play in it if the authorities could be convinced of the wisdom and practicability of this policy. So in 1943 a campaign was launched. The NCSS set up a special committee to review the position and to recommend to the government any necessary changes in the powers and procedures of parish councils. In formulating these recommendations the National Council was determined, in spite of the difficulties of wartime conditions, to give each of the 7,000 parish councils in the country the chance to debate and discuss the proposed changes. It was a formidable undertaking but it was carried out. Conferences were arranged all over the country. Forty-three counties held meetings. The response was encouraging beyond all expectation. Even in remote hamlets a lively interest in the future of village government was stirring; and everywhere proposals for reform were keenly and critically debated, with the help of speakers from the National Council and often with the active co-operation of the women's institutes. Already it was clear that if the new machinery was to be truly democratic the old, discredited way of voting by a show of hands must go; and fresh evidence of the need for change was prepared against the day when elections would once again be held. To many it might have seemed unwise to launch a campaign to renew the springs of local government in the midst of the greatest conflict in history. But enterprise and faith were justified in the outcome, for by this time men's thoughts were already turning in hope to the future.

The burden on the small wartime staff of the Council's rural department grew as the number of parish councils availing themselves of the advisory service continued to increase, and it was decided to encourage the formation of county committees to promote the maximum decentralisation. It was now becoming clear that a National Association of Parish Councils was needed. Steps were taken to work out constitutions for both county associations and a National Association, and by the time the war came to an end these preparations had reached a stage where quick progress could be made when the opportunity came.

Another valuable piece of rural work which the NCSS did during the war was the presentation of evidence to the Scott Committee on the

Utilisation of Land in Rural Areas. One sentence in the report which the committee subsequently made summed up trenchantly the message which the National Council had been preaching for twenty years: 'We are convinced that the cardinal problem is how to re-focus cultural life within the village itself.' Although during the war years the building of village halls was almost at a standstill, the National Council did not allow the practice based on its preaching to lapse. Side by side with the deepening interest in parish councils went plans for the new village halls which would be needed. Schemes already planned were completed, and some extensions were carried out early in the war to cope with the needs of village populations vastly increased by evacuees. Although the full Village Halls Committee could not meet, a sub-committee continued to function and was ready with a new village halls handbook and plans for immediate development almost as soon as the guns stopped firing.

By this time, the NCSS was in touch with over a thousand new schemes for village halls and the number was growing rapidly. To meet a demand of this size at the high cost of post-war building would require a more ambitious scheme than the pioneer pre-war arrangement for interest-free loans from the Development Commission and grants-in-aid from the Carnegie UK Trust, although these had made possible nearly six hundred schemes. It was the Education Act of 1944, extending social and educational provisions to the country as a whole, which foreshadowed a solution. Under this legislation the Ministry of Education worked out with the NCSS a plan whereby all applications to the Ministry for social centres in towns of less than 4,000 inhabitants were to be forwarded to the National Council to be considered for grant and loan assistance; and these plans were to be integrated with those of the local education authorities in their provision of schools and adult education. Here was a unique tribute to the pioneer work of the Council and the opening of a new and very hopeful phase in statutory and voluntary relations.

The new Education Act which held out hopes of great developments in social provision for the countryside was also full of promise for the new housing estates and other urban areas where, towards the end of the war, community associations had been making good progress. The early days of the war had dealt hardly with the movement. Centres were commandeered, or destroyed by bombs, and some associations disintegrated. But later the movement received a powerful stimulus from a widespread determination that the neighbourly spirit of civil defence post and street fire-guard party should be carried over into some permanent peace-time form. In the Forces, too, men and women were learning to do things together and thinking of the better Britain they hoped to make when at last they came back home.

As early as 1943 a national conference had been held in London, to which 630 delegates from all parts of the country came, from central and local authorities and voluntary organisations. The applications to attend far exceeded the capacity of the hall—a startling revelation to the organisers of the opportunities to develop this work which lay just ahead.

Towards the end of the war new neighbourhood groups began to come together, some from civil defence groups, others to plan a social centre as a war memorial; yet others as an outcome of street victory celebrations. By the end of 1945 the NCSS was in touch with over a thousand groups.

Meanwhile the planners had long been at work, designing the new cities which should be built on the ruins of the old. Profiting by the lessons of the inter-war estates, and not a little influenced by the work of a study group of the NCSS, the planners accepted as the basic unit, both for re-developed slum areas and the new estates and satellite towns then being discussed, the small, compact neighbourhood of about 5,000 to 10,000 people; together with its own shops, schools, and community buildings and with its social life focussed in the community centre. This idea had won supporters in many other fields. Educationists had been impressed by the achievements of new informal techniques of adult education in the Forces; sociologists and those concerned for the future of local government by the possibility of reviving disintegrating communities. It was thus a logical development that the new Education Act should lay upon local education authorities the compulsory responsibility to secure the provision of 'Further Education', including in that definition: 'leisure-time occupation, in such organised cultural training and recreative activities as are suited to their requirements, for any persons over compulsory school age who are able and willing to profit by the facilities provided for that purpose'.

With these opportunities in mind the National Council, in May 1944, appointed as head of the community centres department, Frank S. Milligan, former warden of Beachcroft Educational Settlement and founder of Wincham Hall Residential Centre for the unemployed, a pioneer of informal adult education on Merseyside among men in the enforced idleness of the depression, and in the Forces as an army welfare officer and full-time lecturer. It was largely his imaginative, patient efforts to translate ideals into practical achievement within the framework of an active democracy, his grasp of principle, and his understanding of human diversity which, through many difficulties, brought the community associations movement to maturity during the post-war years.

With no immediate possibility of new buildings, attention was focussed on the reservation of sites, plans for temporary accommodation, and the training of community centre wardens and secretaries of community associations. By 1945, the work had reached the stage where a National Federation of Community Associations could be created as an independent autonomous group, working in association with the NCSS, its secretariat and working expenses provided by the Council—a further development of the Council's policy of fostering independent associated groups.

While the community associations were in this way preparing for steadily increasing activity after the war, a parallel branch of community work was in process of transforming itself to meet new conditions in the war emergency and also in its aftermath. The community service clubs, which had been built up from the old occupational centres for the unemployed, suffered badly from the war. With the mobilisation of manpower the number of men using the clubs declined; some premises were commandeered; there was a rapid contraction of the advisory services provided by the NCSS, and a like contraction of funds from both voluntary and government sources. But so well established had the clubs become and such was the part they played in the social life of the community that the movement survived; and the experience gained in them burgeoned also in a new place: in January 1941, the Directorate of Army Education asked the NCSS to advise on the spare-time occupation of troops undergoing prolonged training or on defence duties in isolated areas. Their problem had much in common with that of the men who had lived in enforced idleness in the years before the war, and indeed some of those involved were the same men. So the NCSS agreed to place the services of its most experienced specialists in club work at the disposal of the Army Education Corps for six months. The experiment was an unqualified success and resulted in the widespread adoption by the Army, and later by the Navy and RAF, of a programme of practical activity as an integral part of the war-time education scheme. Units which had shown little interest at the outset were later painting and decorating their quarters, and making gadgets of all kinds to improve their own comfort as well as to fill their time.

During this period the women's clubs remained stable, even increasing in membership and activity. Soon there were over 650 women's clubs, finding in the new needs brought by the war—welfare of evacuees, food production, 'make do and mend'—a new purpose and new activities. Their members, who had received help from the community in the days of the depression, now enjoyed the opportunity of giving help to others. In the small towns they welcomed evacuees from the bombed cities; their clubs became centres for communal feeding and neighbourly help. In Durham they lent their premises for the distribution of welfare foods, and themselves made meat pies and pasties. At Burton-on-Trent they washed blankets for a Red Cross train. In Shropshire they cleaned old houses for evacuees. They undertook food demonstrations and the Make-Do-and-Mend Campaign for the Board of Trade and the Ministry of Food for the whole of the South Wales area. In Scotland they prepared parcels of craft work for invalid prisoners of war. In these and many other ways the women's clubs established a new status in the eyes of the public and their members gained a sense of independence and usefulness they had never known before. The feeling they were part of a national movement began to grow and this was reflected in an increasing demand for a national association. As a first step towards this a Standing Conference of Women's Social Service Clubs was set up in 1942 as a wartime measure.

Established in the years of the depression, when hardship bore heavily on an underprivileged section of the nation, the club movement as a whole was well qualified to cope with other difficulties pressing on other members of the community in wartime, and to emerge into the years of reconstruction with a new-found sense of confidence and purpose. During the closing stages of the war much thought was given to the problems of the returning servicemen and the way in which the clubs might be able to help them. In November 1944, representatives from the areas where the men's clubs, now numbering about 1,000, were situated met in conference. They agreed to recommend that a National Federation of Community Service Clubs, should be established, representing both the men's and the women's side of the movement; that there should be closer links with the community centres movement; and that the clubs should aim to serve the neighbourhood irrespective of employment or unemployment.

The great increase in social service activities during the war helped to emphasise once more the importance of the urban council of social service as a focal point for voluntary effort, but it also illustrated how difficult it had proved to create successfully the right machinery for this collaboration and how comparatively slow had been the development of this vital part of the NCSS pattern of service. By the beginning of the war there were about 120 local organisations, but probably not more than one quarter were councils of social service in the full sense. Though many of them did excellent work during the war and some were able to undertake a wide range of activities, others were specialised agencies with a very limited programme of personal relief work or old people's welfare or citizens' advice bureau work only, and tended to forget their prime function of providing a means of partnership between the voluntary organisations and the statutory bodies and of bringing the social affairs of their districts into the right perspective.

With these considerations brought into new prominence by the pressures of war, and by the prospect of even wider opportunities for co-operative voluntary effort in the changing society likely to follow, the National Council addressed itself with new vigour to the task of resolving the problems of structure and work of local councils. A national conference of councils of social service was held in 1941 which recommended the setting up of a special committee to prepare a report for the guidance of the National Council's policy in this field; and at a second national conference the following year, at which seventy-nine local councils were represented, this report was carefully considered and debated. It was agreed that more effective means of central consultation should be established and a clear lead given to local councils, both on the principles underlying the work and the practical form it should take. The autonomy of individual councils should remain and free scope be left for the working out of local patterns of organisation. At the same time, it was felt that there should be a more general recognition in practice of the broad principles for which councils of social service should stand, and that representation on any central body which might be set up should be limited to those organisations which have evidence of having accepted in their work the broad aims and principles as outlined in the report and amended by the national conference. A Standing Conference of Councils of Social Service should be set up with a representative central committee, which should be accepted by the National Council as the responsible body for the guidance of local councils of social service.

Final arrangements for establishing this Standing Conference were made in 1945, when applications for membership were invited from all local councils and considered with these standards and principles in mind. It was a difficult task. Sixty local societies applied for membership, including six area councils and fifty-four town councils of social service. The committee was able to accept thirty-seven as permanent members; a further seven which had plans for development were accepted for one year in the first instance; decisions on a further five were deferred; while eleven were declined on the grounds that they did not comply with the conditions of membership which had been agreed. Proposals for the constitution and election of a central committee representative of the work in different parts of the country had also been agreed. So the first stage of the new campaign to extend the councils of social service movement throughout the country was completed as the community moved from war to peace; but it was recognised that a great task still lay ahead.

It was interesting that during the war, which severed so many international links, the overseas work of the NCSS should have continued to develop. The Council's first annual report in 1920 had recorded with gratification the visits of social workers from Japan, India, Australia, Mexico, the United States, and other countries, as symbolic of the re-establishment of contacts broken by the first world war. The second world war seems to have increased overseas social work contacts rather than cut them. This was no doubt partly due to the existence of the NCSS as a useful focus for the various interests of foreign social workers and sociologists; partly to a growing understanding in the world about the place of social work; partly to the presence in this country of several exiled governments, anxious to prepare themselves to cope with the immense difficulties of social reconstruction which they would face in their own countries when they returned.

The links between the English-speaking countries were particularly strong, but the influence of the United States was towards a widening of overseas relationships. Miss Bondfield reported on her return from an extended visit to the States that many American groups were convinced that Anglo-American understanding, which was not itself at all complete, did not provide the broad basis for the full international co-operation needed. They wanted to see greater inter-Allied understanding and closer contacts with other great countries such as China and Russia.

The National Council too considered that collaboration in the field of social welfare should be one of the constructive influences working for world harmony when the war was over; and in view of the importance of this side of their work the Emergency Committee decided in 1943 to set up an Overseas and International Committee to guide their policy. To provide an acceptable meeting-place for overseas visitors and temporary residents, who wanted to study British social conditions, institutions, and method, an international common room for social workers was opened at 32 Gordon Square, with the help of a generous gift from the United Office and Professional Workers of America, and under the guidance of Elizabeth Handasyde. Regular meetings were held, addressed by distinguished foreign speakers; discussion groups and visits of observation were arranged. One of the interested foreign observers was Princess (now Queen) Juliana of the Netherlands, who attended several NCSS conferences and committee meetings, and spent many hours visiting citizens' advice bureaux to study their work.

Useful though these meetings, tours, and discussions might be, the National Council recognised that, if true understanding between nations was to grow, there was need for an extension of the work started before the war in exchanging knowledge and experience by prolonged visits by workers in this country to places abroad for study and research. To foster this work the British Committee for the International Exchange of Social Workers and Administrators was set up in 1944, after a visit to America and Canada by Erwin Schuller, a senior member of the staff, who was able to discuss the project with a committee established in the United States. He was also largely responsible for a handbook, *Citizens' Advice Bureaux and Advice Centres in Liberated Europe*, that formed the basis of a course which allied governments in exile here had asked the Council to provide for their senior welfare officers; this was to equip them to establish national information and advice services, operated by local people for the local community, when they returned to their liberated countries.

Later in the same year Erwin Schuller was seconded to the United Nations Relief and Rehabilitation Administration to help to plan courses in America for relief workers training for emergency welfare services abroad. The NCSS had the opportunity to give assistance of more far-reaching importance to another projected international organ when, at the invitation of the Ministry of Education, the Council submitted suggestions on the draft proposals for the United Nations Educational, Scientific, and Cultural Organisation, designed to secure co-operation between public and voluntary organisations.

About this time William Hogarth left the NCSS regional office for London to become secretary of the Council of British Societies for Relief Abroad, which the NCSS had helped to create; and the National Council was able to make a small practical contribution towards the work of his organisation by arranging for a team of craft specialists to visit the displaced persons camps in north-west Germany to advise on the organisation of craft work and similar activities for these unhappy victims of the war.

To fill the key post of secretary to the London Council of Social Service and London regional officer of the NCSS, thus left vacant, the Midlands regional officer, Richard Clements, came to London. He brought with him a wealth of experience in social and political work. He had been one of the pioneers in the Birmingham City Aid Society even before the first world war, and he had come to London as one of the first ambassadors from the great Midlands city to some of the earliest gatherings of the new National Council after that war. He had been one of the first to recognise the social needs of the housing estates and with Miss M. L. Harford, now chief woman officer of the Council, he had helped to initiate some of the earliest experimental attempts to build up the community life of the huge estates which had begun to sprawl out beyond the city bounds in the late nineteen-twenties. During the second world war he had not only been the inspiration and stalwart support of much of the voluntary social work done in his great Midland region but had contrived a remarkably close collaboration with the statutory regional services, which had ensured the full effectiveness of that work.

CHAPTER SIX

Forward Planning

DESPITE the urgent activity stimulated by the war and the sometimes unfamiliar preoccupations involved, more time and opportunity than ever before was given to thinking out the new implications of NCSS policy and to planning its share in post-war reconstruction. Even in the darkest days at the beginning of the war plans were being laid to meet the revolutionary changes which it was felt that the war would bring. There were several reasons for this. Decline in the unemployment problem relieved the NCSS of a heavy burden of day-to-day administration. Working at first hand in swiftly changing social conditions, the Council realised that much previous policy was now outmoded. New ways had to be found of meeting new needs. Moreover, the NCSS itself was being driven to adapt its structure to changing times. Decentralisation under regional officers; the rise of autonomous consultative groups representing specialised interests; the formation of standing conferences: all these were part of the new pattern. And, as before, war and the threat to civilisation were to prove a powerful stimulus to social progress. When the very foundations of their world seemed shaken, thoughtful and serious men sustained their reason and their faith with plans for building a better world tomorrow.

And at that time there were, in the inner circles of the Council, just such a 'company of serious and thoughtful men'. It was their coming together which was to change the future of the NCSS, even though the full results of their work were to be lost through untimely deaths. In 1941 they had been meeting as a Select Committee. Later, as the need for their work became clearer, they were constituted as the Central Planning Committee. Their number included distinguished scholars, men of business, and leaders of social work. First there was Dr Adams, Warden of All Souls, still carrying the responsibility of chairmanship of the Council and bringing to its inner counsels the wisdom which in another war he had brought to the Cabinet Secretariat of Lloyd George. Now, enriched by the experience of another twenty years, during which time he had seen the ideas he had inspired come to fruition in the work of the Council, he guided a committee which included such leaders of public life as the Master of Balliol (Dr A. D. Lindsay), and Professor Ernest Barker, Dr Henry Mess, R. C. Norman, Sir Wyndham Deedes, Margaret Bondfield, Mrs Montagu Norman, A. W. Oyler, Sir Percy Alden, and Leonard Shoeten Sack. To George Haynes, the new secretary, fell the difficult task of translating their ideas into a constitutional framework and a plan of action. One of their earliest acts was the appointment of Dr Henry Mess as part-time director of studies for the NCSS. He was one of the outstanding social workers of his day, who had come to Bedford College, London, from Tyneside, where he was founder and director of the Council of Social Service and where his work, based on the careful social survey which he carried out, had brought some hope and comfort to the derelict towns.

With important studies already in progress the prospects seemed hopeful indeed. The Sir Halley Stewart Trust, through the interest of Sir Malcolm Stewart, then chairman of the Council, had generously given a grant to enable the Council to build up a library for social workers and to appoint a research assistant and librarian. The new department of studies and research, the library, and the international common room were all housed not far from Bedford Square, at No. 32 Gordon Square, a quiet and commodious house in the precinct of London University and admirably suited to the purpose. Although these developments seemed an innovation, they actually fulfilled some of the earliest intentions of the Council.

The department of studies and research concentrated on three main projects. For some time past a group from the Community Centres and Associations Committee, aided by the expert town-planning knowledge of Professor (now Lord) Holford, had been considering how the pre-war experience of the Council in promoting community centres and associations on new housing estates might be related to the problems of post-war reconstruction of the bombed cities. Their report, *The Size and Social Structure of a Town*,* published in 1953, was to exercise an important formative influence on post-war town planning. It used the pre-war experience of the Council to extend and develop in a simple and practical way the earlier idea of the self-contained neighbourhood with its community centre, churches, schools, and shops, as the basic unit for future planning, whether on new housing estates, in new towns, or in the re-development of blitzed cities. It served also to reinforce the views of those town-planners who believed that the ideal population for a town was about 50,000, divided into neighbourhoods of some 10,000 each.

---

* Allen and Unwin. [Out of print.]

While this work was in progress the Council had been approached by the Bank of England to consider the possibility of a survey designed to assess the social consequences which might follow if the Bank decided to make its emergency war-time dispersal of staff to the country a permanent feature. It was not easy to undertake so complex a study in war-time but the Council felt that the question was one of great importance, and the influence of the Bank of England, by virtue of its special position, might be decisive in determining whether or not other bodies would decide to disperse their headquarters staff from London, thus aiding or thwarting the town-planning policy of decentralisation advocated by the Barlow Report* which had just been published. In spite of considerable difficulties the work was carried out, the final draft being completed by Dr Mess just before his death. Although the report,† published in 1944, dealt realistically with the social problems which would follow the dispersal of large office staffs from London, it also pointed out the advantages to be gained from such a move and thus played an important part in hastening the acceptance by all parties of the wisdom and necessity of limiting the further growth of London by dispersing both industry and population.

Closely allied with the survey for the Bank of England, another important project was started by Dr Mess. He was convinced that, while considerable attention had been given to the social problems of great cities with their slums and their housing estates, and also to the life of the villages, the problems of the small towns had been largely overlooked. He therefore planned a survey of some thirty representative towns. In spite of the obvious difficulties of launching such a project during the war, the work was started and survey groups set up in a number of the chosen towns. This large task was never completed, for while it was still in the early stages, the director of studies died suddenly, leaving unfinished much of the work he had planned. Owing to the war-time pressure on the small staff of the NCSS it was impossible to continue the survey in its original form, and but for the patient work of Dr Mess' assistant, Mrs Marjorie Bourne, who collated all the records so far made, this valuable material must have been wasted. Much of it was however preserved by this means and, with the addition of fresh material, it was published some years later.‡

These three war-time surveys (and there were several others of slightly less importance) were to exercise a significant and continuing influence in

---

* *Distribution of the Industrial Population: Report of the Royal Commission.* 1940. Cmd. 6153. HMSO.

† *Dispersal.* Oxford University Press. [Out of print.]

‡ *Small Towns: Their Social and Community Problems.* NCSS. [Out of print.]

the field of social and community planning far beyond the immediate orbit of the NCSS, but other deliberations of the central planning committee were to have a decisive effect on the work and future organisation of the Council itself. As far back as 1941 Dr Mess had begun work on a series of papers in which he analysed critically the history and progress of the NCSS. These were debated and discussed by the Central Planning Committee, which had already set up study groups to consider the future of the rural, urban, and unemployment work; and the whole wide range of the Council's work was now brought under review.

One important outcome of the central planning group's deliberations was to focus attention on certain failures and weaknesses of the NCSS. If the challenge of the future was to be accepted there was urgent need to re-examine fundamental aims and to think out afresh, in terms of the new social order which was emerging, the basic concept of voluntary 'social service' and its relationship to the rapidly increasing statutory services. It was clear that much confusion existed in both the public and the official mind as to the present meaning of the words. Even in the short life-span of the NCSS their meaning had changed considerably. Since the National Council claimed that its principal function was to co-ordinate the voluntary social service organisations and to bring them into partnership with the statutory services, it was obviously a task of some importance and urgency to decide exactly what the words 'social service' meant and what were the implications of attaching the adjective 'voluntary'. There were two special dangers arising from the growing confusion of terms. In the first place, even the enlightened public, upon whom the National Council depended to some extent for its support, were prevented from getting a clear picture of its purpose and intentions. Secondly, there was increasing interest overseas, in the Commonwealth, in the United States and in Allied countries in the work of the Council, and it was particularly important that a clear picture should be presented to them.

But here at the beginning, in the very meaning of words, obscurities arose. No legal definition of the term 'social service' existed. Official attempts at definition had tended to intensify the confusion. The Treasury's White Paper, for instance, which set out 'The Annual Return of Expenditure on Public Social Services', included such services as education, although few teachers would have regarded their calling as a social service. In the public mind, however, the old conception of social service still persisted: that it was work mainly for the relief of the individual in distress, service rendered by the privileged to the less fortunate, and intended primarily to help the poorer sections of society. Although the Council had done more than any other agency to broaden this narrow concept and to insist that social service embraced all the common efforts of the community to enrich normal life, the fact that the NCSS had been so largely identified in the public mind with efforts to assist the unemployed had helped to perpetuate the older and more limited idea.

It was scarcely surprising that the man in the street found the nomenclature of voluntary social service puzzling. There were voluntary organisations and voluntary workers. But statutory bodies such as the children's care committees used voluntary workers, while many voluntary organisations employed salaried workers. The difficulty was intensified by the way that the British statutory social services had developed in a piece-meal fashion. Almost all of them had been pioneered by voluntary action. Once their value was proved and the need for large-scale extension demonstrated, they had been taken over by central government or local authorities. But here again it was impossible to define where the action of the state ended and the sphere of purely voluntary action continued, for in much of the National Council's activities a new principle was seen at work in which statutory grants were given to enable voluntary societies to go on doing the work which might have been taken over by the state. If, however, the criterion of the voluntary organisation was to be that it retained absolute control of its own policy, there were always some people who feared that too large subsidies might endanger that vital independence, and even result in too close an identification of the organisation with the government of the day. And in a more equalitarian society what was to be the relation of social service to the principle of mutual aid? How, for instance, could one classify a community association whose support derived from the mutual enterprise of the residents on a housing estate, advised and assisted by the National Council, and whose centre was later grant-aided by the local authority?

One distinction, however, seemed to emerge with some clarity. Whilst a service was in the pioneer or experimental stage it could claim to be regarded as 'social service'. Thus community centres were still entitled to the term in 1940 while libraries, which had justified this description in the rural areas in the nineteen-twenties when they had formed a large part of the rural community councils' campaign for 'better living in the country', could no longer claim to be described in this way.

These and similar questions exercised the minds of the central planning committee as they analysed critically the history and progress of the NCSS in order to determine the part it ought to play in the new society. From their deliberations it emerged more clearly that there was no one agreed definition of social service and it was doubtful if any agreed definition could be framed. The best that could be done was to bear in mind the breadth of meaning of the term and its different connotations and to be clear in what sense it was used on any particular occasion.

Although uncertainty existed even in the minds of the group as to these exact lines of demarcation, it was evident that one essential to be emphasised was the pioneering character of the venture. Despite the ever-growing area of statutory action, the need for voluntary organisations was obviously as great as ever. They could experiment in controversial fields where as yet the state could not follow; they possessed a flexibility which the machinery of authority could not be expected to show; they could function in areas of service calling for real devotion and self-sacrifice on the part of the workers; they could inspire great resources of volunteer help which the state, except in times of emergency, could not hope to do. Nor did the lessons of continental history pass unnoticed. The Code Napoleon, which influenced so much of Europe, had inhibited the development of autonomous institutions as well as the autonomy of local government. By contrast, the political maturity of the British people was nourished by the liberty of voluntary organisations with their freedom of speech, discussion and action. But the voluntary agencies which had played so large a part in moulding the character of the British people had owed their strength and vitality in the past largely to the fact that they were independent because their finance was private and independent. Now, however, these sources of revenue were declining, and anxious thought had to be given to finding some substitute for the lost income from the wealthy whose support would evidently become more and more precarious.

The group faced once again the old problem presented by the local councils of social service. Why were they so difficult to initiate, to finance, and to keep true to their real functions? Here on the local scale was the same dilemma which faced the NCSS on a national scale. The past twenty years had shown conclusively that bodies whose real function was thinking and planning were not popular with the contributing public who liked to see some practical, direct, executive action for their money. The tradition of the pathetic child on the appeal leaflet still persisted, even if the child was no longer barefoot. (The bare feet are back on the advertisements twenty years later.)

There were striking parallels between the history of the NCSS and many of the local councils of social service. Each had as one of its aims the task of filling the gaps in social provision once it was clear that no other appropriate body existed to carry out the work. This was excellent in theory; in practice it sometimes happened that the gaps took so much filling that insufficient resources of money and man-power were left to do adequately the tasks for which it had been primarily created. The initiation of new experiments was certainly a function of the councils, both local and national. But when they had to struggle desperately to raise voluntary funds it required great wisdom and courage on their part to hand over to other bodies the projects which they had started and which had proved popular with the charitable public. This had certainly been the dilemma with the unemployment work at both local and national levels. Once started it would have been almost impossible to withdraw. But the inevitable consequence had been the absorption of too great a proportion of the available resources to the detriment of the vital over-all functions of thinking and planning.

Another consequence was that once a co-ordinating body itself entered the field of practical action, the bodies whose activities it sought to co-ordinate might come to regard it as a competitor and rival, particularly in the matter of money-raising. It was true that the NCSS had exercised a commendable restraint in refraining from national appeals which might have affected adversely the appeals of many of its constituent organisations, but the suspicion remained.

How was this difficulty to be solved in terms of the new society from which the large scale benefactor was likely to disappear? Superficially the finances of the NCSS appeared healthy enough. Its income had risen from about £1,300 in 1920 to approximately £40,000 and expenditure had rarely exceeded income. But this apparent strength hid serious weaknesses. Of its own income of £40,000 a year far too high a proportion was earmarked for specific projects. 'Free' income amounted to less than £7,000 and reserves were a similar figure, so that it was difficult to embark on new projects, however justified, unless grant-aid from some source could be reasonably anticipated before long.

It was clear to the planning committee that this was a far bigger question than the mere consideration of NCSS finance. It was related to the much wider issues of social organisation and leadership in a modern democratic society. In feudal times this had been a charge on the land. Manor and church, each receiving its dues, had contributed notable leadership until the industrial revolution began to break up the ancient communities, massing the population into rapidly expanding towns, each with its east-end and its west-end into which the respective classes were segregated. For over a hundred years this segregation had proceeded by slow, natural means. But with the coming of the twentieth century it was rapidly accelerated by the transport revolution which electric traction and the motor car brought about, releasing all but the poorest workers from the need to live alongside the factory. The building of the great municipal housing estates in the nineteen-twenties—huge 'one-class reservations' such as Becontree, Dagenham, and Norris Green—meant that the weight of statutory authority was added to the natural forces making for segregation.

The years between the wars had been marked by three great crises in society. The three most outstanding services of the NCSS had been devised to meet these crises. The first was the rural movement, created in the aftermath of the first world war to stem the tide of rural depopulation, and to stimulate the latent resources of leadership in the villages to fill the gap left by the decline of the old order symbolised by the leadership of squire and parson. The second was the community associations and centres movement, aimed at rousing local initiative and enterprise on the new housing estates of the nineteen-twenties which the policy of social segregation had left with many problems. The third was the work with the unemployed, cut off from the normal life of the community by poverty and insecurity and doomed to live out their seemingly useless lives in those grim reservations euphemistically known as the 'Distressed Areas'.

In the new society where both feudal and plutocratic influences were discredited and distrusted, the task of the NCSS was seen to be the creation of a tradition of leadership in those places where it was lacking. With this went the parallel task of providing some kind of premises as a centre for the social activities of the community and a focus for this leadership— village halls, community centres, clubs for the unemployed.

But how would these services be paid for in the new society which was now developing? Dr Mess, writing before the Education Act of 1944, had come to hold out hopes of greatly increased statutory help for village halls and community centres; he argued that the costs of providing the necessary social organisation which the complexities of modern civilisation demanded, and which the unprivileged areas could not be expected to find themselves, should reasonably be regarded as a charge on productive resources. It was impossible to press on the landed proprietors still left in the countryside the claim that they were a continuing privileged class, for they were already so heavily taxed that they were rapidly disappearing. Nor was there much hope that in the urban areas the new companies which had replaced the old resident factory owners might feel under an obligation to help. Equally there was little chance that suburban residents, whose pleasant places remained inviolate because the squalor of industry was usually concentrated elsewhere in congested city centres, would feel a sense of responsibility for the welfare of those about whose conditions of life they could mercifully remain ignorant; since their very segregation prevented them from seeing how the other half of the town lived.

The conclusion to which Dr Mess was drawn was that the work of social organisations in the countryside, in the congested parts of old towns, and in their new working-class extensions, had no popular 'appeal value' and should be aided locally by limited subsidies from the rates to help local councils of social service; and by grants from central sources to aid the central planning and research activities of the National Council itself to carry out adequately a function which it had never had the resources to discharge satisfactorily. Those who questioned whether this might not undermine its independence were reminded that the independence of the universities had never been impaired by the University Grants Committee.

Linked with the problem of finance was the need for better publicity for the voluntary social service movement. A periodical of high quality and yet with a wide appeal seemed to be called for, to replace the old *Bulletin* which had ceased publication during the war. Such a journal would provide the keynote of the Council's publications, helping to link together the special reports, booklets and leaflets provided for different sections of the work; and also supply the basis for a continuous programme of publications which would be much more effective in informing both the social worker and the layman than a series of unrelated specialist papers.

Reviewing the achievements and the failures of the past twenty years, Dr Mess in his critical analysis drew attention to the benefits arising from the co-ordination of voluntary effort which the National Council had made possible—a volume of achievement not easy to measure or assess. He recorded the increase of mutual knowledge between societies working in parallel fields; the lessening of jealousies and misunderstandings; the first attempts to plan in a national way the differing functions and areas of a multiplicity of organisations; the slow evolution of the partnership with local authorities and government departments.

Whilst the central planning committee was hammering out the funda-mentals of social policy, the subsidiary planning groups were also hard at work. The rural committee was preparing its evidence for the Scott Com-mittee on the Utilisation of Land in Rural Areas and the Luxmore Com-mittee on Rural Education Services. The unemployment committee was relating the lessons learnt from the pre-war occupational clubs to the post-war situation. The councils of social service group were studying the work and structure of local councils. The community centres and associations committee had nearly reached its first objective of providing the Ministry of Reconstruction with a review of the factors which should control the size and social structure of housing estates. The Women's Group on Public Welfare were discussing the significance for future family policy of the disturbing results of their survey in *Our Towns* of social problems revealed by evacuation.

The death of Dr Mess was a serious loss to the NCSS; but he had left a valuable legacy in the series of papers and studies which he had produced for the central planning group. Building on these, and with the deliberations of the group to aid his own clear thinking, the general secretary of the National Council produced at the beginning of 1944 an impressive document on the *Future Purpose and Organisation of the NCSS* as a guide to its post-war policy.

After describing the broad purpose of the NCSS, as set out when the Council was established in 1919 and when it was incorporated in 1924, the statement went on to reaffirm the principles on which the Council was based. Its real task was to help forward the advance along the whole front of social life, emphasising that no type of social work was a mere 'benevolent extra' but that all the activities should be related to one another so as to form part of a synthesis.

This principle applied to both the two main interests of the Council. The first of these was the specialised work of organisations, such as those that had largely contributed to the creation of the NCSS, which devoted their energies to the solution of problems caused by personal misfortune or inadequacy. Here the Council's continuing aim must be to help the organisations to keep their work relevant and up-to-date, bringing it into the main stream of social progress and relating it to the changing needs of society.

The second element in the Council's experience, of equal if not greater importance, was concerned not with the individual's problems but with his opportunities: with the chance to develop to the full his personality and his creative impulses, which he could only do in association with others, as in the groups organised on a small local scale and in federations as national bodies which the National Council had from the beginning served or helped to initiate. Through its work with village hall committees, music and drama groups, unemployed men's clubs, and many other projects, and in face of a growing centralisation of social responsibility, the NCSS was more than ever convinced of the supreme importance of the small voluntary group in which the individual citizen had himself a real measure of responsibility. But the aim of the National Council should be not only to encourage the creation of such groups but also to help them to broaden their interests and loyalties and to develop relationships with other groups so that their members might come to understand their place in the whole. The problem in this field was a question of co-ordination and the prevention of overlapping, but it was also a search for 'wholeness of vision', an outlook that respects and welcomes differences of view and function and tries to find ways in which the groups can contribute to one another. An illustration of this principle was the need, to which the Council had persistently called attention, for better community relationships in towns and countryside. 'One of the great needs of the age is the re-creation of community life in terms of new needs and circumstances. This is true whether we think of local, national or international life—the challenge is present throughout. We must discover how to live together as neighbours, as citizens, and as members of a world family of nations.'

One of the Council's special and continuing responsibilities was the promotion of partnership between state and voluntary effort. Voluntary societies had not only a pioneer function, opening the way to state action when the value of a project had been proved; in the social and educational fields the free associations had also a distinctive function of their own. The state should not seek to incorporate into itself all those self-directing group activities which help to make the rich texture of social life; it should rather aid and foster them (a point of view which seems now officially accepted). Though a non-party-political and non-sectarian body, the NCSS should be prepared to give a lead even on controversial matters, provided they were within its own experience and competence, making it clear on whose behalf it was speaking and safeguarding the position of its constituents.

The statement went on to suggest the way in which the organisation of the National Council should develop to meet the changing times. It began by describing the existing, complex structure of the NCSS, with its strengths and also its inherent weaknesses. There was the massive Council itself, comprising nearly 200 representatives of voluntary organisations and government departments, and individual members, which met only once a year for formal business. To provide a forum of discussion for the national bodies in war-time and to secure their support in action taken by the National Council on their behalf, the Standing Conference of Voluntary Organisations had been established in 1938. The executive committee, itself consisting of nearly seventy elected, nominated, or co-opted members, met only once a year in war-time, and its business was being carried out by the emergency committee whose membership was designed to secure better representation of national and regional interests in war-time. This committee also acted for the standing conference, thus providing an executive link. In addition there were a dozen or more sub-committees dealing with the work in town and country (finance, rural, CSS, CAB, etc.); and three autonomous groups (Women's Group on Public Welfare, SCNJO, and Churches Group).

The memorandum pointed out that the existing Council, meeting once a year formally, was quite inadequate for the first purpose of the NCSS, which should be to promote the means whereby all the various elements concerned with social welfare could come together; and that it had become increasingly clear that one executive committee could not be executively responsible for all the work of groups and committees carried out in its name.

The suggested new procedure for the Council was that there should be two meetings a year during one of which the formal annual general meeting should take place and, as soon as circumstances permitted, a summer meeting as part of a National Conference on Social Life and Work.

As to the executive committee, the proposal was that it should be relieved of the burden of approving detailed policy in every field of NCSS work by the progressive development of properly constituted associated groups, representative of well-defined fields of social work, on the pattern of the existing autonomous groups, which were free to determine their own policy, using the National Council's machinery for the exchange of information and ideas and the affirmation of general ideals and purposes, and relying on it for administrative and secretarial services. The types of local groups for which the Council had a large measure of responsibility—community associations, citizens' advice bureaux, community service clubs—should have their own national conferences or groups, responsible for guidance on general matters of policy and organisation, with secretarial and administrative services provided by the Council.

The executive committee would then be free to perform its proper tasks: to consider vital questions of policy which could not be covered by any particular group and which might affect the voluntary movement as a whole; and to devote more attention to extending the services of survey and study, publications and information, which would help forward the work of voluntary organisations generally. The groups would be able to develop their work without the delays and frustrations which reference of every detail of policy to the executive committee must entail.

The most important of the other proposals concerned the regional and local organisation of the NCSS, since it had always been realised that a solution of the problem of collaboration in social service could never be secured by action at national level only.

The regional officers had played so important a role in war-time, keeping headquarters in touch with local developments and helping forward co-operation between statutory and voluntary bodies in their areas, that this system should continue though not necessarily geared, in the different post-war conditions, to the existing Civil Defence Regions.

The councils of social service, rural community councils, community associations, citizens' advice bureaux, village hall committees, which had developed largely as a result of NCSS initiative and which in their different ways promoted co-operative effort in their own districts, formed an extremely complicated and confusing network of organisation, varying in activities, resources, and local influences from place to place; but in considering how better co-ordination between them could be achieved, local spontaneity must on no account be sacrifi ed to a tidy national pattern.

As to Scotland, with its autonomous Council of Social Service; Northern Ireland where a limited CSS was established; and Wales which had no body representative of the Principality as a whole, though the South Wales and Monmouthshire Council of Social Service covered a wide region; the principles suggested were that the NCSS should be recognised as the national organisation concerned with focussing at the national level the interests of England, Scotland, Wales, and Northern Ireland, and that each country should have the fullest measure of autonomy.

With regard to area, county, and local organisation, the basis of any plan of future development must be a recognition of the need for complete coverage of the country and for bringing town and countryside into more effective partnership, both in creating and sharing in community services and activities. Experience had shown that, on the whole, rural community councils on a county basis and councils of social service covering a region or area were on the whole more satisfactory than urban councils of social service covering a single town. There seemed therefore much to commend the pattern pioneered in Kent where the RCC became an overall County Council of Social Service covering both urban and rural needs. Such a county CSS would be a completely autonomous body deriving its authority from its own local constituent organisations. But the NCSS should expect that the county CSS should provide a focus of voluntary effort for its area and that all the major concerns of the National Council should be represented. In the towns, there might be a good case for a council of social service with wide interests and functions working in a county borough; but the original plan of 1920 for a CSS in every town was obviously not feasible, and some simpler organisation, such as a consultative committee of social service would be more likely to meet the needs of the smaller towns. For citizens' advice bureaux, whose development was closely associated with that of town councils of social service, it was suggested that they should have their autonomous national committee, the constitution of which would take into account the responsibility of the area and town councils of social service for the maintenance and extension of the work.

There would evidently be great scope for the development of community associations after the war in 'built-up' areas as well as on new housing estates; and the questions involved touched so many of the constituent organisations of the NCSS that the executive committee should retain the power to review the whole sphere of this work and to set up any necessary sub-committees on policy, while recognising the Consultative Council of Community Associations as a fully autonomous body and continuing to provide the secretariat.

Finally the question of finance was examined. It was calculated that the main part of the programme of the Council reconstituted in this way could be carried out on an annual budget of about £50,000 to £55,000. It was reasonable to expect that a part of this would continue to come from statutory funds for certain specific services; and it was hoped that the invaluable war-time block grant from the Carnegie UK Trust might continue to form a stable part of the Council's income. By now the annual amount disbursed through the Benevolent Fund (formerly called the Charitable Covenants Fund) had reached a total of £400,000 approximately three per cent of which was customarily directed by the donors to the National Council, thus providing another useful source of income. It was not expected that in an impoverished post-war world the volume of small subscriptions and donations would show a marked increase, so there would be a large gap to be filled. An intensive campaign was therefore planned to interest some of the great commercial corporations.

Here was a plan, comprehensive yet practical and flexible, which would go far to create a complex national pattern of services without the dangers of building up a 'bureaucracy of social service'. So large a scheme could not be carried into effect quickly. Long and patient negotiation would be needed with the many groups and interests involved. But the first reactions to it were encouraging. It was unanimously approved at the annual meeting of the NCSS in 1944, a few months before the war in Europe at last came to an end; and with the guide lines thus set for its future policy the Council was ready to use its resources to the full in the new epoch which lay ahead.

CHAPTER SEVEN

Reconstruction

Τ HE epoch which lay ahead in 1945 was new not only because the old epoch of war was over. Already a new era had been foreshadowed by the fundamental reforms of the social services planned when the country was still fighting for its life. The Beveridge Report on Social Security had shown that whatever political party was returned to power a great increase in social legislation was to be expected. The advent of a Labour government with a large majority in July 1945 suggested that this might be in the nature of a social revolution; and before long it was clear that the 'Welfare State' was on the way. What was to be the relationship of the voluntary movement to these new developments?

Despite government spokesmen's assurances about the accepted value of voluntary effort, many people were convinced that the old pioneer services had had their day and that the welfare state, with its plans to care for the individual from the cradle to the grave, would make the work of most voluntary organisations wholly unnecessary. Others thought that state machinery was cumbersome and soulless and that, since voluntary organisations had a duty to bring their unique understanding to human problems, a conflict between statutory and voluntary agencies was inevitable.

The NCSS did not share either of these views. It had been founded to promote a partnership between public and voluntary bodies for the common good, and the new developments in state services offered more, rather than less, opportunity to pursue this aim. First of all, it was certain that, for some years to come, considerations of public finance and the burden of central and local government administration must limit the area of state action, and give voluntary workers the chance and the need to supplement and extend the statutory social services. Secondly, there would always be new ground to till which the state, with less freedom of action and sometimes with less foresight than voluntary bodies, could not or would not undertake. And finally there were certain pieces of work—for example, independent advice services, or leisure-time activities where citizens could best provide for themselves in free associations—which in any foreseeable future would be accepted as more suitable for voluntary action than public control.

Convinced therefore that the advent of the welfare state would bring no diminution of voluntary work, but in fact new and larger opportunities, the National Council went confidently ahead with its plans for the post-war years.

On the rural side, the first essential was to get the rural community councils—the main machinery through which the National Council operated in the countryside—into full working order again after the inevitable dislocation caused by the war. But the problem of finance seemed almost insuperable. Income from voluntary sources which in 1934/5 had represented thirty-six per cent of the total had declined to seven per cent, and although the proportion from local authorities had risen from fifteen per cent to twenty-six per cent this still left a serious gap to be filled. At a critical moment the Council's application to the Development Commissioners brought an encouraging response. Recognising the urgent need, the Commissioners recommended to the Treasury that substantial grants from central government should be made to established rural community councils to enable them to provide efficient administration, especially for their services to village halls and rural industries, for the next three years. The argument for rural community councils has never been better stated than in the Commissioners' reply to the Council's application:

'The Commissioners believe that rural community councils, representative as they are of both the statutory and the voluntary organisations of their areas and claiming no executive functions of their own save those assigned to them by agreement, can make a very special contribution to the economic and social developments of rural areas. They can ensure that attention is not concentrated unduly upon one set of problems alone, but that all the needs and wishes of those who live and work in the country are kept in view and brought into relation.'

Thus fortified, the work for parish councils, village halls, rural industries, informal education, and other activities much curtailed during the war, went ahead with renewed vigour. Now too, there was a chance to consider other needs of the countryside, such as the means of bringing a citizens' advice service more effectively to the village, and supplementing the government's new health service with voluntary work. 'The rural community councils stand on the threshold of great opportunities', said the annual report of 1946/7.

This was certainly true of the work for parish councils, 2,500 of which were already affiliated to the newly established National Association of

Parish Councils. The results of the long campaign were triumphantly shown in the elections of March, 1946, when from all over the country it was reported that 'there were more candidates, more contested elections, more demands for polls and better attended meetings than ever before.' But it was the national conference at Westminster in October, 1947, which really set the seal on the achievement of the past thirteen years. 2,400 parish councillors attended; in the chair was Lord Justice Scott, the president of the new Association, whose wise guidance had contributed so greatly to its foundation; and the principal speakers were the Lord President of the Council and the Minister of Education. It was obvious to those present on this memorable occasion that parish councils had at last established themselves as an essential part of the machinery of local government. It was almost a foregone conclusion that the following year would see, in the Representation of the People Act, the successful culmination of the campaign for the abolition of the vote by show of hands. For some years the NCSS continued to provide the administrative services for the National Association, but by 1951 such excellent progress had been made in establishing its position as one of the local authority associations with wide coverage of the whole country and influence with government departments that the headquarters of the NAPC became entirely responsible for its own administration. A joint consultative committee was set up to consider matters of common interest so as to ensure the co-operation of rural community councils in the work of the county associations, and in non-RCC counties the Council's regional officers provided secretarial services for parish councils associations.

The use of village halls for all kinds of purposes during the war had served to stimulate rather than to dampen the interest of village people in them as centres of social life in the broadest sense and their determination to have their own halls as soon as possible. Soon after the end of hostilities the NCSS was already in touch with more than 2,000 village committees planning to build new halls or to improve existing ones; and two years later the number of hopeful aspirants had risen to 3,000. But rising costs, shortage of materials, periodic bans on building, and the country's financial difficulties, put every sort of hindrance in the way.

Continuing its invaluable pre-war help the Carnegie United Kingdom Trust had allocated a grant of £100,000 to the National Council for the quinquennial period 1946/50 to assist village hall schemes; but owing to increased building costs the whole sum was almost exhausted in less than two years. This was to be the last grant from the Carnegie UK Trustees because their policy had always been to help a new venture to the point where it was no longer an experiment but a service which the appropriate statutory authorities were prepared to take over. They considered that village halls had now reached this stage and that their assistance, most generously given over a period of more than twenty years, must be withdrawn. They were, however, deeply concerned that their work should be continued, and negotiations between the Trustees, the National Council, the Ministry of Education and the Development Commissioners resulted in a new scheme of aid. By this the Ministry of Education and the Scottish Home Department undertook, using their powers under the Physical Training and Recreation Act of 1937, to make grants towards the cost of village hall schemes, on the advice of the village halls committee of the Council which would submit recommendations on individual applications and consider matters of general policy on the development and maintenance of village halls. The Ministry would continue to look to the NCSS and the RCC's for their advisory services to local village hall committees. The Village Halls Loan Fund, which the Council administered on behalf of the Development Commissioners, would also be available in special cases; but this was very quickly exhausted.

It was evident that, in spite of these schemes, the shortage of material and manpower would mean that the need of many of the hundreds of villages all over the country for a permanent hall could not be adequately met for some years; and in an effort to satisfy some of the more pressing needs the National Council, with the co-operation of the Development Commission, was able to start a scheme for the erection of temporary village halls, often converted war-time huts. The Council, on behalf of the Commission, let the premises to local committees for a small rent, and the committees were responsible for the erection of the buildings and the supply of any necessary additional material. A programme of 200 temporary halls was originally set for the next two years for England and Wales and, by 1951, 157 had been opened.

Good as some of these halls were, the scheme was never regarded as a substitute for the permanent centres of village life which had been a cornerstone of the Council's rural policy for thirty years. It was therefore a serious blow to the Council's plans when, late in 1950, the Ministry of Education put a ban on any new permanent halls, as part of a general policy of economy in manpower and materials. Although later this ban was removed, severe restrictions remained: £3,000 was to be the maximum cost of any new village hall, of which £1,000 or one-third would be the normal maximum government grant. Three thousand pounds was obviously a quite inadequate sum for a centre that would meet the needs of larger villages, and many of the smaller places would find the task of raising £2,000 beyond their powers.

While hoping that these restrictions would soon be eased, the Council therefore took active steps to revive the Village Halls Loan Fund which had formerly played such an important part in reinforcing the capital grants provided by the Carnegie United Kingdom Trust; and on the recommendation of the Development Commissioners the Treasury agreed in 1951 to replenish the Fund.

In all this work the village halls committee had powerful help and co-operation of several kinds. First were the rural community council secretaries, who had to keep constantly in touch with local committees, advising on technical problems, securing the interest of local architects and solicitors, negotiating with county authorities and advising local groups on the many building regulations. They not only acted as interpreters between the local groups and higher authorities but also kept the National Council up-to-date with developments.

Then there was the Council's expert advisory panel of architects who continuously studied and advised on the building and architectural problems facing the local committees; and the panel of legal advisers, guiding them on the all-important form of the trust deed under which the hall would be secured for common use, and on the many questions concerning management, rates and taxes, licences for music and dancing, and other matters on which information was needed.

Not least of the advantages which the National Council enjoyed in this work was the knowledge and ingenuity of one individual: their building adviser, Paul Matt. He had learned almost all it was possible to know about temporary halls and buildings for club use from his unique experience in the nineteen-thirties when he had been responsible for advising the NCSS on the development of several hundred clubs and centres for the unemployed. His genius for improvisation which had devised a simple hut that the men themselves could erect was turned in this time of straitened resources to solving the same problem for the villages. Scheme after scheme was drawn up; and as each reached the production stage some essential material would go into short supply; but the staunch and good-tempered architect was undaunted and as soon as one plan was blocked he devised another and finally, after steel and aluminium had failed him, succeeded with forms of construction using a concrete framework.

The village hall often serves as the local theatre, cinema and concert hall, and as more halls opened the opportunities for enriching village life through music, drama, and the arts grew fast. At the end of the war the Carnegie United Kingdom Trust decided on a new policy by which they would make their grants for music and drama direct to county music and drama committees, thus relieving the rural department of the responsibility for detailed administration of the Trustees' Fund and enabling it to turn its attention to forming Standing Conferences for County Music Committees and County Drama Committees, made up of representatives from the various county committees and acting as a central focus for their work. All rural community councils took an active interest in this plan, and many employed officers to guide and encourage local groups.

Up to 1950 the emphasis was almost entirely on rural activities, but it was realised that this was a field where a closer relationship between town and country would help in a better understanding, so much needed, of urban and rural points of view. The Standing Conferences therefore began to consider how desirable and practicable it would be to invite representative committees in county boroughs to join them; but owing to lack of funds from urban sources progress here was slow.

Meanwhile, the Standing Conference of County Music Committees found many ways of stimulating a variety of musical interests. An annual school for rural conductors. was held, and an Advisory Committee on Amateur Opera formed. They sponsored the preparation and publication of *Music and the Amateur*, and collaborated with the Music Schools Association in the issue of a magazine, *Making Music*. The Combined Arts Group of the National Council reconstituted and revised an earlier publication, *Entertain Yourselves*, for which there had been many requests.

Another piece of rural work to which the National Council attached special importance was the study of local history, not only as an educational activity but because an informed interest in the history of a village helps to encourage a sense of community. Late in 1947 the Central Local History Committee, which after some years of good work had been in abeyance during the war, was reformed; and a year later a Standing Conference for Local History was set up. With Sir Frank Stenton, President of the Historical Association, presiding at the first annual meeting, and Sir Frederick Rees, formerly Principal of the University College of South Wales, elected chairman the following year, the high standards aimed at were manifest, even to those who feared that an organisation for amateurs might lower the standards of historical research; and reports from county committees showed growing interest in local history everywhere, though lack of funds made impossible a campaign for more local history committees in the counties during this period. A great deal was done, however, to guide and encourage the existing committees, including a series of pamphlets produced in collaboration with universities and other bodies, on such subjects as *How to Write a Parish Guide, Local History Exhibitions: How to Plan and Present Them*.

Help for rural industries, in which the NCSS had been actively interested from the early 1920s, also developed considerably in the immediate post-war period. Since 1940 the Council had administered, on behalf of the Development Commission, £17,000 for loans to help rural craftsmen to buy new, up-to-date equipment and the scheme had already been of use to more than 2,000 men; but there was now an obvious need to help them to get new or improved premises as well as tools, and in 1946 the Commissioners agreed to put an initial sum of £50,000 at the disposal of the Council to provide loans for this purpose. As interest was to be charged on this new type of loan, the charitable constitution of the Council prevented it from undertaking the administration itself, and an Industrial and Provident Society, the Rural Industries Loan Fund Limited, was formed at the beginning of 1947, to administer both the workshop and the equipment funds. The Council made available the administrative services for the Society; and from 1949, and for nearly twenty years, George Haynes was to be its chairman. Nora Newton, who had most efficiently run the equipment loan fund throughout the war, became the new Fund's secretary.

The development of all these activities threw more and more work on the rural community councils, and their resources did not grow to match the increased responsibilities. Later in this post-war period their income from voluntary sources went up from the seven per cent of the war years to twenty-three per cent, but there seemed little hope that it would ever again reach the thirty-six per cent of 1934/35, whereas their average expenditure rose every year—from £1,125 in 1934/35, for instance, to £4,230 in 1949/50. The Development Commission agreed to extend their help to established rural community councils to April, 1952, but, while accepting with gratitude this further generous aid, the NCSS decided to suggest to the Commissioners that the time had come to consider realistically the permanent financing of the rural community councils.

Accordingly they submitted in June 1950 a memorandum to the Development Commissioners in which, while reaffirming the principle that grant-aid should be conditional on the rural community councils securing the support of the local authorities with whom they were working in partnership, they pointed out that the supreme value of the central grants was that they had been available for those essential overhead and administrative expenses which attracted neither local grant-aid nor voluntary contributions. While suggesting, therefore, the importance of the continuance of central grants and on a higher scale to help rural community councils to meet their larger responsibilities and higher costs, the memorandum also raised the question as to whether such grants should be for a limited period only; or whether it should not now be recognised that some assistance from central government funds was a necessary feature of the successful organisation of community work in the countryside. Considering the great volume of voluntary service which it inspired, the general grant from the Development Fund—only £25,000 in 1949/50—seemed an insignificant figure compared with other items of public expenditure. In terms of money even the whole expenditure of the RCC movement was seen to be very small in relation to the work done by those who gave their services without payment directly to the RCC or to the multifarious activities which it stimulated or promoted. If this work were not done voluntarily it would either not be done at all or would have to be carried out by the public authorities at much greater cost. 'Failure to "prime the pump" is the most false of all public economies', concluded the application to the Commissioners.

To support this application the NCSS prepared a short summary of the results achieved by the rural community councils in the thirty years since the first council was formed in Oxfordshire with the help of the Carnegie UK Trustees. In brief: they had provided the administrative framework for the development of rural industries and for the provision or maintenance of 775 village halls. They had carried the burden in their counties of building up the National Association of Parish Councils, from 1934, when it was generally thought that parish councils had had their day, to 1950 when over 3,500 parish councils were associated in a corporate effort to improve village government. They had earned a tribute from the National Federation of Young Farmers' Clubs for their work in the early days of that movement. In the field of informal education they had made a notable contribution to the growth and quality of village music, drama, and the study of local history. They had helped in the preservation of the countryside, the provision of playing fields, the development of the health service, and the promotion of village produce societies. 'But perhaps their most important work', the memorandum went on, 'cannot be evaluated. Only those who have had an opportunity of seeing RCC officers going their long rounds of the villages, advising, encouraging and helping in innumerable small problems of village life, can appreciate the real value of a service which is both informed and informal, and which can bring the most isolated villages into contact with new ideas'.

But the Council emphasised that the work was still in its early stages. Only about two-thirds of the counties in England and Wales had RCCs or their equivalents. For every village with a suitable hall there were probably three without. For every craftsman with a modern workshop a dozen were working with poor tools; the parish councils were only beginning to use their opportunities; there was still almost unlimited scope for the extension of informal adult education. Meanwhile new problems were emerging from the complexity of post-war life, and so far there had been almost complete failure to bring to country people such advisory and personal services as citizens' advice bureaux, marriage guidance, family welfare, and the care of the elderly. But as 'an efficient, general-purpose organisation able, at short notice, to undertake unusual tasks', the RCCs continued to rise to the occasion unfailingly, whether it was to help the Foreign Office with the welfare of European voluntary workers on the farms; to marshal, for the Festival of Britain authorities, the co-operation of county and local organisations; or to meet the demands of the Colonial Office, the India Office, the Foreign Office, or the British Council, for planned tours of the countryside for overseas visitors who wanted to see something of statutory and voluntary services in the villages.

Although it might have seemed a logical development from the thinking and planning of the war years, the idea that there should be in each county an overall council of social service, covering both urban and rural work, with the country interests safeguarded by a strong rural committee, was not advocated by the NCSS as an universally applicable plan. Progress towards a pattern of this kind had in fact been made in some areas, such as Cornwall, but the Council considered that each county should feel its way towards a solution of this problem without undue pressure from the centre to create neat but unrealistic patterns of administration.

On the same principle the movement towards separate Councils of Social Service for Wales and Northern Ireland had been encouraged to follow its natural course, benefiting from the experience of the Scottish Council of Social Service which was by now firmly established as an essential institution in the life of the nation. Thus, in 1947, the Council of Social Service for Wales and Monmouthshire was established, as an independent body, bringing about a fusion of the old South Wales Council of Social Service and the North Wales regional office of the NCSS; (though the latter continued its responsibility for the regional service in North Wales).

This development owed much to the groundwork done by Sir Percy Watkins who, on his retirement from the post of secretary to the Welsh Department of the Board of Education in 1933, had become the regional officer of the NCSS for Wales. The first director of the new Council was Dr W. J. Williams, formerly chief inspector of the Ministry of Education for Wales, and J. B. Evans was the first secretary.

The position of the three Councils, for Scotland, Wales, and Northern Ireland, in relation to the National Council of Social Service, was clear from the beginning; but it has been spelt out again in this Jubilee Year in an agreed statement. This reiterated that the three Councils are autonomous, self-governing bodies, and are members of the NCSS in recognition of the latter's special rôle in formulating those policies that have significance for the whole of the United Kingdom and in presenting these policies to central government and to other organisations, in the knowledge that they are speaking on behalf of the four Councils.

However, in spite of the difficulty of promoting urban councils of social service when no grant-aid comparable with that given by the Carnegie United Kingdom Trust and the Development Commission for rural work was available, the movement went slowly ahead with the formation of several new councils and regular meetings of the Standing Conference and the Central Committee.

Though the ideal pattern for a CSS continued to be a local version of the National Council itself, carrying out the same co-ordinating function in its area as the NCSS at national level, existing and new councils still varied widely. Some found that they had to concentrate chiefly on one or two services lacking in their neighbourhood; many provided skilled casework and were members of the central body bringing together the voluntary family casework agencies under the leadership of the Family Welfare Association; some, usually those of more recent growth, devoted most of their resources to group activities; only a few were the focus of all types of social work in their area. But a great deal of thought was given throughout this immediate post-war period, both by the Standing Conference and by the National Council itself, to ways in which the whole movement could be strengthened and extended; and as early as 1948 the Standing Conference demonstrated its understanding of the true place of the CSS in the new society by encouraging the establishment of local working parties of constituent members of councils to study the new social services; the ways in which the voluntary organisations could work in partnership with the local authorities, and what new tasks could best be discharged by voluntary effort. There were groups to consider the welfare of the aged and of the chronic sick; children deprived of normal home life; the National Health Service; and the social aspects of town and country planning. Two years later they moved on to study the official development plans then being submitted by the local planning authorities to the Ministry of Housing and Local Government; and to discuss how the efforts of the voluntary organisations in their area could be correlated with the local authority services for the handicapped, so much improved since the war but still failing of their full effect on the lives of the disabled as members of the community, partly because of a lack of co-ordinated work. Reports from the many councils taking part in these various studies were collated at headquarters and were of use not only as a practical demonstration of the real function of a council of social service but also in helping national bodies to understand local problems.

At this time the Council had sadly to accept the retirement of Sir Wyndham Deedes, who had served it so long and with such enlightened devotion, most particularly in the development of councils of social service.

By now, the pattern of NCSS organisation, working through associated groups and committees, was well established. One of the earliest of the associated groups, the Women's Group on Public Welfare, was also one of the most active in this post-war period. Started before the beginning of the war to consider primarily matters arising out of evacuation, from the wide viewpoint of the leading women's organisations, it had steadily expanded its field of interest to cover a remarkably broad range of social problems; and the work at the centre was increasingly reinforced by the activities of the standing conferences of women's organisations in about a hundred towns and cities in Great Britain. These standing conferences not only formed a valuable focus for discussion between local women's organisations and joint action on such current matters as local fuel economy campaigns or the drive to encourage women recruits for industry; but they also supplemented the studies of the Women's Group by the results of their own experience and observations on many questions of social policy—for example, the procedure in matrimonial courts on which in 1947 the Group made important recommendations to the Home Secretary. The links between the Women's Group and the standing conferences were continually being strengthened; and the Group, for its part, provided a service of information and advisory visits to the conferences.

Among the wide variety of matters with which the Women's Group concerned itself in these years was the question of better home-making in all its aspects; the Modern Home-Making Committee taking on the work of the former Council for Scientific Management in the Home and acting as the national co-ordinating body for social studies in the field. Their studies ranged from the preparation of schemes for talks and classes on home-making both for instructors and for housewives to the proper heights for working surfaces in the kitchen; from the quality of utility furniture to the housewife's reactions to the design of pre-fabricated houses—the latter being a careful report prepared for the International Scientific Management Congress in Brussels in 1951. International contacts, indeed, were strong. As early as 1946 the Control Commission for Germany invited the Group to recommend delegates to visit the British Zone to advise on the development of women's democratic organisations and clubs in areas of great unemployment; organised parties of German women later visited this country to observe methods of organisation; and there was a flow of visitors to the Group from Australia, West Africa, Greece, and other countries.

The principles governing child emigration; the economic needs of widows with young children; consumer research and education; accommodation for women and girls in London; the compilation, at the Prime Minister's request, of a list of experienced women to serve on royal commissions and government committees: these are only a few of the other subjects to which the members of the Women's Group put their collective minds during half-a-dozen years. But the work of probably the most far-reaching importance was the preparation and publication of the report on *The Neglected Child and his Family*. The Group had been deeply concerned with the needs of children deprived of ordinary home care ever since their investigations into evacuation problems, resulting in the report *Our Towns: A Close-up*, had revealed this as one of the most important problems; and at the beginning of 1945 it organised a national conference, attended by representatives of voluntary organisations, national institutions, religious denominations, government departments, and local authorities, to call attention to the needs and to the standards of care that should be aimed at. Later in the same year the government appointed the Curtis Committee to consider this same subject; and its famous report in 1946 eventually led to the establishment of an entirely new child care service, under the Children Act of 1948. *The Neglected Child* report, compiled while this new government policy was being worked out, could be regarded as a supplementary study, whose proposals were only to be put into official operation some years later. For, whereas the new legislation was primarily concerned with questions of child care resulting from a breakdown in family life, the Women's Group report attempted to review the problem at an earlier stage, and considered preventative measures which might help to buttress the family and prevent the breakdown which was so often the reason why children had to be removed from their own homes.

The National Old People's Welfare Committee had made itself familiar during the war, through the joint consultations and experience of its member organisations, with many of the problems of the aged certain to develop in the post-war society—the increased proportion of elderly people in the population, especially of the old or infirm; the shortage of suitable housing or homes; the inevitable breakdown of family ties and responsibility as the young people moved to new towns or new jobs in another part of the country. The work of the Committee in its early days had won the confidence of the government. It was therefore in a strong position in the post-war period to help in meeting these problems, and to influence the new social legislation and administrative schemes, particularly in the field of national insurance and assistance and the National Health Service.

The National Committee was strengthened year by year at this time by increasing support from national organisations particularly concerned with the welfare of the elderly, some of which, such as the Salvation Army, the Women's Voluntary Service (now the Women's Royal Voluntary Service), the Church Army, were individually making a notable and increasing contribution in this field. In the first post-war year the number of bodies represented on the NOPWC increased from thirty-nine to fifty-seven. And the movement came alive throughout the country in the creation of regional, county, and local committees constituted on the same lines of co-operation and linked to the central Committee. Regional committees soon covered all the twelve regions; county committees grew from eight to thirty-six in four years, and local committees from 150 to over 700. These local committees were at the heart of the work, with the chance to mobilise the resources of all the interested organisations and individuals in their neighbourhood in personal service for the old who were infirm, under-nourished, ill-housed, or just bored or lonely. Not all committees, of course, were equally enterprising or successful; but many of them provided communal meals or mobile canteens; ran clubs; arranged home-help schemes; or planned rotas of regular visitors to the home-bound; and some of them provided homes for old people who could no longer look after themselves or formed housing associations for the purpose. In the first post-war year alone, these local committees provided forty-eight homes with accommodation for over 1,000 residents, in addition to homes established by other voluntary organisations.

Indeed, accommodation was, as the National Committee had foreseen during the war, one of the greatest needs; not only suitable housing for the able-bodied but proper provision for the care of old people who became infirm or chronically sick. The Committee had constant consultations with the Ministry of Health on this subject; and in particular its reasoned proposals, backed by close knowledge of conditions in many parts of the country, were able to effect several amendments and additions to the National Assistance Act of 1948, which was to prove of cardinal importance to the welfare of the old, providing the foundation for a new range of social services. The National Committee, for example, had long been concerned about the standards of homes, and the Act now provided for registration and inspection; and about preserving some feeling of independence as well as security for the residents, and they would now receive adequate payments for their personal expenses. Power was given in the Act to local authorities to assist voluntary homes in meeting the cost of maintenance, and to contribute towards clubs and meal services provided by voluntary organisations; and a series of Ministry circulars to local authorities helped in strengthening the partnership between statutory and voluntary efforts by commending the NOPWC's work, stressing the value of the co-ordination of local welfare activities by means of county and other committees, and drawing attention to the powers of the local authority under the Local Government Act and National Assistance Act of 1948 to grant-aid such work. Of great value to the Committee in all their work in connection with the National Assistance Act was the fact that their chairman was Alderman Fred Messer, a most knowledgeable and indefatigable member of Parliament, who took a prominent part in debates in the House of Commons on the Bill.

Meanwhile, having encouraged the provision of more homes, both statutory and voluntary, the National Committee foresaw the paramount importance and difficulty of staffing them adequately. In consultation with the Ministry of Health, it worked out plans for a six-months' course of training for wardens and matrons, with an experienced tutor in charge and the help of experts from different fields. This experiment was financed by a generous grant from the National Corporation for the Care of Old People which the Nuffield Foundation had set up in 1947 with the co-operation of the Lord Mayor's Air Raid Distress Fund. This first course was a great success. Twenty-two wardens of local authority homes and twenty-three of voluntary homes took it, and twice as many failed to get places. A second course was organised next year, in 1951; and, in addition, over 250 wardens and matrons had by then attended short refresher courses also arranged by the National Committee. This was pioneer work which was to develop remarkably in many fields of social work over the next twenty years.

No subject concerned with the welfare of old people was too complex or too small for the NOPWC to take up in this period, or since. They assailed the Ministry of Information about wireless licence concessions, the Treasury on income tax and the cost of tobacco, the Ministry of Fuel and

Power over fuel restrictions, the Ministry of Health on the difficulties of getting hospital treatment or nursing care at home. And understanding of all this work for the welfare of the old was spread by conferences and meetings, national and regional; by publications; by exhibitions and talks. Of the first edition of the handbook, *Old People's Welfare* (later revised and enlarged as *Age is Opportunity**), a practical manual for those working with the aged, 4,500 copies were sold and it had quickly to be reprinted; and new editions issued in 1947 and 1949 also ran to several thousand copies. Nor was interest confined to this country. More and more visitors from abroad wanted to learn about this partnership of statutory and voluntary in what was to most of them a new field of social work; and in 1951 the secretary of the NOPWC, Dorothea Ramsey, was invited to the United States to give an address to the Second International Gerontological Conference at St Louis.

The decision of the first national conference of citizens' advice bureaux in 1945 that a service originally set up to meet the emergencies of war would be all the more needed to meet the problems of peace was quickly justified in the early years of reconstruction. Certainly the number of bureaux dropped in the first twelve months from the peak figure of 1,060 to 639; but many of those closed were small offices serving a limited population which it would have been difficult to maintain or justify under peace conditions; and, in any event, the original pre-war estimate of the number which might give sufficient coverage of the country had been only about 500. And though the actual number of enquiries fell at this time, the questions became on the whole more complex and time-consuming, since they more often involved personal or domestic problems or help in adjusting to the increasingly complicated social system. The fact was that people had learnt during the war to rely on the help of this independent, informal but informed source of advice and information in all their problems and perplexities; and though many men and women returning from the forces or the factories to ordinary life might make some use of the Resettlement Advice Service which the government had set up for them or the official information centres now provided by some local authorities, with which the bureaux themselves were working very closely, most people preferred to take their questions in the first place to an unofficial bureau, or even in the second place to check the exact meaning of what 'They' had said.

---

* Replaced 1968 by *The Elderly*. NCSS.

The importance of this service became even more evident as the new and complicated social legislation—National Insurance, National Assistance, National Health Service—came into operation, bringing within its scope millions of people not previously in touch with any public service, who wanted independent advice and information about their new rights and duties and the application of the new rules to their particular case. With a constant supply of information and help from their headquarters and the most friendly relations with their local authorities and local offices of government departments who were only too glad of their co-operation, the bureau workers were able to carry out with real success their function of 'interpreting the State to the individual'; and to play their part also in 'interpreting the individual to the State' by keeping the Ministries informed of the practical effects of legislation and the way it was in fact working. The total number of enquiries dealt with in that first year of the welfare state rose to over a million and a half, of which more than a quarter were concerned with the new social services.

The record of the bureaux in the early years of peace was good, but it had not been easily achieved. When the war was over the Central CAB Committee faced two outstanding problems. First, would it be able to retain or recruit enough voluntary workers of adequate quality to man the bureaux, in some places with the support of the very small core of full-time staff, once the emergency was over? This anxiety was fairly quickly removed. Many experienced workers who had learnt their craft in war-time stayed on, and new volunteers from many walks of life were eager to fill a regular place in this interesting service and to take pains to equip themselves with the necessary knowledge and experience. They realised that it was exacting work, not just giving guidance or advice, though that was hard enough, but helping people to think for themselves; and many of them felt the need for more understanding of the causes underlying the problems brought to them and a wider knowledge of the services which might help. The Central Committee tried to meet this need with a constantly expanding series of training courses and conferences, aided by experts from both the statutory and voluntary fields; by continuing the regular supply of information in *Citizens' Advice Notes* and frequent information circulars; and by a handbook, *Advising the Citizen*, which set out the place of the CAB in relation to other social agencies, outlined the functions of central government departments and local authorities, and dealt with bureau organisation and techniques of interviewing and giving advice.

The second main problem was money. At the end of the war the Ministry of Health withdrew the central grant from which the NCSS had been able to grant-aid individual bureaux, and they were left to find their own funds. A few could not manage to do this; but it was soon clear that, in the aggregate, bureaux were going to receive more in cash and kind from their local authorities than they had had under the central grant system. This was most encouraging, not only as a practical help but also as a recognition from the authorities of the permanent value of the service.

More serious was the decision of the Ministry under the stress of economic conditions in 1950 to halve the grant for headquarters services in the current year and discontinue it entirely the following year. Immediate and drastic economies had to be made in the central and regional services. The gravest result was the loss of most of the travelling officers whose work in helping to launch and sustain the bureaux, to act as links between them and the centre, and to assist in maintaining the high standard of work by means of advisory visits, courses and conferences, had been invaluable from the early days. This decision of the government was a severe blow to the service; yet in the event it called forth a demonstration of the strength rather than the weakness of the movement. First, at the very centre of affairs, members of all political parties paid a remarkable tribute to it when they found an occasion during a late sitting of the House of Commons to urge strongly the claims of this work to continued support from Exchequer funds—though unfortunately without success. Secondly, in the country the workers and voluntary committees of the bureaux responded with great energy and loyalty to the challenge, most of them contriving to raise enough money to make a contribution towards the cost of the central services as well as maintaining themselves; and devising bit by bit methods of servicing their county or regional CAB committees for the discussion of local or national policy questions and the planning of training days, or of using the most experienced workers to advise the smaller bureaux in their area. The staff at headquarters, reduced to a minimum, continued somehow to keep up the regular supply of information to the bureaux; to improve still more their good relations with government departments, local authority associations, and professional bodies such as The Law Society with which they worked so closely on preparations for the government's Legal Aid and Advice Schemes. But the central services were inevitably curtailed; and, as the local committees correspondingly grew in importance, sharing more responsibility for the development and maintenance of the national service, the Central Committee adopted in 1950 a new name—the National Citizens' Advice Bureaux Committee—and a new constitution giving greater weight to members representing local bureaux.

The spirit of neighbourliness engendered by the common sharing of troubles and efforts during the war did not fade away when more normal conditions of life returned. Indeed, it gave a remarkable impetus to the community associations movement in the early days of peace. The term 'community centre', previously almost unknown, became a household word, although there was still a good deal of misunderstanding on the part of both authorities and the public about what it really meant. Not only from the municipal housing estates where the movement had begun but from prosperous suburbs, from down-town areas of great cities, and even from ancient market towns with their own strong pattern of community life, came enquiries about this new social institution. Schemes developed in almost every town, some as war memorials, some as the result of victory street parties, others on the initiative of the local education authorities upon whom the Education Act of 1944 had placed the primary responsibility for the development of community centres as part of their wider schemes for further education. In fact, such was the enthusiasm for the new idea that just after the war it was popularly supposed that community centres would be provided in every neighbourhood as automatically as schools. If they had been, they would certainly not have been

A community centre

the kind of centres for which the NCSS stood. For it visualised centres springing from the expressed needs of the people and run by a community association widely representative of all the interests of the neighbourhood —its statutory authorities, its voluntary organisations, and its residents as individuals.

But, as events turned out, there was little risk that centres would be provided too quickly and on the wrong basis. As with village halls so with community centres, the post-war years were a long record of delays and frustrations in almost every building project. In spite of this plans went hopefully forward, and details of new schemes from all over the country came to the NCSS so fast that the small community centres staff at head-quarters, seconded to the newly founded National Federation of Community Associations, could scarcely keep pace with them. Before long the Federation was in touch with nearly 1,000 schemes, though probably less than half had fully representative associations qualifying for the minimum basis of membership of the Federation. All of them, however, showed an earnest wish to bring greater harmony into neighbourhood life and find ways of working together for the common good and pleasure; and the Federation did its best to help them all, with plans for temporary buildings, advice on negotiations with local authorities, guidance to new and in-experienced committees on the solution of everyday problems and the maze of regulations and controls which seemed to frustrate any attempt to secure premises of their own. Information circulars were regularly sent out, and a series of pamphlets produced on such subjects as *Community Associations and Local Authorities* and *Building Possibilities and Achievements*. One of the biggest tasks in the early post-war years was that of advising local education authorities, as well as local voluntary groups. Although the authorities were keenly interested in the possibilities of the new Act, they were only just beginning to appoint specialist officers of their own and welcomed the accumulated experience of the National Council. At a critical point a grant from the Ministry of Education made possible the appointment of travelling officers, who were able to go to all parts of the country, maintaining personal touch with leaders of local work, collecting information, and giving advice.

The Federation attached great importance to the employment by community associations and centres of qualified full-time secretaries and wardens; and, like other groups associated with the National Council in their own special fields, it devised many methods during this period of providing training for them, and of co-operating with other bodies concerned with further education and with the Ministry of Education on future training policy. With the help of the Community Education Trust (whose grants unhappily came to an end in 1950), week-end schools and longer courses were held, and a post-graduate specialist course was planned; and the Federation was represented on the committee of the Ministry which, after long consultation, issued a statement on the Training of Youth Leaders and Community Centre Wardens that made an important advance in official recognition of the status of community centre leaders.

It was never easy to explain in words the idea behind the community association nor how this idea should be worked out in practice, but an exhibition, 'Living Communities', prepared by the Federation which for five years toured the country, did something to clear up public misunderstanding. As far as the local authorities were concerned, most of them by this time were appreciating fully the value of the association as the living spirit which brought the centre—a mere building—to life. As the provision of the centres was to be increasingly the responsibility of the education authorities this was an important achievement. Moreover, there was a new appreciation of the part which the community association could play in the wider field of further education.

If it had been possible to provide community centres during the early post-war years when the educational world was showing so much interest in them as potential vehicles for adult education, it is probable that the emphasis of the movement would have turned towards its educational side. But the limitations imposed by building controls, culminating in a virtual ban on the building of community centres in 1949 and 1950, encouraged the associations to look outward towards the unresolved social problems of their neighbourhoods, rather than limiting their attention to the day-to-day problems of administering and financing their centres or to the provision of narrowly educational facilities. It is significant that the community centres handbook published at this time should be entitled *Our Neighbourhood*. The theme of the outstandingly successful annual conference of 1951 was the citizen's part in social planning, and this again illustrated the tendency to turn outwards to the wider fields of community service. There was evidently plenty of scope here, for it was clear that many of the post-war estates, in spite of the warnings of the prophets in the nineteen-thirties when the first new housing estates were being built, were going to be as deficient in social provisions as their predecessors. Although the ban on the building of community centres had at this date been partially lifted, the deepening economic crisis meant a gradual reduction in the scale of grant-aid. Immediately after the war grants from statutory sources had been approximately seventy per cent, leaving local communities to find the remaining thirty per cent. By 1951 the proportions had been reversed. It is true that this gave an impetus to the use of voluntary labour schemes, which was good, but it also meant that the possibility of starting new associations and centres in unprivileged areas, where money and leadership might both be lacking, had much diminished.

The community centres idea was proving during these post-war years to be yet another concept in the National Council's work which attracted great interest overseas. Through the international department of the NCSS, with its links with the Foreign Office, the British Council, the Colonial Office, and the Commonwealth Relations Office, large numbers of overseas visitors and students came to ask for information and to look at community centres of different kinds so that they might see how the idea could be adapted to conditions in their own countries; and the Federation's representative on the Colonial Social Welfare Advisory Committee was able to make a useful contribution to its plans for the social development of colonial territories.

This representative was Frank Milligan, 'philosopher-statesman' of the movement, who combined the secretaryship of the National Federation of Community Associations with the leadership of the community centres and clubs department of the NCSS. He had had from the start of the Federation the support of Edward Sewell Harris, formerly secretary of the pioneer Watling Community Association, whose long experience and enthusiasm had been invaluable in the post of chairman. When Sewell Harris retired from the chairmanship in 1951 he had the satisfaction of knowing that in spite of frustrations and disappointments the work was expanding steadily, for forty new local associations had joined the Federation that year bringing the total to 250.

He was succeeded by Dr (now Dame) Mabel Tylecote who for seven years was to give her energetic leadership as chairman and, on her retirement in 1958, as president of the Federation.

The development of community centres and associations was only one branch of the neighbourhood work of the NCSS. In addition there were nearly 1,000 'community service clubs' of various kinds, originating in the unemployed club movement. Since the nineteen thirties many of them had broadened out from their original purpose and become real centres of neighbourhood life in the smaller industrial towns of the north-east, the north-west, the Midlands, and South Wales. During the war the Assistance Board had provided grants at a level sufficient to secure the continuance of the machinery established in the days of unemployment and had helped the National Council's unemployment committee with the difficult problems of administration over the war period. In view of the uncertainty about the demands likely to be made on the clubs in the transition from war to peace, when the employment situation was doubt-ful, the Board agreed to continue its grants-in-aid till 1947; but thereafter it became clear that it would be more appropriate for aid to come from the local education authorities, since the clubs' chief function was now in the field of informal adult education. To tide them over the gap till this help materialised, the Ministry of Education made a special grant for the following year—a fitting sequel to their long story of service to the unemployed.

Frank Milligan, on the right next to Dame Mabel Tylecote and Edward Sewell Harris
(with Arthur and Lillian Davis)

Although the men's clubs had dwindled in numbers and influence the women's clubs and sections continued to grow though, like every other organisation, they suffered from the economic conditions of the early post-war years, with a reduction in the number of organisers who had given so much help in supporting or promoting clubs, and even some decline in membership where the demand for married women in industry was high. Even so, in 1949 there were nearly 700 women's clubs with a membership of some 24,000; and their National Standing Conference felt that the time had come when a national association would serve to express better their unity of purpose and help to make them into a stronger collective force for women's welfare. The National Association of Women's Clubs was therefore formally established in September 1950—a sign of the greater maturity of outlook of the club members and a reward for the long, patient work of Lucy Butcher. In the worst days of the unemployment crisis she had come from her work as a trade union organiser to help Richard Clements in the Midlands Office of the NCSS. There she had seen the latent possibilities of women's clubs and realised how much could be accomplished by local groups of working-class women, backed by the help of the National Council. It was largely due to her lively faith, enthusiasm, and persistence that the movement had grown so well in such seemingly unpropitious times; and when the National Association was formed she became its first secretary.

The National Council had always attached special importance to the rôle of the churches in social work; and the Central Churches Group, set up in 1942 to bring together representatives of the principal churches and religious denominations in this country with the NCSS, provided a most apt medium for joint consideration and planning of that rôle in the early post-war years. Through discussions with church leaders and through a series of publications and conferences the Group was able to give guidance to clergy and ministers of religion on all the main problems and opportunities of the day. A series of printed letters, *In the Service of the Community*, was circulated, advising on such questions as the churches' part in the organisation of schemes to help men and women returning from the forces or factories to adjust to civilian life; and the principles of partnership between citizens' advice bureaux and the churches. Other subjects of special interest to the National Council which were successively studied were the churches' co-operation in old people's welfare, and their part in the provision of new centres of community life. A conference was convened in 1947 on the problem of the child deprived of normal home life; and the following year the Group devoted much of its time to considering, from the standpoint of the church, the social needs of the projected New

Towns and other newly developed urban areas.

The Churches Group was concerned equally with social workers as with social work. To encourage more church people to take up paid social service posts in the undermanned statutory and voluntary organisations, they produced a pamphlet on *Social Service as a Religious Vocation*; and in 1951 an important paper on the moral principles underlying social work, at the request of social workers who felt the need for some authoritative statement. At the same period the Group was beginning to give renewed attention to the formation of local churches groups, so as to spread the influence of its work more widely.

It was a severe loss to the Central Churches Group when Dr Malcolm Spencer, the secretary from its inception and the inspiration of much of this development, died in 1950.

The NCSS had for many years had excellent relations with the National Playing Fields Association. Now, in this post-war period, these links were strengthened by an arrangement whereby the regional officers of the Council acted as advisory officers of the NPFA, thus helping to build up and develop a number of county and local playing fields associations. In return, the NPFA made a substantial contribution towards the cost of this advisory service. Here was an excellent example of co-operation between two national voluntary organisations to give a service which, by this means, could be provided both efficiently and economically.

The Education Act of 1944 had made possible a considerable extension of youth work, largely through the local education authorities. This increased the importance of the Standing Conference of National Voluntary Youth Organisations (formerly called Juvenile Organisations), the oldest of the Council's associated groups, as the focus of the voluntary organisations, providing not only a means of consultation and joint action but also a link between statutory and voluntary effort at a time when a partnership between the two was vitally important if the youth service was to develop on the right lines.

The Standing Conference was able to take full advantage of this opportunity because, while striving to achieve a consensus of opinion among its member organisations on general principles and often on detailed action, it always recognised the need for variety of approach in work with young people and respected the individual contribution which each organisation could make in accordance with its own traditions and methods. This pattern of co-operation and compromise was in part repeated at local level, where there were by now fifty local standing conferences similarly constituted and able to work with their local authorities as the national body worked with the Ministries of Education and Labour and other central departments.

Much of the work of the Conference was done by 'ad hoc' groups set up to examine particular problems and report to the Conference. Like the Churches Group and other groups associated with the NCSS, the Conference was indefatigable at this time in pursuing a great variety of subjects which had special and topical relevance to their interests: the relationship of youth organisations to those community centres which were springing up all over the country; research into the day-to-day lives of young people in industry, and into the leisure-time activities of school children; the influence of the cinema; the teaching of homecraft; sex education; the effect of conscription on young workers. Many of these reports formed the basis of recommendations by the Standing Conference to government committees considering the subjects concerned, not the least important being the Ministry of Education committee on the recruitment, training, and conditions of service of youth leaders and community centre wardens, with which the NFCA was also actively associated.

A piece of work which helped to set the British youth organisations squarely on the map of the post-war age, and not only the map of Britain, was the part which SCNVYO and the local standing conferences played in the Festival of Britain in 1951. The core of this was the Festival Centre of Youth at St Anne's House, Soho, where an attractive series of displays was arranged which demonstrated the aims and activities of the member organisations of the Conference to thousands of visitors from this country and overseas. It was made possible by a great deal of hard work on the part of the youth organisations, and that generous combination of money and co-operation from a variety of sources—here, from the King George's Jubilee Trust, the City Parochial Foundation, and the *News Chronicle*—which has so often demonstrated the interest and confidence that National Council ventures can attract.

More positive overseas contacts had meanwhile been part of the work of the Conference ever since the end of the war. As early as 1946 the secretary was invited to visit Belgium, Holland, and France; and the Control Commission for Germany asked the Conference to appoint a delegation to visit Germany to survey the situation of youth work in the British Zone. This resulted in an important report, *Young Germany Today*. In subsequent years the Conference, at the request of the British and United States governments, made arrangements for several parties of German youth leaders from the British and American Zones to visit this country for brief training courses—a not unimportant contribution to the re-education of German young people.

But the most far-reaching of all the overseas youth work which developed at this period was the establishment of an international youth assembly. With the end of the war many enquiries came to the NCSS from other countries about the work of voluntary organisations in Great Britain and, in particular, about the methods used in this country to secure full co-operation between the statutory and voluntary services, and youth work attracted special interest. As a result of contacts and discussions with boards and conferences for youth work, similar to SCNVYO, in other countries, the suggestion was made that some means should be established at international level to provide a focus for these consultative bodies. The NCSS, in view of its experience in this kind of work, was asked to take the initiative in convening an international assembly when the matter could be discussed. A preliminary conference was held in London in 1947 and a more widely representative one in August 1948, with delegations from twenty-five countries and sixteen observers from international movements and UN agencies. Its preparation, under the supervision of an international advisory committee, entailed a great deal of difficult organisation. That it was successfully done was in large measure due to the then head of the youth department, Violet Welton, with her lively understanding of the NCSS concept and an informed enthusiasm for this project.

The conference did not come to its conclusions without long discussion and argument, but with the help of many organisations and individuals it reached a successful outcome: the decision to establish a widely representative international youth assembly, for which the National Council would provide the secretariat until a properly constituted international committee could take responsibility for the organisation. The World Assembly of Youth was thus set up; and a British National Committee formed, on which very many of the SCNVYO organisations were represented. During the first year the British Committee spent much time in preparing a plan for its activities, considering how the finance could be found to enable it to develop the work of WAY in Great Britain, and in briefing a delegation for the Council meeting held in Istanbul in 1950. By the following year the British Committee was able to become independent of the NCSS, and to send a large representative delegation to the first meeting of WAY in the United States, though problems of finance and other organisational difficulties still persisted.

One of the most outstanding trends in the post-war activities of the NCSS was the rapid growth of its overseas and international work. In spite of the dislocation of international relations caused by the war the Council had been able to maintain a remarkable number of contacts with foreign social workers during those years, for it had long recognised the valuable part which voluntary organisations could play, given the opportunities, in fostering a spirit of understanding between countries through their work for education and social welfare. But it was the situation in the post-war world which, for three main reasons, provided the opportunities and the demand for the Council to give a lead in this work. The desperate need for relief and reconstruction in many countries, and the social problems which the war had left behind everywhere, required a marshalling of knowledge and experience of social service from every source. The development of the United Nations organisations concerned with welfare and education offered the opportunity of extending the co-operation between government and voluntary agencies into the international field. And the possibilities of travel once again and the universal wish to renew old contacts and to make new ones, to discuss, compare, and learn, brought visitors and students to Britain from all over the world and stimulated plans for exchange and study visits.

Interest in the new 'welfare state' in Britain, and in the unique partnership between statutory and voluntary institutions and in the National Council, which had contributed so much to the creation of that partnership, meant that an increasing number of these visitors came to the NCSS, often at the instigation of the Foreign Office and other government agencies which found in the Council a convenient means of consultation. In one year alone visitors for whom the Council provided contacts or arranged tours and visits of observation included people as varied as the President of the Court of Appeal of the Lebanon and a Swedish youth leader; a Cypriot civil servant and students of Belgian schools of social work; and diplomatic and consular officials home on leave. On the other hand, as early as 1945 British social workers and administrators began to make study visits or lecture tours abroad; and the secretary of the National Council himself spent some weeks in the United States and Canada, renewing contacts with the leaders of public and private agencies and discussing the possibilities of closer co-operation on international questions.

But plans for the direct exchange of social workers through the British Committee for the Interchange of Social Workers and Administrators, set up by the NCSS during the war, developed rather slowly in spite of some financial help from the Nuffield Foundation, partly because of travel and currency difficulties, and partly due to the lack of similar committees with which the Council could work in most other countries. However, the British Committee was able to arrange in the next two or three years several study visits for probation officers, social-work tutors and administrators, community centre workers, public health officers, and others, to and from France, Canada, Australia, as well as the United States; and by 1949 firm plans had been worked out with the USA for long-term direct exchanges of psychiatric social workers and almoners. The following year the British Committee's links with Western European countries were strengthened by an agreement, made at the request of the UN Division of Social Affairs at Geneva, to co-operate in a plan for the interchange of social workers within Europe on a short-term basis. The pioneer work of the National Council in this field was at last fairly launched.

From the early post-war days the overseas and international department worked in close touch with the relevant UN organisations on world problems of reconstruction and social welfare. In 1947 George Haynes was asked to chair a small conference of international voluntary organisations at UNESCO headquarters in Paris to discuss their future plans for relief and reconstruction following the closing down of UNRRA; and he presided also at another meeting called by the Relief and Rehabilitation Section of UNESCO to discuss educational relief. In the same year the Social Affairs Division of the UN invited the Council's help in the placing of UN Fellows visiting Great Britain for social studies; and though lack of finance made it impossible for the Council to appoint the additional staff needed if it were to take responsibility for this difficult work, an arrangement was made to co-operate fully with the British Council which took on the task of organising it. In order to facilitate co-operation with the UN Division of the Foreign Office in providing information on various aspects of British social work which the Social Commission of the UN often required, joint working parties were set up to prepare reports on such subjects as the part played by voluntary organisations in child and youth welfare and in the care of homeless children. A particularly valuable report was prepared by a special panel of experienced people, under the chairmanship of Professor Richard Titmuss, when the government asked for the help of the British Committee in presenting this country's views on the subject of professional social-work training, in relation to an international survey made by the UN. Here was yet another way in which the National Council was able to channel the experience of voluntary organisations in this country to make their contribution to the deliberations of the United Nations.

The most important development in this field, however, was undoubtedly the revival of the International Conference on Social Work, which had been founded in the nineteen-twenties by the eminent Belgian, Dr René Sand, at that time Secretary-General of the League of Red Cross Societies. The National Council had not played a significant part in the first three meetings held by the organisation; but, through a British committee, it was to have been responsible for the British share in the fourth international conference which would have taken place in Brussels if the war had not intervened. Now, in 1945, contacts with the United States and in particular with Dr René Sand, president of the International Conference, were renewed; a National Committee with over seventy leading voluntary organisations as members was established; and the next year a strong British delegation took a prominent part in an international reunion in Brussels when it was decided to rebuild the organisation, and at The Hague, a year later, when successful discussions on the methods of establishing the international conference on a secure footing enabled the participating countries to plan for a plenary conference in the United States in 1948. Here again a representative British delegation, which had prepared careful statements on British experience in the international field and on the future constitution of the conference, took a notable share in a series of meetings drawing together representatives of organisations and workers from many parts of the world. A constitution was adopted and the framework of the future organisation was set up. Important discussions took place with the Social Affairs Division of the United Nations, and the conference was invited into the fullest co-operation with the UN in its work for international welfare.

Participation in these meetings had an important influence on British organisations. The British Committee extended its membership, strengthened its contacts with the government departments specially concerned with the development of the UN agencies, and decided to assist in international studies by forming representative working parties to prepare reports on work in this country. In considering these matters the committee came to the conclusion that something more was needed to secure the widest possible collaboration here of those organisations engaged in some form of social work and community organisation; and that an attempt should be made to set up a national conference which would enable both workers and organisations, statutory and voluntary, to review their problems together and take stock of new trends and purposes. It decided, in association with the National Council, to convene a British Committee on Social Work at which the establishment of a permanent conference could be considered; and, as a result of a preliminary conference of representatives of many national organisations and leaders of social-work practice and training held in 1948, the British National Conference on Social Work was set up. Such a conference, it was agreed, would not only enable this country to play its full part as a participant in schemes for international co-operation but would also be a great stimulus in providing a focus for British thought and effort.

The first meeting of the British National Conference, held in Harrogate in April 1950, proved an admirable beginning to the fulfilment of these aims. It was most carefully organised and prepared with the help of ninety-two working parties in different towns and cities in the United Kingdom who had studied the main subjects of the conference and whose reports formed a basis for the discussions. And the theme, 'Social Services in 1950: the Respective Roles of Statutory Authorities and Voluntary Organisations', was broadly the theme of the international conference to be held in Paris three months later, and so helped to brief the British delegation for their part in the wider deliberations. The Harrogate meeting was attended by some 450 delegates who were drawn from many interests, including national and local voluntary organisations, local authorities, government departments, university schools of social studies, from the preparatory working parties, and from other countries.

The Fifth International Conference in Paris, where the French National Committee, with characteristic charm and practicality, acted as host to some 1,500 delegates from forty-nine countries, was an outstanding event in the development of international social work. It owed much of its success to the skilled leadership of George Haynes, secretary of the NCSS, who had been unanimously appointed president of the International Conference—a tribute to his intense personal commitment to the cause of international understanding, and a recognition of the British contribution and of the special part played by the National Council. The main theme was the subject of a number of addresses at plenary sessions, and was also studied by representative commissions. In addition, some fifteen open discussions were arranged for delegates on such subjects as the welfare of the disabled, neighbourhood work, the care of old people; but delegates thronged to them in such unexpected numbers that the groups proved rather too large for fruitful discussion, although they gave useful opportunities for enlarging views: a problem of organisation that was to recur again and again in later years.

At about the same time the National Council was taking the initiative in organising another piece of international work, consequent on the approaching end to the activities of the International Refugee Organisation. An acute problem still remained in the Displaced Persons camps in Germany, Austria, and Italy, and the IRO was appealing to every country to carry a share of the burden of re-settling the remaining refugees. Both the Foreign Office and some of the leading voluntary organisations which had been engaged in relief work abroad asked the Council to see what could be done to set up an organisation here which would care for the displaced persons already in this country and others who might be brought here later; and after a series of discussions with the Foreign Office and representatives of IRO under the auspices of the Council, the principal voluntary bodies concerned agreed to establish a British Council for Aid to Refugees as an independent voluntary organisation with an independent board of trustees responsible for funds from IRO. Of this organisation Dame May Curwen was, and remains, the chairman.

In 1953 the then United Nations High Commissioner for Refugees asked her to convene a meeting of all the organisations that were engaged in the 'adoption' of individual refugees in camps, with a view to co-operation between them by which camps as a whole might be helped rather than only individual inmates; overlapping eliminated; and organisations encouraged to think of new plans to lift the morale of these too often 'forgotten people', as well as helping to meet some of their material needs. As a result, a small Standing Conference of British Organisations for Aid to Refugees was formed, the British Council for Aid to Refugees undertaking the secretarial work at first, and the secretary of the National Council working as a most active chairman.

Such were the small but important beginnings of the National Council's co-operative work on behalf of refugees which, with the then unforeseen growth of this tragic problem, has since become a major part of its international programme.

To reinforce the leadership of George Haynes in all this work the NCSS was fortunate in having Miss M. L. (Letty) Harford, who had been connected with the Council from almost its earliest days. Her experience of social work went back to the times when there were few professional caseworkers, who had to do their job in virtual isolation; and she was therefore able to put its full value on the idea of co-operation and partnership which she had first seen develop in councils of social service in the north of England and had herself served for many years in Chesterfield with the enthusiasm, sympathy, and knowledge which were to inform all her work, in whatever sphere. She had come to NCSS headquarters first to specialise in women's work and eventually to become head of the overseas and international department at the period of its most important developments.

Of the plans made during the war for the reorganisation of the NCSS the first—the development of the associated groups—had met with good success. The second—the strengthening of the Council's corporate function by providing certain central services for its constituent members and groups—had had more varied fortune.

The library made an impressive start. A collection of 8,000 books on social service matters was built up in five years in what appeared to be ideal premises in Gordon Square, with a highly skilled librarian, Miss F. M. Birkett, who was able not only to keep abreast of all important publications on the subject in papers, journals, and annual reports as well as books, but to advise many organisations and individuals on literature relating to their work. But in 1946, just as this service was establishing itself with the prospect of becoming an increasingly important instrument for better knowledge and understanding of social problems in this country and overseas, it was learned that the landlords would not continue to allow public access to the building. The usefulness of the service would have been lost if books could no longer be loaned or used on the premises; and no other suitable accommodation could be found. With great regret the Council had to release its librarian and transfer the books and further purchases to Bedford Square for internal use and very limited lending, with oversight on a 'caretaker' basis.

The Council had long been convinced that one of the most useful services it could render to the voluntary organisations and to all those engaged in social work was the production of publications, giving information and views based on practical experience, in an attractive and easily accessible form. In the early post-war period the publications department made a most promising beginning, first under the direction of John Morgan, who had played a large part in building up the whole concept of an information service and, when he left to take an important post at Toronto University, with the enthusiastic guidance of Harold King, formerly a National Council regional officer. By 1947, in spite of paper and printing difficulties, the department was able to report a large increase in the number of publications issued and, most notably, the launching of a quarterly periodical, *Social Service*, to take the place of the pre-war *Social Service Review*. The following year, in view of the growing importance of this field of the Council's work, a publications board was set up under the chairmanship of Sir Horace Wilson, to be responsible for general oversight and planning.

The volume of work can be indicated by the record of a single year: fifteen new important publications and several minor ones; reprints and revisions of six earlier publications; nineteen leaflets, reports, and material for free distribution prepared at the request of various departments of the Council; and five periodicals. The subjects covered over the years ranged from old people's welfare to amateur opera; town and country planning to adoption legislation; 'Reflections on Leisure' to the history of the school meals service. They included handbooks and conference reports for every department and group of the NCSS; and research studies like the National Association of Girls' Clubs and Mixed Clubs' *Hours away from Work*, or surveys of social policy such as *New Towns*, prepared for the Council by L. E. White. Their readers were as various as their matter: leaders of social work and fledgling students; parish councillors and foreign academics; clergy and cabinet ministers.

But behind this success difficulties were mounting. Many of the publications were necessarily designed for a special interest, limited in its appeal, and purchasers had to be sought out. The number of copies of a particular publication might have to be small, though nevertheless of value in a restricted but important field. Most of the publications had to be produced as cheaply as possible to help various groups and departments of the Council; prices were kept low, as many were bought by students and social workers with little money to spend on books; and profits were therefore often negligible. Meanwhile costs of paper and printing were rising steadily, and the margin narrowed. The Council's general finances were, by 1951, in a difficult state and it could not afford to meet any considerable drop in revenue. So it was regretfully decided, on the advice of the publications board, to limit the publications programme for the time being to the production of two quarterly journals, *Social Service* and *The Village*; and the revision and current development of such essential features of the information service as *Citizens' Advice Notes*, *Voluntary Social Services*, *Public Social Services*, and other handbooks of information required by the various groups and departments. Nevertheless, the publishing service had proved of real value and the experience was to stand the Council in good stead when more favourable conditions eventually returned.

Citizens' Advice Notes, under the skilled and experienced direction of Geoffrey Redmayne, who had worked on the Council staff since 1932 assisted mainly by expert volunteers, continued to be one of the most important activities of the information department. Indeed, the flood of new social legislation, in the broadest sense, involved much increased work in preparing the *Notes* and a wide expansion in the field covered and in the subscribers for which they catered. But this up-to-date précis of government legislation and regulations was not the answer to scores of the questions which came every day to the department by telephone or letter or word of mouth, from other departments of the Council, from statutory and voluntary bodies, and from individual social workers or puzzled members of the public who could not always be appropriately referred to a local citizens' advice bureau.

Some of the questions came from CABx themselves and arose often out of the application to individual cases of laws and regulations and provisions set out in CANS or in the information circulars sent to them at frequent intervals. These problems were difficult enough and involved very close contacts with government departments and other statutory authorities or voluntary organisations, and up-to-the-minute knowledge of new administrative procedures or social provisions. Still more complex, however, was the vast variety of the enquiries from outside organisations. The scope of these can be guessed at from the record of one day when, in addition to the ordinary run of questions, enquiries came from a New Town Corporation, the British Council, a government commission, the Library of the House of Commons, an export firm, and a Service benevolent institution. Equally important was the task of keeping other departments and groups of the Council supplied with information that might be of use to them and of relating their more specialised information services to one another and to the central service, in order to avoid gaps or overlapping in the collection and distribution of material.

The information department was attempting, indeed, to provide a centre for that co-operation within the NCSS and with both voluntary and governmental institutions outside it, which was the main principle of the Council's work. But its staff was extremely small and, as the financial crisis bore more hardly on the National Council, even this was reduced; and as with the other departments, plans for expansion of its services at the beginning of the nineteen-fifties had to be postponed.

After the death of Dr Henry Mess in 1944 the plan to set up a central studies department remained in abeyance. The need could have been met only by a team of really high calibre, and continued financial stringency made it impossible to provide the necessary funds. This was unfortunate, for there was a growing realisation in this post-war period of the need for social research and of the very little which was being done in this country compared, for example, with the United States. Nevertheless, although there was no permanent research department, groups and working parties continued to act as laboratories for the study of a wide range of current social problems. In 1945 the results of an enquiry into the future use of the experiment of British Restaurants, which had played so useful a part in community feeding in war-time, were ready for publication; and a draft report was prepared on a survey of the reading habits of young people, which the Carnegie UK Trust had asked the Council to undertake.

Two years later a report was published on a problem of great and continuing significance to the whole voluntary movement and indeed to social work in general: the salaries and conditions of social workers. Many forms of social work and voluntary activity were of necessity becoming increasingly specialised and required staff with professional training; but the supply of adequately trained social workers was far short of the demand for them largely because facilities for training were still inadequate. If voluntary organisations were to be in a position to attract sufficient numbers of trained full-time workers, they would have seriously to reconsider the question of salaries. A joint committee of the National Council and the British Federation of Social Workers under the chairmanship of Professor T. S. Simey was set up to study the problem; and it came to the conclusion that drastic steps were needed to improve salary scales for whole-time social workers in the voluntary field: a conclusion which, in view of the acute financial difficulties that most bodies were facing, obviously pointed the importance of persistent joint consultation and planning among the principal voluntary bodies, such as the National Council existed to facilitate.

Of equal importance for the future of voluntary work was the major enquiry which the National Council promoted in 1950, with the financial help and co-operation of the King Edward's Hospital Fund for London, into voluntary service and the hospitals.

Much of the Council's work at this time was naturally directed, through study groups, conferences, and meetings of all kinds, to an evaluation of the changes in the social structure which the new legislation had brought; but the executive committee finally came to the conclusion that a comprehensive study was really what was needed to discover how, both at the centre and throughout the country, voluntary service was being affected by the new state and local authority services. Was the trend moving away from voluntary participation and initiative in favour of an all-competent state, or were new opportunities being created for voluntary action? Was the citizen becoming an active partner in shaping and maintaining the new services or merely the recipient of what was provided? Did the social pattern taking shape faithfully reflect the intentions of the legislature? In the light of what was happening, was a new philosophy of voluntary service needed? These were large questions concerning every aspect of the social provisions; but since the changes in the hospital service were perhaps the most striking, it was thought that these might offer the best field for immediate study.

A joint advisory committee was set up under the chairmanship of Lady Norman to assist and guide the study, with John Trevelyan, former

Director of Education for Westmorland, as director of the enquiry. It ranged over the fundamental concept of voluntary service and society; the historical development of the hospital service; the problems of voluntary service within the hospital administration; the appointment, composition, and functions of regional hospital boards and hospital management committees, and their relationship to the Ministry of Health and to each other; and voluntary service to the sick and infirm both within and outside the hospital.

The report, *Voluntary Service and the State: A Study of the Needs of the Hospital Service*, was published in 1952 and was immediately recognised as a valuable contribution to thought on the future place of voluntary work not only in the hospitals but throughout the social services. The main practical conclusion was that 'nationalisation' of the hospitals had rather increased the need for voluntary service than lessened or ended it, as many people had once expected; that, indeed, 'new demands, both national and local, are made on voluntary societies, and it is true to say that, at the present time, although there is a national health service financed almost entirely from public funds, there is more voluntary service given to the sick and infirm than ever before'. As for the 'philosophy' of the matter, the report described voluntary service as 'something which none but a free society can produce . . . a partnership in which the state provides and yet calls for its citizens to play their part to the full. This we believe is the way in which freedom can be preserved within an ordered structure under central direction. . . . The preservation of voluntary service in society is of the utmost importance. . . . We believe then that the voluntary spirit that inspires true voluntary service is something that is of the essence of greatness in man, and that a nation that fails to make use of this gift can never be a great nation.'

In addition to these specific studies and surveys the NCSS, because of its central position among the national voluntary organisations and its close relationship with government departments, was able in 1949 to sponsor discussions and action which were to lead during the next decade to a complete re-interpretation in modern terms of the place of charity, in its widest sense, in the welfare state.

This enterprise began as far back as 1947 when Lord Beveridge asked the help of some of the leading national voluntary organisations, with the good offices of the National Council, in preparing his book on *Voluntary Action**. Published in 1948, this book did much to focus attention not only on the contribution to British life which the voluntary associations

---

* *Voluntary Action.* Allen and Unwin. [Out of print.]

were making but also on the unprecedented difficulties that faced them in the post-war world, and the uncertainties about their effective role in the future. The National Council invited some of the main national organisations to join in considering these questions and, reinforced by these consultations, looked hopefully for an occasion when the government would be able to state its general attitude to the work of voluntary bodies in such a way as to remove their uncertainties.

A debate on voluntary action and social progress initiated by Lord Samuel in the House of Lords in June 1949 fulfilled the Council's most optimistic hopes. The peers were unanimous about the value of the work of voluntary organisations, and the need to encourage voluntary effort for social welfare through the spontaneous groupings of individuals which had always been an important feature of British community life; and at the conclusion of the debate Lord Pakenham stated the view of the government in striking terms. 'We consider,' he said, 'that the voluntary spirit is the very life-blood of democracy. We consider that the individual volunteer, the man who is proud to serve the community for nothing, is he whose personal sense of mission inspires and elevates the whole process of official governmental effort. We are convinced that voluntary associations have rendered, are rendering, and must be encouraged to continue to render, great and indispensable service to the community. I hope that the deliberate expression of our basic governmental attitude will carry far and wide. I hope that it will establish firmly in the public mind the value of voluntary service as we see it, and in particular, I hope it will prove decisive for good with any citizens, young or old, who are thinking of joining or starting voluntary bodies but are wondering whether such activities are now adjudged really significant; who are wondering whether their own sacrifices are really wanted in the Britain of the present day. I want to remove all possible doubt from their minds, speaking from this place in the most emphatic manner.'

Nor was the debate confined to a discussion of general issues but was given a practical turn by Lord Samuel's proposal, welcomed by the House, that the government should consider the establishment of 'Common Goods Funds' whereby 'dormant funds' lying in banks, the Court of Chancery, and certain charities no longer able to allocate their funds to useful purpose, might be used to finance voluntary effort.

Recognising the great opportunities for the voluntary movement which were thus opened out, the NCSS circulated a summary of the debate in pamphlet form, and convened a conference in October where a general discussion could take place as a preliminary to an approach to the government. Over 180 national organisations were represented and at the conclusion of the meeting, which was addressed by Lord Samuel, a resolution was unanimously passed welcoming the statement made in the House of Lords by Lord Pakenham on behalf of the government, and requesting the NCSS to inform the government of the views expressed at this meeting; to keep the national bodies closely informed of any steps which might be proposed; and if necessary to convene a further meeting and 'to take any other appropriate action having regard to the diversity of needs and purposes of voluntary organisations'.

A small deputation, led by Lord Samuel, subsequently reported these conclusions to the Lord President of the Council, who welcomed the initiative which the NCSS had taken in the recent discussions and was able to say, on behalf of the government, that it was proposed to establish a committee to enquire into the law relating to charitable trusts in England and Wales. Although the problem of 'dormant funds' would be outside the scope of this committee, the government promised to enquire into the position and consult further with the National Council.

The committee, under the chairmanship of Lord Nathan, was set up in 1950 with these terms of reference: 'To consider and report on the changes in law and practice (except as regards taxation) relating to charitable trusts in England and Wales which would be necessary to enable the maximum benefit to the community to be derived from them.' The National Council again convened a conference to give the national organisations an opportunity to discuss some of the issues which the Nathan Committee would consider and which might vitally affect their future, and made a report to them on the initiative taken on their behalf and the statement of views submitted to the committee. This statement suggested that the committee might consider:

(a) a new definition of charity;
(b) registration of all charitable trusts and bodies formed for charitable purposes only, with a view particularly to periodic reviews of the practicability or desirability of such trusts;
(c) a new definition of the jurisdiction of the Charity Commissioners;
(d) modification of the *cy pres* principle;
(e) the establishment, nationally and locally, of general charitable trusts for the reapplication 'inter alia' of property becoming available under (d) above; and
(f) codification of the law of charity.

So complex were the issues involved that the Nathan Committee took nearly three years to produce its report; the government did not announce its policy on the subject for another twelve months; this was not embodied in legislation till 1960, more than a decade after the National Council took the first initiative; and all the implications of it are still being slowly worked out in practice. But it remained, throughout that long period and since, the work which, in the words of the annual report that first referred to it, 'provides perhaps the most striking example . . . of the way in which the Council can serve as a forum of discussion for the voluntary movement and of the will to work together which has been such a happy feature of the relationships of voluntary organisations during and since the war'. And, because of this, it remains also the best example of the way in which the National Council has been instrumental in creating a true partnership between the voluntary movement and the state and in profoundly influencing policy.

This summary indicates only the main lines of the undertaking. The full development belongs to the later chapters of the history.

In the meantime an example of a more immediately practical service which the NCSS was able to provide for voluntary organisations was developing most satisfactorily. This was the Social Workers Pension Fund which the Council established in 1946, at the invitation of the Standing Conference of Voluntary Organisations, as a major contribution towards raising the status and improving the security of professional workers engaged in social service. Considering the qualities demanded and the exacting nature of their work, they were amongst the worst paid sections of the community and few enjoyed the right to a pension. Any organisation primarily concerned with social service might belong to the new scheme which was to be on a contributory basis and ensure retirement pensions based on annual payments calculated as a percentage of salary. During the first year nineteen organisations joined the scheme, and the number rose rapidly year by year. By the time of the first quinquennial valuation the actuary was able to give a most favourable report. Contributors numbered 1,067 drawn from over 240 participating organisations, whilst administrative expenses were well below the figure of five per cent for which allowance had been made by the actuary. Moreover reciprocal arrangements were being made with government departments and local authorities whereby workers could transfer from voluntary to statutory service or vice versa without loss of pension rights.

It was not only individuals engaged in social work who were facing financial difficulties in the post-war period. For voluntary organisations in general and for the National Council in particular it was a time of grave financial crisis. Salary scales were rightly rising. Expensive but essential equipment and premises needed renewal or repair after the war years. The work in which the Council specialised and was pledged to develop—consultations, research, and so on—demanded a comparatively large administrative machine. But voluntary subscriptions were falling; and, because the Council was composed of representatives of many organisations each seeking public support, it was precluded from making a general appeal for funds. The steep rise of living costs and the redistribution of income by heavy taxation reduced the numbers of those who could give substantial subscriptions to good causes, or afford to give their services without payment. Moreover, many people thought at the time that the new statutory social services would reduce the need for voluntary action, and were reluctant to give to organisations which they believed might be 'taken over' by the state. The popular misconception that the NCSS received most of its income from the government still persisted, though in fact for every £2 received from this source £5 had to be raised from voluntary sources and no public grant at all was made for a number of the Council's activities.

Consequently, for those responsible for the finances of the NCSS, the post-war years were times of grave anxiety. It was fortunate that the Council had, in its finance and general purposes committee, a number of devoted financial experts under the chairmanship of Sir Edward Peacock, whose outstanding knowledge of finance and clear judgment, as a leading banker and trusted counsellor in the City, and deep interest in social work, were put at the service of the Council with generosity and vigour over a long period of years.

Grants from government departments and trusts were a considerable financial help, and welcome also as showing the widespread understanding of the Council's work and its difficulties. In 1945 grants from the Development Commission for rural work, the Ministry of Health for citizens' advice bureaux, and the Assistance Board for old people's welfare (this aid was later taken over by the Ministry of Health), accounted for approximately thirty per cent of the total income. The following year the Ministry of Education made its first grant towards community work which was particularly encouraging and useful. In the early post-war period several trusts gave grants for special purposes, such as the Sir Halley Stewart Trust's help for library and information work; and a little later the Nuffield Foundation offered a grant for two years towards the cost of administrative services for the National Old People's Welfare Committee. The Carnegie UK Trust continued to maintain the support it had given steadily for very many years with a generous grant that was all the more valuable for being allocated in advance for considerable periods and given for the general administrative expenses of the Council, not tied to some special work. There were also many contributions from individuals and firms; and a special appeal to industry in 1945 had a good response.

But costs were continually rising, and there was increasing need for the Council to expand its services. The budget for 1944/45 showed that expenditure had reached nearly £46,000, and income fell short by some £900. The following year the expenditure was more than £62,000 and there was a deficit of over £5,000. Another disquieting trend was the falling off in the sums subscribed to the Benevolent Fund for distribution to charities. In 1946 this figure reached a peak total of £557,000; but the annual amount began to decline after the 1946 Finance Act had abolished the surtax concession in respect of seven-year covenanted subscriptions. In the same year the expenditure of the NCSS had risen to £75,000, but income fell short by over £13,000. As it was providing services for the equivalent of ten national organisations, this figure was not in any sense extravagant. But the situation was critical, for the Council's carefully accumulated reserves were almost exhausted. Though the deficit was reduced in 1949/50 it rose again the next year, and it was clear that, unless considerable additional funds could be raised, the activities of the Council would have to be drastically curtailed.

These were dark days; and in the midst of them the Council suffered a loss of a different quality from any financial loss. For at the end of 1949 it had to accept, with profound regret, the resignation of Dr W. G. S. Adams, still affectionately known as 'The Warden' from his All Souls' days, who had been its chairman almost from the beginning. Throughout this long period he had presided over the affairs of the Council with unfailing wisdom. Without his wide knowledge and his glowing faith in the capacity of men to achieve better things, the Council could never have reached that influence in the community with which he now left it. Yet there was inspiration to be had, as well as a sense of bereavement, in looking back from the end of this span of history which he had so largely made. For the Council had begun its new and complex work with scarcely any resources; yet in thirty years it had accomplished more than would have seemed possible even to its founding fathers, full of faith and hope. It had taken the risks against which the old Chinese saying, quoted by the Warden, warns the over-ambitious: 'He who raises himself on tip-toe cannot stand, he who stretches his legs far apart cannot walk'; and it had belied such sombre expectations, going steadily and far. Still with the encouragement and interest of Dr Adams in his new role as vice-president, it could be confident of going farther, whatever the odds.

CHAPTER EIGHT

The Welfare State on a Shoestring

THE financial odds against the work of the National Council were indeed great; but the immaterial assets heavily outweighed them. The importance of voluntary organisations was now definitively recognised, and the authorities were prepared to regard them as important instruments of community life, not merely as useful agents. The acceptance by the state of responsibility for minimum standards in health, education, and economic security had removed many of the deprivations and inequalities which in the past had often claimed a disproportionate amount of voluntary effort; so that it was now increasingly possible for the voluntary bodies to take into account the total aspect of social development and to measure their plans by longer-term values. At the same time there was plenty of evidence that the individual citizen, freed by the new statutory services from many day-to-day difficulties, far from losing his initiative and the willingness to help himself was more and more ready to take his share of social responsibility. Often through the small, spontaneous groupings which the National Council was specially concerned to foster, he was eager not only to improve the state services but to contribute to overall social development by his interest in the quality of community life.

None the less, this very position of responsibility and influence which was now open to the voluntary organisation and the volunteer required a higher standard of performance to match the new standards of the welfare state if the status of voluntary work was to be maintained and its full worth proved; and there were many hindrances in the way.

More social workers were needed to administer the work of voluntary organisations and to guide and support the efforts of voluntary workers. But there was a general shortage of social workers; the voluntary bodies could not compete in salaries or security of employment with the statutory authorities; and though there were established training schemes for some forms of social work, others had no acceptable basic training courses at all. At a time when it was essential for small groups and large organisations alike to be certain of their legal status as charities, many questions in this field were still undecided. Reviews of income tax concessions and of rating assessment procedure threatened their already precarious finances.

Here were problems affecting the present and future of every voluntary organisation where the NCSS, because of its central position in relation to voluntary bodies and government departments, was in a unique position to help. During these difficult years, when the welfare state was beginning to develop in poverty and some perplexity, though every department of the Council's work grew and multiplied both nationally and locally its most significant efforts were concentrated on trying to remove obstacles that might prevent charities from using their resources to the best advantage for the public service in the changing conditions of the time.

The first of these efforts, of basic importance to the whole voluntary movement, was concerned with the review which the government had undertaken of the law relating to charitable trusts. The initiatives and the beginnings of this process, with Lord Beveridge's book on *Voluntary Action*, the debate in the House of Lords, the representative meetings and deputations arranged by the Council, took place in the post-war years already described. The fulfilment belongs to the last section of this history and beyond. But it was during the period covered by the present chapter that some of the most crucial points in the long story were reached.

In December 1952, the Nathan Committee published its anxiously awaited report.* This succeeded admirably in stating some long-standing problems in terms of modern conditions, and in providing an essential point of reference for further study and discussion. But on so difficult a subject the recommendations were bound to be controversial and to lead to widely divergent views. To help voluntary organisations in their detailed study of the document the Council convened another meeting, attended by 220 representatives of national voluntary organisations and charitable trusts, and addressed by a member and by the secretary of the Committee, to consider some of the report's salient points; and, at the invitation of the government, it later prepared a paper giving a detached summary of the views expressed by about fifty of the leading organisations, without any comment of its own except on detailed points affecting village halls. In this way the Council was able to give the authorities an unbiased account of the reactions which the report had aroused among voluntary organisations generally. On one point above all there was widespread agreement: that local responsibility should be preserved and that nothing should be done which would seriously affect this essential condition for

---

* *Report of the Committee on the Law and Practice relating to Charitable Trusts.* Cmd. 8710. HMSO.

effective action. This extract from the Council's summary sets out the point clearly:

'The view is widely held that an essential condition for the survival of voluntary action is a secure confidence that it will be left free to act, if occasion arise, independently of momentarily popular moods and views. It is maintained that it would follow from this that legislative and official provisions should be of such nature as to involve the minimum of interference with the wishes of benefactors and trustees, and that mere administrative convenience or tidiness would not justify harmful restrictions on that freedom. At the same time there is a general recognition that the responsibilities falling on trustees require constant vigilance to ensure the most effective administration of their trusts in the light of current needs.'

It was clear that members of the Committee on Charitable Trusts and very many other bodies shared these sentiments. The issue turned on the answer to the question as to how this condition of freedom and responsibility could best be provided in the modern age.

In July 1955 the government issued a White Paper setting out their policy on the problems considered by the Nathan Committee. They endorsed the main intention of the report, which was to liberate the administration of charitable endowments from some of the technical restrictions that had accumulated over the centuries; and they accepted some, though not all, of the main recommendations. One of the most important points was their rejection of the proposal to provide a new statutory definition of the term 'charity', since it would necessarily be 'new in substance as well as in form'. This declaration of policy mitigated another anxiety for voluntary organisations which a recent report of the Royal Commission on Taxation of Profits and Income had aroused when it recommended that a new definition of charity should be enacted for income tax purposes which would rule out a large number of bodies enjoying income tax concessions—another uncertainty about the legal position of voluntary organisations, involving serious financial consequences, which was of deep concern to the Council.

It was four years later that the government embodied its policy in a Charities Bill which eventually became law in 1960. Throughout this time the National Council, with the help and full confidence of the national voluntary organisations, maintained close contact with the Home Office which was in charge of the measure, and with members of both Houses of Parliament, to ensure that the main lines of thought on the voluntary side were taken fully into account. In the debates on the Bill both the Lord Chancellor in the House of Lords and the Home Secretary in the Commons acknowledged the assistance which the Council had given in discussions leading to the drafting of the Bill; and its main provisions and intentions were widely welcomed by the voluntary organisations.

In the meantime two other measures concerned with charity law had illustrated the impact which voluntary bodies, consulting and working out their policy together, could have on legislation.

The first was in fact a whole series of measures concerned with the rating of charitable properties which, though not of comparable importance with the review of charity law, involved the possibility of an increased financial burden which must have seriously impaired, or even terminated, the work of many organisations. The consultations, discussions, and proposals which the Council led on this problem spanned an even longer period than those which culminated in the Charities Act, 1960, for they had their origin in the Local Government Act of 1948 and finally came to a permanently favourable conclusion in the Rating and Valuation Act, 1961.

When assessment for rates had been in the hands of local authorities their practice had generally been to give sympathetic consideration to the amount of rates payable by voluntary organisations for the property and land they occupied; but the 1948 Local Government Act transferred assessment duties to the Board of Inland Revenue which had no power to give sympathetic assessments. Well before the new rating lists were to come into operation the National Council instituted negotiations with the government and the local authority associations in order to try to secure an agreement under which the position of voluntary societies would not be less favourable than before. These negotiations, reinforced from other quarters, resulted in the Rating and Valuation Act of 1955 which provided local rating authorities with discretionary powers to remit or reduce the rates on properties occupied by organisations 'whose main objects are charitable or otherwise concerned with the advancement of religion, education or social welfare', and included almshouses and playing fields occupied by non-profit making clubs. In addition, it postponed for three years the dates from which the rates of these properties could be increased.

These were useful provisions, enshrining in law a procedure which many local authorities had formerly adopted without express legal sanction, and thus strengthening the position of a wide range of voluntary bodies. But it was obvious that putting the new law into practice would bring innumerable problems for the local authorities and the voluntary organisations. How should the words of the Act, covering a wider range of interests than those of purely legal charities, be interpreted in individual cases; what was the position regarding appeals; above all, what would happen in two or three years' time when the remission of rates would be entirely at the discretion of local authorities?

Through discussions, pamphlets, and direct correspondence with very many organisations, the Council tried to shed light on these problems; and when the government set up the Pritchard Committee in 1958 to advise on a permanent policy for the rating of charitable properties, the Council resumed its consultations with a wide variety of organisations in order to obtain a broad consensus of opinion to put before the Committee. The Council's main points were that, as the work of these bodies was for the benefit of the community, they were justified in seeking rating relief, without which their activities would have to be seriously curtailed or ended; and that, in order to provide some greater measure of security and uniformity of treatment, legislation should be passed providing a statutory partial remission of rates, with freedom for rating authorities to grant further concessions. The Pritchard Committee, reporting in 1959, advised the government broadly on these lines; and the principles were eventually embodied in the Rating and Valuation Act of 1961.

This was a happy conclusion to a long and arduous enterprise in which the National Council had contrived to maintain the confidence and good-will of national and local government, as well as of the voluntary bodies, in a partnership on which, it was convinced, the efficiency and development of the social services as a whole depended.

The other matter concerned with charity law where the NCSS played a useful part arose from the House of Lords decision on a single case—the case of the Commissioners of Inland Revenue *v.* Baddeley in 1955—but far-reaching in its implications because it gave rise to serious doubts about the charitable status of a large number of voluntary bodies providing educational, social, and recreational facilities in towns and villages all over the country. The National Council felt itself directly concerned, both as an accepted forum for the discussion of such issues of importance to the voluntary movement, and as the provider of certain model trust deeds and constitutions for the guidance of many local bodies.

As in so many other instances, a careful study of the issues was carried out with a number of leading societies and in close contact with the government departments most concerned with the problems; and the Council's general conclusion was that new legislation might well be needed in the changed circumstances of the times, if many activities for social welfare were to remain within the ambit of English charitable law and enjoy the privileges which this status provides. The government finally agreed; and the Recreational Charities Act of 1958 went far to remove the legal uncertainties which had arisen in this field during the last few years. The Act, with which the National Council was so closely concerned, is one of the rare direct interventions of the legislature to define the lines of interpretation by the Courts in matters of legal charity; and a measure of great interest to all involved in the conduct of charitable effort.

For many years the Council had provided advice on questions affecting the status and constitutions of voluntary societies, particularly in the case of village halls, community centres, and similar institutions; but, as the developments just described make plain, the work had recently grown to such proportions that the Council decided to establish a special legal department. Many organisations were, and are, well served by their own legal advisers; but some of the issues arising obviously required consultation between different bodies so that views and experience could be shared, and a focus provided for more precise and professional study. Moreover, the rapid growth in the number of village halls, community centres, and other local organisations requiring legal advice on trust deeds, draft conveyances, and so on—and the prospect in the near future of the increased importance to local bodies of assuring their charitable status when the new legislation on charity law was formulated—meant that the calls on the legal advisory services of the Council were bound to increase.

The Council was able to initiate several other services of general use to voluntary organisations during this period. For example, the steep rise in electricity charges created additional financial burdens, especially for small local organisations; and the NCSS prepared information on ways in which electricity could be used more economically; encouraged negotiations with Regional Boards on the possibilities of special tariffs; and submitted evidence to a government committee examining the structure of tariffs and the role of the consumers' consultative councils, with some marginally helpful results. The charges made for the playing of gramophone records and the uncertainty about their collection had long discouraged many groups for which they were a vital part of recreational and educational activities; and here, evidence on the incidence of licence fees on the work of voluntary organisations prepared by the Council for the government's Copyright Committee, and negotiations with Phonographic Performances Ltd., the body controlling the issue of licences, after a long campaign in which the Council was supported by over eighty organisations had a useful influence on the amending legislation which was eventually passed.

But the work concerned with charity law, the rating of charitable properties, and the position of recreational charities remained the most important of the National Council's general services in these years; and its effects were felt not least on the Council's own special interests in the countryside. Ever since the Baddeley case judgment in 1955, for instance, a great many village halls had found themselves in difficulties because of the doubt thrown on their charitable status and new hall committees were unable to formulate their trusts. The passing of the Recreational Charities Act made it possible for the Council to revise the model trust deeds and confidently to advise hundreds of villages on these fundamental matters. Indeed, in the first few months after the legal department was set up the requests from village halls alone were so numerous that additional barristers had to be recruited to the staff to make up the backlog of the work, and the Development Commission made a grant of £2,000 towards the cost.

These were by no means the only difficulties, and encouragements, which village halls met with in the stringent nineteen fifties. In the early years of the period, the plan for erecting 200 temporary halls in England and Wales was nearly completed; and for Scotland the village halls committee, in close co-operation with the Scottish Council of Social Service, was able to expand the programme. But government grant-aid towards building permanent village halls and community centres was not restored till the end of 1954, and it was the end of the decade before the maximum grant was raised sufficiently to help the larger villages to meet the increased cost of building adequate centres; and that the small villages were given the chance to qualify for grants of up to one-half of the cost instead of one-third.

Nonetheless these difficulties did not quench the interest and enthusiasm of a great many local groups. Some went ahead with entirely voluntary labour, the National Council giving advice and help on types of suitable material and construction—another example of the self-help which the adverse conditions were encouraging in many fields of voluntary work. Others were able to adapt existing buildings to village hall purposes, or to make improvements to prevent halls from falling into disuse. And even when the Ministry of Education grant was restored, the effort to raise more voluntary funds did not slacken. £220,000 raised locally, for example, was spent on the 117 schemes put in hand in 1955. Even so, the gap between the total cost of providing and equipping the hall and the amount raised by local effort and grant-aid was widening all the time because of rising costs, and help from the Village Halls Loan Fund was in great demand. In 1953 the Treasury made a further advance of £15,000 to the Fund; and four years later the Fund stood at £102,000, most of which was on loan to local committees.

Another important impetus was given at about that time to village halls by the generous decision of the Carnegie UK Trust to provide over the next few years £100,000 for equipment grants for pre-war halls outside the scope of Ministry grant. The scheme was administered by the Trust with the help of the RCCs or, where these did not exist, of the Council's regional staff; and by the end of the first full year's working 1,000 applications had reached the Trust and over 550 grants had been offered.

This help with the re-equipment of old halls encouraged many committees to turn their thoughts actively to the possibility of structural modernisation and improvement. But many village hall committees looked further and began to explore new ideas for the best *use* of their premises; and a number of surveys showed plainly that there was a need for all committees to study with a fresh eye the changing needs of village life if they were to ensure that their centres were really playing a vital part in the welfare of the community.

In all this work the rural community councils of course took a leading part, encouraging, advising, making links between scattered villages. In several counties they took the initiative in calling conferences of village hall committees, which helped to direct attention to practical work that could be done, and to share the experience of one place with another's. Financially the RCCs were now in a better position than most of the National Council's other interests, for in response to the carefully reasoned application of 1950 for more adequate and long-term aid, the Development Commission recommended to the Treasury, after considerable study of the work of the RCCs, that grants should be made available from the Development Fund over a period of years and on a scale sufficient to provide, with local support, a sound basis of finance. As a result the Treasury decided in 1953 that, subject to the sanction of parliamentary votes, grants could be made annually for a period of seven years. The National and Welsh Councils would be expected to provide an effective national service; to maintain close contacts with the work in all the counties; and to do everything in their power to reinforce the efforts of the rural community councils to take advantage of the new opportunity. It was a generous policy which gave a challenge as well as a chance to the Council and the rural community councils alike.

Coverage of the whole country by rural community councils was developing steadily. New county organisations were established in 1952 in Hampshire, Surrey, Northumberland, and Cumberland; and the next year in Staffordshire largely through the support of the county council, and one more definitively planned for Bedfordshire. By 1954 forty-five counties had the services of their own RCC and there were hopes of establishing one soon in each of the remaining counties.

Their work also was expanding steadily. The provision of good personal services for those in the small, scattered rural communities who needed them had always been a difficult problem; but the rural community councils with the help of their member organisations and the National Council's headquarters staff were increasingly finding the way, or a variety of ways, of doing this. Services for the old or the handicapped were developing all over the countryside; and in 1957 the Carnegie UK Trust made available a sum of £5,000 to be spent during the next few years in developing various experiments already initiated by rural community councils to bring the services of the citizens' advice bureaux movement into more intimate contact with the personal needs of country folk.

In broader fields of social policy, too, some interesting enterprises were undertaken. Rural community councils in the East and West Midlands encouraged and collated the opinions of voluntary bodies in their counties upon the effectiveness, from the consumer's point of view, of the existing local government structure, for submission to the Local Government Commission which began its reviews in that area. The Northumberland RCC devised the means of finding out and making known the needs and wishes of the community in an even broader context than their own county, when they made a study of rural transport in mid-Northumberland, which was recognised by the Ministry of Transport and others in authority as of real value to the national consideration of this major policy question.

Meanwhile the earliest interests of the rural community councils were by no means neglected. They continued to play a notable part, acting in co-operation with the Rural Industries Bureau and the Rural Industries Loan Fund, in the development of small-scale businesses and of many new types of industry, so essential in providing various forms of employment and in making full use of local resources. During the fifteen months to the end of March 1955, alone, equipment to the value of over £75,000 was supplied to rural craftsmen through the Equipment Loan Fund, and amounts totalling approximately £45,000 were paid out under the Workshops Loan Fund.

Work for music and drama also made striking progress, in spite of the difficulties of the times. Early in this period there was some tendency to question whether grants from public funds could be justified in present conditions; and some county councils reduced their aid to county music and drama committees. But there was no widespread support for the view that these activities were an unnecessary 'trimming' to life; and the Carnegie UK Trust continued its steady aid. This was obviously a field where a little money and a great deal of thought and hard work could make opportunities for people to do things for themselves rather than depending on others for their entertainment and informal education; and during the nineteen-fifties the Standing Conferences of Music and of Drama with their affiliated county committees not only provided their usual advisory services for local choirs, orchestras, and dramatic societies but established their position as experts in the very fundamentals of this exercise. In 1954 for instance, the Standing Conference of Music Committees produced a pamphlet on the training of teachers which aroused great interest in the profession; and they were later invited by the Ministry of Education to give evidence to a government committee on the training of music teachers in schools. Meanwhile the Conference was studying all aspects of the music facilities in schools. Efforts were made to secure more satisfactory conditions for making and listening to music in the numerous multi-purpose new school halls; and in 1957 the National Council, at the request of both Standing Conferences, set up a joint committee to prepare a statement on the design of new school halls for music and drama. The large variety of expert experience which the Conferences could draw upon in both these activities enabled them to produce suggestions of practical assistance to educationists and architects in designing halls which could be of use not only to the schools but also to their neighbourhoods.

Still concerned with the roots of music appreciation and practice the Music Conference produced a booklet on *Youth Makes Music*, which led to rapidly expanding contacts with musical activities among young people and to the organisation of a pioneer training course for leaders of young musicians.

But these wide-ranging studies and experiments did not lead to neglect of the practical help and guidance which the local groups immediately needed. Demonstrations and discussions of techniques were arranged; legal, technical, and occupational enquiries answered; practical questions, such as the cost of royalties which were a hardship to some dramatic societies, were taken up.

The Standing Conference for Local History and its affiliated county committees were also rapidly developing their work in a field of interest which was making an increased appeal to the public. The number of representative county committees grew from twenty-four at the beginning of the decade to thirty-five by the end. Many of them issued bulletins on work in their districts including, for example, the preparation of an historical atlas, a photographic survey of buildings and local customs, preservation by means of tape-recordings of local dialects, and the organisation of local history competitions and recording schemes. Individuals and village groups could look to their county committee for help in the sort of activities they wanted to undertake: preparing a local history, training a guide-lecturer, campaigning for the preservation of historic sites; and in their turn the committees had at their disposal, through the Standing Conference, the expert advice of some forty national organisations and authorities. With their assistance the Conference provided such central services as a quarterly news bulletin, training courses, and a series of aids to study; pamphlets, for instance on *Discovering the Past, Armorial Bearings of the Sovereigns of England, Handlist of Medieval Ecclesiastical Terms*; and it was able to undertake pieces of work of such national importance as collaboration with the director of the National Portrait Gallery in a scheme to maintain a national index of historic family portraits. New contacts resulted from enquiries stimulated by BBC programmes on local history and archaeology, in which the Conference cooperated; and the scope of the Conference continued to broaden through these years to include every aspect of local history, as may be illustrated by the last accession to membership in the decade—the Business Archives Council.

Indeed, in spite of the general atmosphere of economy and retrenchment, the work with which the rural department was concerned grew largely at this time; and the rural committee, with the help of the rural community councils gave a good deal of its attention to problems of organisation and administration in this varied and complex section. They reconsidered, for example, the administration of the work for the development of rural industries; and the position of some of the smaller county voluntary organisations who were looking more and more to RCCs for help as their financial position and the difficulty of replacing retired voluntary workers with long service made their future uncertain. But in 1959 priority in these tasks was given to an objective assessment of the whole work of the rural community councils, to provide a basis for the evidence which the Development Commissioners required for their review of the way in which the government's block grants towards the general community work of rural community councils was being used. This survey strikingly revealed the scope and strength of their activities and the confidence with which it was being undertaken.

Not a little of the credit for the position which the rural work had reached belonged to John Smeal, the Council's chief rural officer for sixteen difficult years, throughout most of the war and well into the period of reconstruction. He always attached paramount importance to the contribution made by the co-operation of a host of voluntary bodies; by individual men and women both as leaders, particularly the RCC secretaries and the committee members, and as modest helpers; and by the aid of trusts and government departments. But all these would have failed of real success without the highly knowledgeable and sensitive leadership, with its special quality of understanding salted with humour, given over so long a time by John Smeal; and when he retired in 1957 his loss was keenly felt all over the country. Luckily, H. S. E. Snelson, a colleague with long experience of the work, first with the National Council itself and later as an outstanding secretary of the Yorkshire RCC, was ready to take his place.

The Central Committee of the Standing Conference of Councils of Social Service had a much harder row to hoe. There was still no central grant-aid for this work and local authorities were seldom ready to help anything except the specific services—old people's welfare, advisory work, and so on—which the local CSS might be doing. The financial stringency of these years, heavy taxation and rising costs made the position even more difficult. In many places new undertakings had to be postponed, and in others it was found impossible to initiate new social experiments or to plan for a systematic expansion of existing services.

Yet it was obvious that councils of social service had an essential part to play in the development of the welfare state; and the argument for this was so irresistible that over these years public opinion began to recognise it to the extent that, towards the end of the decade, it was largely the local people who took the initiative in starting each one of the new councils then set up. For the partnership in effort between the authorities and the voluntary organisations and within the ranks of the voluntary agencies themselves, which the CSS existed to create, was plainly essential if the new social machinery was to be made to work. There were so many complications to be worked out: problems of administration for the statutory authorities; difficulties in relations between specialist bodies; gaps in the new social provisions; confusing variety in the needs of different areas; shortage of workers, both paid and voluntary, and of opportunities to train. And, as a National Council annual report said at the time: 'No individual problem or social situation can be treated in isolation in this highly organised world.' A properly constituted council of social service with adequate resources could act as a focus for the consultation and joint action of voluntary organisations and the authorities. It could study the needs of a town; bring organisations into close touch with one another; and help groups and individuals to make their maximum contribution to community life. It could see where overlapping was wasteful and should be prevented, what new problems were appearing and how best they could be met. It could help voluntary societies to make their work better known, help in recruiting new volunteers, and provide common services to improve the efficiency of smaller organisations which were not able to find all the means necessary for their work.

The Central Committee of the Standing Conference made great efforts, with little means, to encourage the formation of new councils and better public understanding and support for them, and to give a lead on the kinds of new work which existing councils might do. They were convinced that the closer co-operation of the councils with other members of the NCSS 'family' was important—citizens' advice bureaux and old people's welfare committees (for which some of them provided the secretariat), rural community councils, local standing conferences of women's organisations, women's social service clubs; and as a first step they arranged a joint conference of councils of social service and citizens' advice bureaux, with plans for a similar joint meeting with rural community councils later. In consultation with another associated group, the National Federation of Community Associations, the question of the contribution which the CSS could make to the many new centres of urban life—in new towns, new housing estates, expanded small towns—was explored; and there was a warm welcome for the establishment, towards the end of this period, of councils at Harlow and Crawley.

The welfare of overseas workers in this country began to be a question of concern and, in response to a request from a number of cities, the Conference set up a group to study the position; and used joint discussion as a means of strengthening local work in the many towns where CSS had initiated, or were co-operating in, work in this field. Mental health, following the report of the Royal Commission, was another problem new to most councils where there was obviously work for voluntary societies of many kinds to do, and a conference was convened in London to study the ways in which councils of social service might help.

As a final example of central services may be quoted the publication by the National Council of an account of an experiment in the raising of voluntary funds for charities in Liverpool, the home of so many social experiments. This scheme had at the time been in operation for only three years and it was too early to apply with confidence its lessons to the conditions and needs of other towns; but it was a very interesting experiment, so successful in Liverpool that it was evidently well worth considering carefully. Through the leadership of the council of social service and the personal service society, a number of local charities had come together in a carefully planned and publicised single approach to wage earners for regular financial support. No effort had been spared to secure the goodwill and the co-operation of the representatives of firms and trade unions and to keep the contributors informed as to how their money was being spent; and at the date of the report 42,000 workers in over 300 firms had responded to the appeal and the number was growing steadily.

In the same year the councils of social service were recipients of some additional support when the National Council for the first time was able to appoint a secretary, Elisabeth Littlejohn, JP, to the Standing Conference and its central committee; a strengthening of the headquarters which was to have a significant effect on a movement that had so far been run on an even slenderer shoestring than most of the Council's work in this period. At the same time, however, the Conference lost the chairman who had carried much of the burden of the work for the past ten years when Richard Clements retired after the best part of a life-time of outstanding work in social service, first in the Midlands, where he had been secretary of the Birmingham Citizens' Society and then chief NCSS advisory officer for the Midlands; and from 1945 in London, as general secretary of the London Council of Social Service and for the last seven years as deputy secretary of the National Council. His exceptional knowledge and many-sided interests had been a great asset to the Council; and his skill and enthusiasm as administrator, speaker, and writer were appreciated by all kinds of groups at home and abroad for, as secretary for some years of the British National Conference on Social Work and as editor of *Social Service Quarterly*, his influence was widespread. But the concept and development of councils of social service had always remained one of his special concerns, and his departure from the chairmanship of the Standing Conference was keenly felt. The Conference was fortunate in his successor, Sir John Wrigley who, as a former Deputy Secretary of the Ministry of Health and of the Ministry of Housing, had a particular concern for the relationship of councils of social service to local authorities.

The central services which the Standing Conference was able to give were useful, especially to the smaller councils with few resources of staff and experience, and they expanded with the strengthening of the headquarters. But most of the matters for discussion and planning were brought up by the local councils of social service themselves, as a result of their recognition of new problems and opportunities in their own areas. Wherever large numbers of Commonwealth immigrants settled, for instance, the local council started or shared with the authorities schemes for trying to bring them fully into the community, through information and advice, club activities, co-operation with trade unions on employment, and so on. Where the pattern of people's lives and relationships were upset by the sudden expansion of their home-town, bringing in hundreds of strangers, or by their migration from a familiar slum which they knew to a new town bare of amenities and neighbourliness, there was an obvious opportunity for some organisation like a css to help provide the community services they needed and especially to help to stimulate public opinion and resources of leadership that would work to create a real community life.

The quality and extent of the service which the councils could give still varied widely from place to place. Some concentrated most of their energies on personal service which, at a time when so many families were feeling the pressures of changing economic and social conditions, was still an urgent need in spite of the provisions of the welfare state. Indeed, here was another problem on the ground which stimulated new consultations at headquarters, for in 1957 the Central Committee decided to co-operate with the National Council of Family Casework Agencies in appointing a joint committee to review the whole position of family casework societies and how it could be strengthened in relation to other developments in the voluntary services.

On the other hand some councils, and not necessarily only those in large cities or urban areas, were able to act as the focus for all the voluntary work in their districts, like the rural community councils in the countryside: as centres of information and advice; meeting places for social workers; promoters of clubs and music and drama groups; initiators of training for voluntary workers; co-ordinators of work with the old, the handicapped, or the mentally ill; forums for consultation on the development plans for their area.

Though the citizens' advice bureau service suffered severely from the economic stringency, it was on the whole better off, at least locally, than the councils of social service movement because both central and local government could not help but appreciate the help which bureaux could give in making the welfare state work. As more and more sections of the new system of social welfare came into operation there was more and more need for people with knowledge, impartiality, judgment, and a great deal of patience to explain to the puzzled citizen how the provisions worked and how they applied to his particular circumstances. And not only this, but also to show him how one service dovetailed with another to cover his needs; to point out the long-term consequences of a decision on alternative courses of action; and, in the light of all these individual problems, to assess the impact of each piece of new legislation in itself and in relation to the other provisions of the welfare state. 'The work of the bureaux', said an annual report in the middle of this decade, 'is directed to a steady interpretation of public policy and action—by explaining why and how "authority" is doing its work, by encouraging respect for "authority" and an understanding of the need to balance the good of the community against the needs and wishes of the individual; whilst at the same time reserving the right to support and help the individual when "authority" acts arbitrarily or is otherwise seen to be at fault.'

This was a tall order and citizens' advice bureaux grew to it gradually and some, of course, more fully than others. But the general success of the movement can be gauged by the growing extent to which its co-operation was sought by government departments and local authorities. The work in two sectors newly brought into the category of social service at this time will illustrate this: housing and legal aid and advice.

In the sphere of housing there was a spate of new legislation concerned with slum clearance; rent control and later a gradual decontrol to help to make more property available for letting; improvement grants to encourage landlords to modernise old houses; and so on. This was all aimed at helping to ease the desperate shortage of reasonably priced accommodation, but it immensely complicated the letting, renting, maintaining, buying, or selling of house property for every landlord and tenant. The Ministries concerned (sometimes the Lord Chancellor's Department as well as the Ministry of Housing) produced explanatory leaflets and forms, and local housing authorities did what they could to help the public; but the independent bureaux, used to interpreting legislation and regulations in simple terms and relating them to individual cases, were so gratefully welcomed by the authorities that the Ministry asked for the assistance of CAB headquarters in drafting their publicity; provided advance information about every new measure; and sent officials to address training schools for CAB workers all over the country.

As to legal aid and advice, years before the CAB service began and long before government aid was thought of, social workers had seen that a close working partnership was needed between them and friendly lawyers prepared to help in cases where the enquirer's limited means or inexperience hindered him from consulting a solicitor on a matter which had legal as well as social aspects. In many towns the local Law Society set up Poor Man's Lawyer schemes whereby one or two solicitors or barristers volunteered to give free consultations on neutral premises, or in larger cities a rota of lawyers staffed a part-time centre. Many CAB organisers had been able to arrange for such sessions to be held at their bureau or, where there was no PML scheme, for some local solicitor to see people there or in his office. But makeshift voluntary schemes could not solve the whole problem, and the CAB service had warmly welcomed the setting up in 1943 of the Rushcliffe Committee on Legal Aid and Advice*; and their evidence obviously influenced considerably the recommendations that the committee made for a state service of free or assisted legal aid and advice, administered by The Law Society but assuming a close collaboration between such a nation-wide organisation as the citizens' advice bureaux and the legal aid centres.

Though the government approved the recommendations in principle, owing to economic and other difficulties it was some years before any of them were put into effect. The efforts of bureaux to maintain and improve the informal services in the meantime brought them into even closer partnership with The Law Society, which encouraged provincial Law Societies to co-operate more effectively with bureaux; this paved the way for a real partnership in the localities when the Legal Aid and Advice Act, 1949, at last gradually came into operation with all its complicated application forms, income tests, and contribution rates which the bureaux were well briefed to explain. Even then it was not till 1959 that the vital advice provisions of the Act were implemented, after years of pressure by the voluntary organisations working through the National Council's Standing Conference on Legal Aid and Advice, set up in 1953; by members of both Houses of Parliament; and by the Lord Chancellor's Advisory Committee of which the secretary of the NCSS was a member. It was in this year that the final accolade was given to the CAB share in all this work when the Lord Chancellor spoke at the National CAB Conference on 'The Law and Social Work: A Pattern of Partnership'.

This was a tribute not only to the work of the local bureaux but also to the central organisation which briefed them and in addition collated their experience so as to produce for the authority reasoned reports on the impact of their measures on the citizen. CAB headquarters gave evidence, for example, to a sub-committee of the Parliamentary Select Committee on Estimates on the working of the Legal Aid Scheme; and from other sectors of their experience they were able to contribute useful information for the Quinquennial Review of the Ministry of Pensions and Social Security; for the Board of Trade War Damage Department on claims still outstanding; for the Inter-departmental Committee on the Rehabilitation of the Disabled; for the National Council's evidence to the Royal Com-

---

* *Committee on Legal Aid and Legal Advice in England and Wales.* Cmd. 6641, 1945. HMSO.

mission on Marriage and Divorce (family and personal problems coming to the bureaux at this stage outnumbered even those concerned mainly with housing); direct to the Minister, at his request, on the working of the Rent Act 1957; and through a group which they formed with the Women's Group on Public Welfare and the National Council of Family Casework Agencies, on the social effects of hire purchase.

The National CAB Committee was very much aware of its increasing responsibility, in face of this broadening out of the work and this increased recognition and respect for it in all quarters, to maintain high standards of work and workers. Throughout this period the headquarters staff had to be reduced to a bare minimum, since no grant for central costs was available and the National Council itself was in financial straits; and though in some cities a council of social service or family casework agency was able to provide the leadership and guidance of a limited number of full-time trained workers, most of the work was wholly maintained by the devoted service of volunteers drawn from all walks of life who needed, and increasingly asked for, more and more briefing and training.

There was no shortage of people eager to do this interesting but exacting work, and there was the opportunity therefore for careful selection, with an eye to personality as well as experience or specialised knowledge, and for careful and continuous training. A basic course was devised and no new bureau was opened until the workers had completed it. Headquarters and county and regional CAB committees organised residential week-end courses; one-day and half-day schools; study sessions at established bureaux; lectures on specific subjects, such as legal aid and advice or the provisions for handicapped people, or on new legislation (in one year there were twenty-nine training courses on the Rent Act alone).

The National Committee was also concerned to see that the coverage of the country was adequate in view of the responsibilities of the service. The number of bureaux remained now around 450; but progress was made with plans to extend the work in the countryside when in 1957 the Carnegie UK Trust made available £5,000 to be spent during the next few years on developing experiments already started by rural community councils; and temporary or longer-term bureaux were set up to help in several national emergencies during this period. There were the disastrous floods in the West Country and in Eastern England in the winter of 1952–53 when CAB was able promptly, with the aid of skilled volunteers from different parts of the country, to man centres which assisted the local flood committees to deal with urgent cases of distress; and gave advice and help to all manner of people with personal problems, sometimes long-term, arising from the devastation. The general secretary of the NCSS and the head of the CAB department served on the Lord Mayor of London's Relief Fund Committee, and for many months, with the experience of the emergency workers to guide them, were able to help with the complicated administration of the Fund.

Next came the abortive rising in Hungary and the Suez crisis, which brought to Britain hundreds of refugees, and expellees, British as well as foreign, but all totally unused to the circumstances and language in this country. Citizens' advice bureaux were set up at the headquarters of the British Council for Aid to Refugees to help the Hungarians, and at the large reception centres; and at the urgent request of the Anglo-Egyptian Resettlement Board, on which the National Council was represented, a trained CAB worker was provided at each reception hostel. But the re-settlement of these strangers was a long-term problem and involved bureaux all over the country, as homes and work were gradually found for them in various places. For years the CAB service had a part to play in helping them to find their place in the British community—a useful rehearsal for their work in the next decade with Commonwealth immigrants.

Visit of the Queen to the flood areas

Nor was the CAB idea confined to this country. Many visitors from overseas—in one year, from Nigeria, Lebanon, and Israel—came to study the work of the bureaux in the hope of starting something similar in their countries; and seven bureaux were opened in Bombay in 1956, and some planned in the Netherlands.

About halfway through the decade, the National CAB Committee received with profound regret the resignation of its chairman, A. A. Garrard, who for eight difficult years, during which the service had emerged from the status of a war-time organisation to win a permanent place in social life, had guided it with unwavering faith and a rare devotion. Leslie Farrer-Brown, director of the Nuffield Foundation and vice-chairman of the National Council, was warmly welcomed as his successor.

Meanwhile the Women's Group on Public Welfare and the Standing Conferences of Women's Organisations were showing what extra point could be given to the contribution of women's societies to social welfare when a wide variety of them came together to work side by side. Their share was not so much to explain the welfare state or to reveal its gaps and misjudgments as to study the broad range of things, large and small, that would determine its quality and turn its provision to the best advantage.

The Women's Group report, for instance, on *The Neglected Child and His Family*, already described, had an influence on the Children and Young Persons (Amendment) Act of 1952, where one of the report's main recommendations was adopted in the new and broader definition of the phrase 'in need of care and protection'. Better homes, with happier families, were priority aims of social welfare; but the Women's Group saw in the shortage of teachers of homecraft something that could spoil the best plans, especially for those poorest families where the mother found it difficult to cope. So a working group was set up to study the position with the help of the Ministry of Education's Inspector of Further Education for Women; and as a result a memorandum was circulated to all women's organisations, followed by a broadcast, making known the possibilities of training as full or part-time teachers, in the hope of encouraging some of the organisations' members to undertake an interesting job and also to meet a community need by passing on their knowledge and experience to the younger generation of housewives.

The Council for Scientific Management in the Home, a special committee of the Group, convinced that social progress would be speeded up through a more sensible application of scientific principles in the domestic sphere, undertook among its other activities a survey, together with the Department of Scientific and Industrial Research, on the equipment and tasks involved in the preparation of family meals in local authority post-war houses. The report they produced proved to be of great interest to local authorities and house-planners. But there were some families who seemed unable to find or keep even the most elementary housing accommodation—no house, in fact, in which the wife could practise her craft. The Group, much concerned about this comparatively small but worrying problem, produced in co-operation with a number of statutory and voluntary bodies a memorandum with recommendations, many of which were incorporated in a circular sent by the Ministries of Health and Housing to local authorities on the subject.

Not that the Group's interests were limited to women in the home. The question of students' grants, the youth service, standards of textile goods, care in food handling in shops, traffic in horses, the low standards of advertisements, were a few of the topics on which they made their views known; and this in spite of the fact that for reasons of economy the number of meetings of the Group and its various committees had to be curtailed and the staff reduced.

The local standing conferences of women's organisations, whose numbers grew steadily during the decade to not far short of 100, were equally catholic in their interests, arising generally from direct experience in their own towns and cities. The subjects discussed in groups or at their annual conference ranged from the care of the aged sick and the housing of the homeless to the control of unsuitable toys and publications for children and road safety for the under-fives; from waiting time in out-patients' departments to the litter nuisance. Nor did they merely discuss and recommend. They did a great deal of practical work in their own areas; co-operating with the management committee of a mental hospital, for example, in the provision of friendly visits and social evenings for patients; gaining the support of the chamber of commerce in a campaign to ensure the control of the sale of flick-knives; trying to improve the system of allocating dates for street and house-to-house collections.

But the enterprise of the Women's Group which best illustrates the way they worked and the chief aim of their work was their study of the problem of loneliness. It was undertaken because they felt that, in spite of the increased provision for social welfare, loneliness in the community was growing and assuming the proportions of a major social problem which threatened the quality of that carefully improved social life. The study was thoroughly done, in the fashion which was a hall-mark of National Council survey work. A representative group made contacts with many organisations and individuals in all parts of the country and received both written and oral evidence from those in a position to observe and judge; and it set out the conclusions* clearly and forcefully.

The Group found that loneliness afflicts all kinds of people of all ages in all kinds of situations, but that modern conditions, many of them created by planners with the best of motives, much aggravated the problem. Large-scale organisation of society; the break-up of small communities; the rapid growth of cities and towns; the weakening of the family circle through a move to a new town by some of its members, the mobility of labour, or the growing independence of the young, were all influencing factors. In a quarter of a century the number of people living alone had doubled. Some were able to make such social contacts as they wished and to contrive a satisfying life for themselves. To others this solitude was an affliction which they were helpless to overcome. They had none of the assets and consolations which a varied community life could offer; and in its worst form their loneliness might lead to mental or physical breakdown.

Their careful study convinced the Group that much could be done, and by all kinds of people and organisations in all kinds of ways, to check this increasing isolation and suffering. Since the lonely person is out of touch, he often does not know what facilities exist for him or how to set about finding them. Authorities and voluntary organisations could help by persistent efforts to make the opportunities known. Societies should have open meetings; clubs for one sex should encourage some mixed activities; youth organisations could keep the old in touch with the young and, for their own young members, should provide some interests that could be pursued at home. Good neighbour schemes, already doing admirable work in some towns, could be increased. Churches might be more welcoming and outgoing. Employers could often help by understanding treatment of the lonely-minded who do not fit in easily with the routine of a large factory.

Here, indeed, was a call to the community which the National Council through its wide contacts with statutory and voluntary bodies and individual citizens, with the churches, industry, and the professions, was in a unique position to broadcast and itself to help in answering. It was a call that had a direct bearing on much of the practical social work with which the Council was concerned; and it directed attention to the kind of social policies to which the Council was mainly committed: the improvement of the quality, as well as the material circumstances, of life, and the pre-

---

* *Loneliness: An Enquiry into Causes and Possible Remedies.* NCSS. 1957. Revised 1964.

Front cover of the report on loneliness

vention of social waste and of heavy demands on the expensive curative services.

In no field of work were these principles and practice more clearly seen than in the activities of the National Old People's Welfare Committee. The thousandth local OPW committee was started early in this period (marking an increase of 169 in one year). By the end there were 1,431, and, where there was no local committee, a regional or county committee, or a county correspondent, provided a link with local contacts. And all these committees, representative of local voluntary organisations and individuals interested in the old, and in close touch with the authorities' work, sometimes as their agent for special tasks, were devoted to trying where possible to make it easy and happy for the aged to stay within the community, maintaining a measure of health and independence. The services to this end multiplied imaginatively. As well as lunch clubs and meals-on-wheels, home-helps, and day visiting, a good many committees provided chiropody to keep old people literally on their feet; mobile libraries, holiday schemes, laundry services, night attendance for the sick, sheltered workshops for those able and anxious for a little light employment. The National Corporation for the Care of Old People continued to give aid, and for three years they set aside a sum specially directed to helping a limited number of chiropody schemes.

Above all was the growth of all kinds of clubs which might entice even the solitary and lonely out of their homes for a chat, a cup of tea or a light meal, a chance to exchange experiences; or to get some informal advice, games, an entertainment now and then, perhaps a bit of work for others by knitting children's garments, carpentry, toy-making. As early as 1953 there were at least 3,600 clubs, over double the number at the beginning of the decade. Next year the movement received a great impetus when the King George VI Foundation allocated to the National Committee a substantial block grant, under the King George VI Old People's Clubs Scheme, for distribution to clubs in England and Wales as a memorial to the late King. In the course of two years just on £90,000 was given to 183 clubs, and by 1957 the allocations were nearly complete and most of the new premises for which grants had been approved were open. Similar grants were made to the Old People's Welfare Committees in Northern Ireland and Scotland and to the British Red Cross Society and the Women's Voluntary Service (now Women's Royal Voluntary Service) for their old people's clubs. In addition the Unilever Fund continued to make an annual block grant from which small grants could be made towards the initial expenses and equipment of new clubs and additional equipment for clubs where activities had expanded.

But not all old people are able, even with many kinds of help, to maintain their own homes or live with relatives. Many old people's welfare committees were intensifying their efforts to provide different types of suitable accommodation to supplement the provisions by local authorities and national voluntary organisations. The number of housing associations grew; and there were several experimental schemes in the form, for example, of houses adapted into flatlets. Boarding-out schemes developed slowly, but in the last year of the period two more counties started a plan, specially helpful in rural areas where it could provide homes for elderly people near their own village instead of accommodation in a far-away institution. A good deal of thought and experiment was given also to the special needs of the infirm and frail, whose numbers were growing with the increasing longevity of the population.

There were plenty of volunteers ready to work on local committees or in the clubs and the activities associated with them; and a fair number of women and some men interested in residential care work; but as the work in both these fields became heavier, more complex, and more important, with the increase in both the numbers and kinds of local projects and of homes and group dwellings, the need for training grew more and more urgent. It was plain that a good matron or warden having the right aptitude for the work, in touch with developing thought and practice in geriatrics, and ready to take part in general planning for the welfare of old people, was a real source of strength throughout the whole work as well as in her particular home; and a renewal of the generous grant and co-operation from the National Corporation for the Care of Old People, first given for an experimental course in 1950, enabled the National Committee to continue the training courses for matrons year by year. The students themselves frequently paid tribute to the experience they had gained in these months, and a considerable number of appointing bodies, statutory and voluntary, turned to the National Committee to recommend suitable staff.

The very success of the work convinced the Committee that some more permanent means must be found of providing this initial training. The answer came when the King George VI Foundation arranged to provide, not only the grant for clubs already described, but under its Social Service Scheme (Old People) an extremely generous grant for training; which meant that the training and refresher courses for matrons and potential matrons could be financed and assured for several years under the careful terms of an arrangement worked out with the Foundation.

This arrangement and grant covered also the inauguration of vacation, refresher, and short courses for voluntary and paid workers in the field, who would provide a cadre of efficient, trained leaders and workers, properly equipped for the care of old people; and a limited number of bursaries for the training of new recruits to old people's work and for those wishing to specialise. Here was a new development of great importance. New attitudes to ageing, modern methods of rehabilitation, complex legislation, and the growing demand for more communal homes, suitable clubs, meals, and other services, meant that volunteers already at work, as well as new recruits, needed more information and preparation if they were to use their abilities and their enthusiasm to the best advantage. Services must be efficiently planned, managed, and directed; committees adequately serviced; clubs well run; methods of co-operation with all the organisations concerned thoroughly understood and practised; and, like the CAB workers in their own field, the OPW workers themselves were most anxious to have the chance of learning 'how to do the right thing in the right way'. The courses soon became a regular part of the work of old people's welfare committees in many areas of the country; and by the end of the decade the total number of leaders' courses which had been held was fifty-four, of leaders' follow-up courses eight, and of local courses, 184. Many residential courses for tutors and for secretaries and organisers responsible for planning work and training voluntary workers were organised nationally.

The negotiation, planning, and developing of all these activities, national and local, threw an increasing weight of responsibility upon the National Old People's Welfare Committee (which in 1956 became the National Old People's Welfare *Council* to mark its growing status). 'It is now established,' declared the Minister of Housing at the 1954 conference, 'as the accepted focus and centre to deal with the diverse and often difficult problems relating to the welfare of old people.' At the eighth national conference over 500 people attended, representing government departments, county and county borough councils, regional hospital boards, old people's welfare committees and other voluntary bodies, and several overseas visitors. There were old people's welfare committees in Northern Ireland, Scotland, and Wales on the same model, with which very close contact was maintained.

All this meant that the National Committee felt a duty to keep the whole position regarding the welfare of old people under constant review, with the help and experience of its member organisations and its local committees, and to adapt policy to changing needs. Seeing the need for more detailed information about the social and economic circumstances of old people, for instance, the National Committee set up a group to conduct a pilot survey in a selected area; to study in detail the ways in which the elderly were using existing services, in order to provide a guide for future policy and action; and published a report on their findings, *Over Seventy*. One of the early national conferences was largely devoted to the employment of the elderly, a problem which the committee considered was not receiving adequate attention; and representatives of both the government and the Trades Union Congress spoke about the new approach needed by employers, trade unions, and the public.

Regular visiting of the lonely and housebound was obviously one of the most important services which a local committee could organise, and as the years went by more and more people (including the elderly themselves) volunteered for this work. But it was known that the effectiveness of this service varied considerably from place to place and was difficult to assess. During the last year of this period the Council had discussions with the Ministry of Health about the future of voluntary visiting, which the government considered an essential service; and appointed a group of experienced people, representative of statutory and voluntary bodies, to review the organisation of the schemes, clarify their purpose and function, and encourage local committees to reconsider the effectiveness of their own work of this kind.

Old people's welfare exhibition organised by Sheffield Council of Social Service

Two final examples of the Council's continuing review of policy and practice may be given. In 1959 a review was undertaken of the extent to which the new club buildings under the King George VI scheme were helping in the development and expansion of club activities; and how far organisers were taking advantage of the specially designed buildings to provide imaginative facilities which would really meet members' needs and wishes. In the same year two surveys were made to find out what proportion of old people belonged to clubs. This amounted to only thirteen per cent; and though the Council realised that many elderly people preferred to join less specialised organisations or none at all, they felt that they ought to give serious thought to the way in which provision for leisure activities and club programmes might develop in the future so that a larger section of old people might benefit; and they decided to rewrite their literature on the subject.

During the greater part of this decade, the NOPWC had the great advantage, besides the co-operation of its member organisations and central and local government which it shared with other groups of the NCSS, of that direct appeal which attracts funds, in addition to the support of an annual Ministry of Health grant for administration and considerable financial help from the NCSS. The National Corporation for the Care of Old People continued to give most welcome aid. The King George VI Foundation made very large allocations for training services and club work. Unilever Ltd gave grants for club equipment. The survey of the social circumstances of old people was made possible by a grant from the Sir Halley Stewart Trust. More than one BBC appeal brought a generous response. All this was another proof of the growing interest in the welfare of old people and the growing confidence reposed in a national organisation that brought together all the voluntary and statutory resources to work in their service.

To this confidence the NOPWC and its secretary contributed much; and it was fortunate that when Dorothea Ramsey, who had been the very able secretary since the beginning of the reconstruction period, decided to retire in 1952, Marjorie Bucke, with pre-war experience in the Council's community work and some years as assistant to Miss Ramsey, was there to take her place.

The National Federation of Community Associations was one of the groups of the NCSS which definitely had few financial advantages in this period. In the early part it had to face not only a further cut in its budget due to the economies which the National Council was compelled to make, but also the effects of the national economy measures on the work of its member associations.

As to this second difficulty, the Federation sent the Ministry of Education a memorandum suggesting ways in which the necessary economies might be applied in their case with the least harm; and it much welcomed the renewal of the Ministry's modest grant and encouraging co-operation. It also prepared a paper as documentary support for a deputation from the National Council which made representations to the Ministry of Housing and Local Government about the social and recreational needs of the large housing estates and the new towns.

To help to meet the first problem the Federation had to decide to increase membership fees; but in spite of the difficulties which the local associations were facing and which meant that a few had now to withdraw from membership, new applications came in and resulted in a small net increase.

A little later the NFCA undertook discussions with the Ministry of Housing, in co-operation with the Central Churches Group which was equally concerned with the need for community centres and other communal provision; and these produced an offer of increased building licences to the value of £1½ million for churches and community buildings. Such licences could only be taken up, however, if there were sufficient money to buy the labour and materials set free by them. Community associations, though willing and able to raise voluntary funds, could not find enough to meet the whole cost, and the Ministry of Education refused to relax the ban on grant-aid for any except voluntary labour schemes. As local education authorities were of course bound by the Ministry's restrictions, only housing authorities if they were willing to put the cost of building on to the rents and rates, and voluntary organisations able to raise the full cost, could take advantage of the new position. One of the major difficulties was that it was impossible usually to prepare schemes and raise the money required within the period for which the licences were offered because the restrictions had been in force for so long that authorities and voluntary organisations had scarcely thought it worthwhile to prepare schemes.

It was naturally difficult to keep up the interest of groups when year after year their plans for even the most elementary community centre were constantly deferred; and though there were plenty of married women on the new housing estates, in new towns and the central wards of cities who were anxious to help in shaping a new community life there, they needed some encouragement and guidance in the difficult circumstances of the time; and the Federation staff was so small (two or three at headquarters and two travelling officers) that it was not easy to keep pace with the need. Even so, between 700 and 800 visits were paid to local groups all over the country during each year of this decade; and the number of associations and groups grew slowly, from about 1,460 at the beginning of the period to 1,650 at the end, though the number which qualified for full membership of the Federation never rose above 400.

Some had to use schools or private houses or to hire halls as their centres. Others managed to build their own premises with voluntary labour and the use of uncontrolled materials. One of the most encouraging methods of provision at this time was in Bristol where the local education authority was prepared to meet the bulk of the cost of materials and to provide skilled technical advice if the local association could demonstrate that it had the interest and support of its members and could provide at least one competent person to supervise the erection of a simple building. Several centres were built in this way in the Bristol district, and some in other places where the local authority adopted a similar plan. Excellent help in building operations was given in several towns by groups of young people from overseas, organised by the Society of Friends. The London County Council built on some of its estates small 'tenants' rooms' which provided useful centres but also a problem for the Federation as to how they could be related to the development of a community association. The use of school premises, which many associations without premises of their own had to make, also raised many difficulties. The Federation, after a survey of the evidence sent in by more than 100 groups, suggested to the Ministry of Education that the addition to schools of a separate wing for adult use would be a useful compromise. When the Ministry at last relaxed the restrictions on grant-aid and removed the ban on new community buildings, the Federation, like the rural department and village halls, though grateful for some mercy found that the amount available was so limited that it was difficult for voluntary bodies on new estates, where the need was greatest, to prepare suitable schemes.

However, the number of associations with their own premises steadily grew and with them the importance of full-time wardens to help them to make the best use of the centre as the focus of neighbourhood work. But year after year, in spite of much pressure, the Ministry of Education failed to implement the recommendations of the Fletcher Committee on the recruitment, training, salaries, and conditions of service of youth leaders and community centre wardens, to which both SCNVYO and the NFCA had contributed valuable proposals, and there was still no adequate scheme for finding and training the right people for these key posts. In 1957, however, that stalwart supporter of NCSS enterprises, the Carnegie UK Trust, offered to provide funds for a modest scheme on lines to be prepared by the education committee of the Federation, and two six-month courses of theoretical and practical training were worked out. The Trust also made possible the extension of shorter courses for voluntary leaders which had been held from time to time; and in co-operation with a number of local education authorities, councils of social service, and local federations of community associations, a series of experimental courses were arranged directed particularly to the needs of new housing estates.

No less important for the content and quality of the work were the week-end and one-day conference courses for leaders and representatives of community associations; the area conferences and meetings; the Ministry's residential course at the University of Reading planned and run in close co-operation with the Federation; and the annual conferences of the NFCA where such subjects as 'Initiative and Responsibility in Public Affairs' were thoroughly debated. In the last year of the decade nearly 1,400 people attended these conferences and courses, compared with less than 700 at the beginning.

It was clear that, apart from their interest in securing adequate centres and in planning useful pieces of neighbourhood work, the members were becoming increasingly concerned with the spirit and purpose of the movement. This wider interest was matched by the appreciation which central and local government authorities, educationalists, sociologists, civic leaders, and many voluntary bodies such as councils of social service and planning associations, were showing for the contribution that community associations could make to informal education, a sense of civic responsibility and the whole problem of community activity and voluntary service at a time when so much was apparently 'laid-on'. The Federation was well aware of this; and not content with the progress made it set up a research committee of social workers, sociologists, planners, and educationalists to re-examine the place of the community association and the community centre in relation to developing social policy.

At about the same time the Federation, realising the social and educational possibilities of the new medium of television, established a National Advisory Committee on Television Group-Viewing with the idea of encouraging a more critical and creative use of it. This enterprise made rapid progress. By the following year many organisations were already asking for its help in their efforts to use television programmes as an aid to study and discussion among their members. Short courses were arranged for leaders of existing groups; the BBC and Independent Television authorities helped the committee with advance information about programmes; a bulletin of information and suggestions was regularly sent to interested centres. A national conference, attended by delegates from many organisations, local authorities, and university extra-mural departments, unanimously expressed the view that this pioneer project of the Federation, so far carried out mainly by volunteers, ought to be placed on a more secure and permanent basis. The NCSS fully agreed that this was an important piece of work meriting widespread support and gave much thought to how it could be strengthened and financed. The open conference after the National Council's annual meeting in 1958 was devoted to discussion of the theme 'The Social Implications of Television' and it attracted a record attendance from all over the country. The following year it was possible to complete arrangements for a reconstitution of the committee on a more formal basis; and yet another NCSS offspring became independent, working in close association with the National Institute of Adult Education and sharing its offices.

No more practical and energetic way of helping to make the welfare state run successfully on a shoestring was shown in these years than by the members of that other neighbourhood organisation, grown out of the days of adversity between the wars: the National Association of Women's Clubs. The members were mainly busy housewives of small means, often harassed by the rising cost of living, shortages, lack of accommodation, and even in some areas by the anxieties and deprivations of unemployment once again. But they saw in these difficulties only another reason for making time to get together and help each other, not only with the aid of classes in cookery and dressmaking, budgeting and such-like chores, but in relaxing and enlivening doings—singing, acting, music, talks on interesting subjects outside the daily round. And not for themselves alone. By drawing into their practical and sympathetic fellowship the lonely housewife stranded in unfamiliar surroundings in a new town or housing estate, the inadequate mother unable to cope with her family, the woman harassed by a higher rent and hire purchase repayments on equipment for a new home, they were able to do useful 'preventive' social work which helped in its small way to forestall juvenile delinquency, ill-health, the lowering of living standards, the creation of more 'problem families'.

They began, too, to use this direct experience of all kinds of problems as a springboard for action on more than a local scale. Resolutions to be debated at their national conference and requests to the National Association for representations to ministries and national bodies about various questions flowed up to headquarters: the high price of children's clothing, lack of nursery schools, visiting of children in hospital, married women at work. 'Members are doing things in their clubs, in their localities and nationally', said the secretary of the Association in the mid-fifties, 'which a generation ago would have seemed impossible; and furthermore are doing these things with a growing ease and confidence which promises well for the future.'

It was the secretary herself and her handful of helpers—a single travelling officer was restored to the staff in 1953—who were the real inspiration of this work; but throughout the decade headquarters never had enough resources to give half the promotional and advisory services they knew were needed. Nevertheless, they contrived to extend their advice on the planning of programmes, to produce booklets with hints on *Club Management* or describing *Clubs for Housewives*, and some numbers of a club newsletter; to take up with the relevant government departments important questions like the need for better home-making education and the damaging increase in fees for local education authority classes; and to widen the interests of their members by preparing national conferences on such themes as 'Colonial Education and Welfare' the Wolfenden Report on Homosexuality and Prostitution and, in the final year of the decade, the key theme of 'The Welfare State—Our Opportunities and Responsibilities'.

But the very limitations of money and aid from the centre helped to develop that self-help which became a pattern of club life. In one year there was an increase of eleven clubs (to a total of 571) and 777 members (to a total of over 21,000) and this was largely due to the hard work of the twenty affiliated associations of clubs. They not only made special efforts to form new clubs, but also to provide members with the kind of services they needed. In the absence of paid organisers they found and trained voluntary leaders, organised schools and conferences, arranged music and drama festivals and exhibitions of club work. At the worst moment the clubs even managed to make contributions to the National Association amounting to nearly £700, in spite of the fact that the members were mainly working housewives and that their own clubs were not only self-supporting but contributed very generously to the finances of their local association.

It was a small movement that did not grow much in size during these years, but it certainly grew largely in significance, giving to a group of sterling citizens a voice, a place of their own to think and act in, and the confidence to use both faculties in the service of the community. Very sadly in 1958 they had to accept the retirement of their secretary and 'inspiring genius', Lucy Butcher, but her indomitable leadership for thirteen years, and indeed her life's devotion to the interests of working-class housewives, had set their movement far on the way she had planned for it; and her successor, Norah Phillips (now Baroness Phillips of Fulham) who had worked with her at headquarters, was ready to carry it even further.

The collaboration between the neighbourhood work of the community associations and clubs and the churches was particularly close because the Central Churches Group was equally convinced of the very urgent need for more meeting places, both lay and religious, which would encourage the growth of community life in modern circumstances, more especially in the new housing areas and the new towns, the London County Council's out-county estates, and the expanded towns. They feared that this tremendous movement of population from the over-crowded cities to better material conditions would solve one set of problems only to create another, if no adequate provision was made for the social needs of the new communities; and it was obvious that the programme for churches and other centres of community life was in fact falling far behind the housing programme.

Here was a great new venture of the welfare state which was in danger of falling short of half its fine potential for want of the means to use all the social resources waiting to be mobilised. The Group held a conference at the beginning of the decade, attended by representative leaders of all the religious denominations, social workers and administrators, central and local, to discuss the problem. It made a vigorous contribution to the Churches' Main Committee's representation to the government, and to the National Council's deputations to the Ministries of Housing and of Education, urging that it was essential for permanent, or at least temporary, buildings to be provided; and that a simplified administrative procedure and a simple division of financial responsibility between housing authority and education authority would speed the process. The release of a number of building licences following these urgent approaches, while being of little use to community associations for the reasons already known, did enable the churches to make considerable progress with their schemes. But they continued to be mindful of the lay needs; and while pressing the case for community centres they also sponsored a plan for erecting simple buildings where necessary which could be used by both lay and religious organisations.

This was only one facet of the complete involvement of the Central Churches Group with modern society. What was needed, said their chairman, the Bishop of Colchester, at one of their conferences in the mid-fifties, was close co-operation between the churches and the statutory authorities and voluntary bodies, so that the original religious inspiration

208

should not be obscured and lost, but carried over into the social life of the present. This might well prove to be a contribution of outstanding importance in the relationship between the church in its widest sense and the state. That it was an initiative welcomed by statutory and voluntary social agencies was proved by the growing number of requests from both to the churches for their help in all kinds of social problems: the adoption of children, for instance; mental health visiting; care of the elderly; the religious upbringing of children in the care of local authorities.

The best way to widen and strengthen this co-operation was obviously by the development of regular area meetings between leaders of the local clergy of all denominations and officers of the statutory and voluntary services, to explain and discuss the operation of the welfare state and the opportunities and problems it brought. Experiments of this kind in Cornwall, Cumberland, and Hampshire started early in the decade, and they aroused widespread interest. They were discussed at diocesan conferences in several districts, and working parties were set up to consider the machinery of collaboration. In Derbyshire, for example, a joint committee to promote co-operation was established by the Bishop of Derby and the rural community council. In Manchester a churches group was formed with the support of leaders of all the religious denominations, the council of social service acting as convenor. And so the movement spread and though progress in forming new groups was not rapid it was none the less positive.

Youth should not have ranked as a problem to the welfare state, like infirm old age or uprooted families; but the increase of children in the population since the war, the changing relationships within the family, the changing attitudes of the young to recreation, work, money, and life in general, all helped to make young people's contribution to the community and their opportunities for growth and activity less predictable and more difficult to guide. All the resources of experience and initiative in the field of youth activity and youth leadership were needed. The Education Act of 1944, making possible a real expansion of youth work in a partnership of statutory and voluntary, should have opened the way to a rapid development of the youth service. In fact progress was slow. But there was mounting concern in the government and among the public about this question, and the Standing Conference of National Voluntary Youth Organisations was able to do a good deal to stimulate it, taking every opportunity to help its member organisations to put forward their ideas.

For instance when, partway through this period, the King George's Jubilee Trust launched an enquiry into the influences affecting the upbringing of young people, all the organisations on the Standing Conference submitted memoranda to the various working parties making the study, and the secretary of the Conference was a member of the group on Leisure Time Activities; and when the report, *Citizens of Tomorrow*, was published, the conference arranged meetings to study the recommendations and to make them more widely known. A deputation from the Standing Conference to the Minister of Education promptly followed up the Select Committee on Estimates' report criticising the limitations of the youth service; and a little later they gave evidence on the subject to the Central Advisory Council for Education. At the end of 1958 the government, disturbed by these criticisms, set up the Committee of Enquiry into the youth service under the chairmanship of Lady Albemarle which was to have such important repercussions in the future, and the Conference presented evidence at an early stage of the study. In the final year of the decade there was a lively debate on the question in the House of Lords; and when the two major political parties decided to make their own investigations, both invited the views of the voluntary youth organisations through the Standing Conference.

But useful though all this widespread interest and discussion of the future was, and important the contribution which the Standing Conference could make to it, there were urgent tasks which it could and did tackle immediately. Convinced, like the National Federation of Community Associations, that the youth and community service would never be equal to its work until a real start had been made in establishing an adequate basic training for leaders, the Conference eagerly welcomed the opportunity of preparing proposals for the Leadership Training Memorial Fund which the King George VI Foundation decided in 1954 to form, as a major part of the youth side of the memorial scheme; and was happy to see its proposals as the basis of the plan finally produced. The grants which the national voluntary organisations received from this fund made possible good progress in developing training courses for voluntary youth leadership; and by the end of this period the Standing Conference had launched various experimental courses, such as a higher level course for training staff run in collaboration with a university college, and week-end refresher courses for leaders of under-fifteens.

Another aspect of the efforts of the Standing Conference to relate the whole service more realistically to the new conditions of the age was illustrated in the Conference on Terminology in the Youth Service; here members representing all the chief bodies responsible for youth work in

Britain set themselves to examine the terms so long commonly used in this field of work and to assess how far they really conformed with present conditions.

Moving from phraseology to practice, the Conference looked at ways in which established youth movements could do more for school-age children; briefed its constituent organisations on emergency building schemes to help them in advising their local units needing premises in new towns and housing estates; and, concerned with the needs of young people in industry, made plans to co-operate with interested industrialists in a few experimental projects. Seeing that new leisure-time occupations with a real purpose and close relationship to the activities of the adult community were more likely to appeal to the new generation of young people than the standard doings of most youth clubs, the Conference welcomed the Thames Youth Venture, a scheme for encouraging rivercraft among the young in Greater London, financed by the City Parochial Foundation, to which it gave much practical support; and, on a larger scale, helped to plan and to work the Duke of Edinburgh's Award Scheme, designed to develop character and initiative in young people by offering awards for achievement in a wide variety of fields, from adventure to social service.

The Standing Conference had a good deal of success in reaching its aim of giving the national voluntary bodies opportunities to pool experience and ideas, discuss and influence policy, and stimulate action. Local co-operation and confidence between youth organisations was proving on the whole more difficult to achieve. In this period much time was given to strengthening the work of the area and local standing conferences, which try to provide for their districts the kind of consultative service that the national Standing Conference provides for the national youth movement. By the last year of the decade it was possible to report that the number of local standing conferences had increased, and that many of them were concentrating vigorously and harmoniously on new plans for guiding leaders, taking part in the Duke of Edinburgh's Award Scheme, and devising ways of reaching the 'unattached' who scorn ordinary youth clubs.

The international contacts of the Conference, already reaching out in the immediate post-war period, spread and strengthened considerably in the fifties. British youth work had a special attraction for many foreign visitors and students, and the Conference served as a useful focus for enquiries about the wide variety of youth organisations and their work, programme planning, and explanation of methods and aims. It continued to take an active share in building up good relations between organisations and leaders of youth work in the United Kingdom and the German

Federal Republic. Arrangements were frequently made for study visits of representatives of German youth organisations. The Festival of Britain youth exhibition was sent to tour centres in the British Sector for a whole year, so great was German interest in it. A large group from national youth bodies in this country was mustered, at the request of the Foreign Office, to respond to an invitation to a big festival of youth in Germany.

But the overseas work was by no means confined to Germany. The secretary of the Conference made a lecture tour in the United States; was a member of the official delegation to a conference in France to study youth questions; and of a seminar on citizenship education at the UNESCO Youth Centre at Gauting. Collaboration with the Soviet Relations Committee of the British Council in its effort to develop cultural relations with young people and students in the USSR led first to a small-scale exchange of adult representatives which paved the way in the last year of the decade, after considerable difficulties, to a fortnight's visit of two British parties to Moscow and Leningrad, and the hope of a return visit by a group from Russia. Negotiations were also set on foot at this time with the Polish National Committee of Youth Organisations in the hope of arranging exchanges between youth groups of the two countries.

In 1952 the Standing Conference had regretfully to say farewell to Dame May Curwen as its chairman—a severe loss, for not only had she been at the helm during the critical three years that bridged the post-war period and the opening era of the welfare state, but her wisdom and great experience of young people had been at the service of the Conference ever since its inception sixteen years earlier. Professor Norman Haycocks, armed with an interest in the young and a wide knowledge of them, as Head of the Department of Education of Nottingham University, stepped into her place. Another break in the ranks of those who served the Conference came a few years later when Jean Marindin who, with her deep concern for young people and her gifts of advocacy, had been an outstanding secretary of the Conference for a number of years, resigned on grounds of ill-health, and was succeeded by R. W. J. Keeble, formerly of the headquarters staff of the National Council of YMCAS.

As will be evident from these reports, every department and group of the NCSS was every year getting more visitors from overseas. Many of these were people who came to them direct or through the Foreign Office, the British Council, or other body, being interested in the group's specific subject—youth, advice services, welfare of the old, or whatever. But the majority of visitors were channelled through the overseas and international department, which was each year faced with more and more complicated problems in sorting, guiding, advising; arranging talks and programmes of visits, with the responsibility for ensuring that each person or group got the appropriate contacts, the most useful briefing, a carefully dovetailed time-table (not the least difficult of these tasks since it takes two sides to make a time-table work and time means something different in different languages).

Some of these visitors had a general interest in the social services of this country, and especially in the role of the voluntary bodies. Others were students from universities, colleges, and schools of social work in foreign or Commonwealth countries pursuing their studies abroad. Many were UN Social Welfare Fellows, Colombo Plan Scholars, and the like, seeking guidance about the studies they were making in England; and the department kept specially close contact with the British Council by means of representation on the Technical Advisory Panel concerned with the UN Fellows and on the Standing Committee on the Welfare of Colonial Students. It was plain that other countries were even more deeply interested than they had been in the immediate post-war period in what was being done here, some of them having gained their first inspiration for social welfare from this country and others with more advanced schemes being eager to see how other and different methods from their own, in perhaps comparable circumstances, were working out. Since the NCSS was the only national society whose interests reached out to all the main fields of social work, it was natural that students should come to it as a sorting house, or a centre for all-round appreciation of the British social services. All the government departments were well aware of the value of this.

But the traffic was by no means all one-way. The activities of the British Committee for the Interchange of Social Workers and Administrators developed rapidly in this period, first under Sir Wilson Jameson who had been its chairman from its inception in 1942, and then under John Ross. Each year it selected candidates for social-work posts in hospitals or in the psychiatric services in the United States; and was able to arrange also some direct exchanges of social workers between the two countries, which it was hoped would be further facilitated by the formation in the mid-fifties of an American Exchange Committee. Co-operation with the US Educational Committee in the United Kingdom was strengthened by representation on the Advisory Panel on Social Work set up by the committee to assist in developing the Fulbright scheme of travel grants, which were a material help to those going to the United States to work or study. The Interchange Committee also became responsible for selecting annually the candidates for training scholarships at the Lighthouse Settlement, Philadelphia, offered to English settlement and youth workers; and, in co-operation with the National Union of Students, for choosing young people each summer for a three months' visit to the us as counsellors in children's camps.

Study visits or jobs in Canada and other parts of the Commonwealth were also arranged for social workers from this country, and in reverse. But probably the largest development in these years was in the work of the Intra-European Exchange Sub-Committee, set up at the beginning of the decade as a means of British participation in the special interchange scheme established by the UN Geneva Office. In the first two years of its existence this committee arranged programmes for over fifty social workers and administrators from Britain for short-term study visits in Europe and for a similar number coming to this country, on an exchange of hospitality basis. Already Austria, Belgium, France, Germany, Holland, Italy, Norway, Sweden, and Switzerland were taking part in the scheme; and other countries joined in later. The government showed its sense of the importance of these exchanges by making a grant, renewed annually, to enable the National Council to maintain and extend the project at a time when financial difficulties had made continuation doubtful. The interest of the International Labour Office made it possible to include the industrial, as well as the social, field; and later the scheme was extended to cover social workers who wished to have their programmes planned but preferred to pay their own expenses rather than to share in reciprocal hospitality.

These exchange visits were only one aspect of the work of the Interchange Committee. An interesting extension of the European Social Welfare Programme at this time was the organisation of a number of study groups and seminars held in different countries on a variety of social and industrial subjects. The British committee not only had the responsibility of selecting the British delegates to attend these meetings but was also asked by the government to organise several seminars to be held in this country. The venues of the seminars ranged from Germany to Sicily, Finland to Yugoslavia; and the subjects from children of incomplete families to welfare on isolated building sites, from playground facilities to social research. But none were more significant than the series of three seminars arranged in Britain, which had as their respective subjects the main types of social work; the principles and practice of casework, groupwork, and community development. Typical of these expert seminars was the first, on the advanced study of social casework, which was attended by fifty people from Europe and twenty from this country for the most part distinguished as teachers or supervisors or key workers in their agencies, who worked through advanced group discussion and through lectures by members of the teaching staff from Canada, USA, and the World Health Organisation, under the direction of a member of the UN Technical Assistance Administration. This was work at a high level for a handful of experts. The department was able, through the British National Committee for which it also provided the administrative services, to continue and expand the opportunities it could give to a very much wider body of people to discuss and contribute to social work and social policy through the British National Conference on Social Work held every three years, which had been so successfully initiated at Harrogate in 1950. The subjects chosen reflected the dominating preoccupations of those years: first 'The Family'; then 'Children and Young People'; and at the end of the decade a move outwards to study the modern world at grips with new conditions—'People and Work: Co-operation for Social Welfare in Industrial Communities'. But the unique value of these conferences lies perhaps in the methods of preparation for them which, through scores of small study groups in towns all over the country, often organised by councils of social service, bring together a great variety of people—some at the centre of statutory or voluntary social work, administering or teaching; some on the fringe; others, with different experience and motives, on the outside looking in— to consider at meetings continuing through a year or more some aspect of the conference subject which interests them. To help these groups an expert central studies committee is set up to prepare a guide to studies which lays down lines of thought and questioning on the various topics within the main theme; and the basis of the discussions at the conference itself is provided by a handbook that summarises the findings of the group —findings that are varied in kind and quality but of great value to the members themselves who have had the chance to work them out together and to the conference which receives them welded into a coherent whole, ripe for argument, enlightenment, or disagreement.

But the British National Committee is the British part of the International Conference of Social Work, and as such it has the responsibility among other tasks of preparing the British material for the international conferences which since 1948 have been held every two years, and of selecting the British delegates. This brings social work and social workers in this country into touch with the whole world movement: a fact sharply illustrated by the far-flung meeting places chosen during this decade— Madras, Toronto, Munich, Tokyo—and the broad scope of the themes chosen, most of them emphasising the practical ways in which peoples with few resources, or many, might increase their own capacity for co-operation and self-help. The British committee became skilful at the preparation by experts of papers giving an account of British ideas and experience on various aspects of the conference theme; and at planning, with the help of the publications department of the NCSS and the government's Central Office of Information, exhibitions illustrating by photographs and charts and a selection of books and pamphlets the characteristic features of British social work. The huge number of delegates—usually over 2,000 from more than seventy nations—continued, and continues, to present problems of organisation and feasibility; but a real exchange of thought and experience, in the commissions and groups and even through the formal presentations at plenary sessions, is somehow achieved, and the British members have been able to make a worthwhile contribution.

The catholicity of interests and contacts of the British National Committee is well illustrated by the diversity of experience of the three men who successively served as chairman during this period following Dr. J. H. Nicholson the eminent first chairman: Sir Wilson Jameson, distinguished civil servant; Alan Moncrieff, Nuffield Professor of Child Health at the University of London; and John Marsh, Director of the Industrial Welfare Society.

Exhibit at the 1968 International Conference on Social Welfare, in Helsinki

Early in the decade Miss Harford retired from her position as head of the international department—the last of the many branches of the National Council's work to which she had given such distinguished service over a period of fourteen years. The successful establishment of the British National Committee was largely due to her great zeal and her skill in bringing together many British organisations in friendly co-operation; and its influence in world counsels owed much to the confidence and esteem which she had won from organisations and workers in many countries. Richard Clements, deputy secretary of the National Council, added the secretaryship of the BNC to his many other tasks until his retirement from the Council in 1958, when Nancy Rice-Jones who had been responsible for the work of the international department since 1953 also took over the direction of the British National Conference.

Though financial stringency limited the programme of the publications department during the early years of the decade, the literature which it continued to produce, since it was essential to the work of the various groups and departments and to the central purpose of the NCSS—the two quarterly journals, the two directories of public and voluntary services, *Citizens' Advice Notes*, handbooks, pamphlets, and reports—reached an increasingly wide readership and played an outstanding part in the Council's work of interpreting the voluntary-statutory partnership of the welfare state. Partly this was due to the quality and scope of the material. This was perhaps particularly noticeable in the expert articles on a broad range of subjects in *Social Service Quarterly*, which by now had subscribers in every continent and was studied by staff and students in schools of social work all over the world; while in this country extracts from it were frequently reproduced in other papers and the articles quoted and discussed at conferences and meetings.

Partly the growing success was the result of the policies which the publications department worked out during these difficult years for controlling production costs and increasing sales, since income must be made to match expenditure. The resources and charges of various printers were carefully assessed; circularisation campaigns undertaken; bookstalls and displays at conferences, international as well as national and regional, introduced large audiences directly to this activity of the National Council; and thousands of letters were sent to groups and individuals about books or pamphlets which might specially interest them.

The number of these publications was bound to grow all the time, however strictly limited to the essential requirements of the Council, be-cause the work of its departments and groups was also growing continu-ally and the interest in them increasing. The handbooks of information about specific types of work—*Age is Opportunity*; the village hall series; *Our Neighbourhood*; the councils of social service handbook; and many others—needed constant revision and new editions often sold out so quickly that it was difficult to keep pace. The long negotiations which the Council led on matters of such general importance to voluntary organ-isations as, for example, rating, required the production of explanatory material; and in one year 15,000 copies of the two pamphlets dealing with *The Rating of Charitable Properties* were sold. The methods of preparation devised by the British National Conference on Social Work entailed the publication in advance of each conference of a *Guide to Studies* and a summary of the study groups' reports as well as the final report of the deliberations at the conference itself. The National CAB Committee began to produce pamphlets on such subjects as *Buying a House* and *Hire Purchase: Do's and Don'ts* as part of the policy of making its advisory services readily available to an even wider public (in one year the sales of the first reached 13,000 copies and of the other 32,000). The local history committee added steadily to its handbooks; and the National Council now published its own major reports and surveys.

In all this the publications department not only produced what the other departments asked for (sometimes after much discussion and some argu-ment) but was able to relieve them of a good deal of trouble by know-ledgeable advice on the problems of publication and the best and most economic methods of presentation. And towards the end of the period, by keeping in touch with developments in typography and printing and studying the resources of different kinds of printing houses, the chief publications officer had built up a body of information and experience which enabled the National Council to give a lead to other voluntary organisations also on inexpensive methods of producing attractive publi-cations. The direction of the small department had by now been taken over by Gerald King, who had worked on the staff of the NCSS since before the war in various capacities in Birmingham and London, and for a number of years had devoted himself with a lively and penetrating interest to the problems of publishing during this difficult and crucial period.

The *Citizens' Advice Notes*, the digests of social legislation and adminis-trative regulations, originally devised to serve the newly established citizens' advice bureaux at the beginning of the war, but quickly recog-nised as an infallible guide by all kinds of organisations and individuals, continued to be the most outstanding of the Council's publications. It is not, like the Council's other reference books, revised at intervals when time and resources allow, but amending as well as new digests are issued regularly and frequently to maintain its accuracy and usefulness as a current guide. In one year of this period, for example, digests of nineteen new Acts of Parliament and sixty-nine statutory instruments were published as they came into operation, together with summaries of reports, White Papers, and circulars; and the sections relative to national insurance, transport, and the armed forces were completely revised. Early in the decade its subscribers already included most government departments, 500 local authorities and a larger number of commercial and industrial firms; universities, professional, and voluntary bodies of many kinds, and individuals, in addition to the 500 bureaux.

This was a remarkably practical form of partnership with the welfare state, publicising and explaining its provisions over so wide a field. A remarkable example also of the contribution of voluntary organisations and voluntary workers, since CANs still relied, and continues to rely, on a very small expert staff assisted by a small band of highly skilled volunteers; and depends not only on their ability to distil the essentials of new legislation but also on the exchange of ideas and information between them and other departments of the National Council. In this way the departments' experience of the actual impact of the law in individual cases, whether of individuals or organisations, often illuminates for CANs the ramifications and the significance of current social legislation; and the more theoretical approach of CANs helps to provide a basis for the more practical activities of other departments of the Council.

With none is the exchange more frequent than with the information department for, though the accumulation and exchange of information on its own subjects is part of the work of each department and group of the NCSS, the information department must act as a central focus where developments in legislation, administrative action, or voluntary effort in the changing social field can be related to the varied interests of the groups and of the voluntary bodies associated with them. To help further in this aim *Nacoss News* was started in the mid-fifties: a monthly (later bi-monthly) commentary on social trends and developments, voluntary and statutory, giving information and views which the factual or specialised circulars of the NCSS departments did not normally cover, or did not relate to one another and to the whole scene in a general way. Intended primarily as a service to councils of social service and rural community councils, *Nacoss News* was soon extended to all the member organisations of the National Council; and many government departments and local

219

authorities, when it came to their notice, many libraries, schools of social work, and a wide variety of people interested in social trends, later asked to receive issues regularly.

The circulation was not limited to this country: a good many copies went to other parts of the world and helped to maintain the National Council's exchanges with social work abroad. More directly the department was frequently at this time asked to supply information for foreign agencies interested in the British experience. The Council of Europe, for example, required a list of institutions in this country concerned with social research. A health expert engaged on a survey of social workers for the United Nations asked for information on their numbers, training, and employment in this country. A Swiss social worker wanted material for a research project on holiday provision for families with small means.

Such enquiries required special research in addition to the continuous study of parliamentary reports, publications of voluntary societies, newspapers and journals, proceedings of conferences, and so on which were routine tasks of the department; and it was also still responsible (until 1958), in co-operation with the information department of the neighbouring London Council of Social Service, for the preparation of information circulars for citizens' advice bureaux and for answering difficult questions from bureaux all over the country on the application of the new provisions of the welfare state.

There was of course no chance of setting up a central studies department in this period when money was short and staff in existing departments cut to a minimum. But the Council continued to find ways of bringing together the experience and views of interested parties on some important questions of current social policy to form a synthesis of information and ideas for the future. One way was through the enterprise of an associated group of the Council, as in the case of the Women's Group study of *Loneliness*, already described.

Another method is illustrated by the memorandum on *Housing the Homeless*, produced in 1954 after an enquiry undertaken in collaboration with the National Council of Family Casework Agencies. Though a comparatively small piece of work it was of importance both as a useful contribution to a long-standing problem and as an example of the way in which the experience of a number of organisations could be concentrated and distilled by such a central body as the NCSS. For some time the Council had been troubled by the evidence, coming mainly from citizens' advice bureaux and the casework departments of councils of social service, of the problems in many large cities of homeless families evicted for a variety of reasons from private or publicly owned accommodation; and living in social conditions which made decent family life almost impossible and contributed to the actual break-up of families. Some councils of social service and casework bodies were already working closely with the authorities in experiments to improve the situation; and this experience, assembled in the report together with an appreciation of the grave social consequences of the present situation, offered to the Ministry of Housing and Local Government a pointer to constructive action on a wider scale which was to have a useful influence on policy.

The third method used was a full-scale study, with a grant from a charitable trust, guided by an expert advisory committee and conducted by a person of outstanding competence and experience in social affairs. Such was the enquiry into the future development of voluntary services for handicapped people undertaken by a joint committee of the National Council and the Central Council for the Care of Cripples (now the Central Council for the Disabled), with Dr J. H. Nicholson, formerly Vice-Chancellor of Hull University as director of the enquiry. The chairman was Mr L. Farrer-Brown, then director of the Nuffield Foundation, and the members were appointed by both organisations, with advisers from the Ministry of Health and the Ministry of Labour. The finance for the project was provided by the Nuffield Provincial Hospital Trust.

Since the war a great move forward had been made over the whole field of work for disabled people. The Tomlinson Report* of the war years had opened the way. The Disabled Persons (Employment) Act, 1944, which followed had laid the foundations of a service that could be outstanding among all the services of the welfare state. This achievement was made more likely by a considerable change in attitude towards disablement, both by society and by the handicapped themselves, encouraged by new methods and successes of medical science. To relieve suffering and to help the disabled had been for centuries the main sphere of service for voluntary bodies; and in the last few years there had been a resurgence of interest in it, resulting in fresh work and new organisations. But what was to be the place of all this voluntary effort in relation to the expanding services of the authorities and the whole development of work for the handicapped? It was plain that, as statutory services grew, it became more important that voluntary effort should be well directed, that the relations between the societies should be good, and that each element should play its proper part. The Piercy Committee on the Rehabilitation, Training, and Resettlement of Disabled Persons was reviewing the work primarily

---

* *Report of the Inter-departmental Committee on the Rehabilitation of Disabled Persons*, 1943. Cmd. 6415. HMSO.

from the angle of authority and official action (the committee was still sitting when the Nicholson study was planned), but its report* confirmed the need for an enquiry into 'the nature of the contribution which might best be made by voluntary organisations in present circumstances'.

Here was an obvious task for the NCSS to initiate, for, as Dr Nicholson said in his final report, 'if voluntary action is to continue to make its traditional contribution to policy-making the voluntary bodies must think ahead while practice is flexible—as it still is over a large part of the field'; and the Council was by its very nature apt to encourage and assist this thinking ahead.

The task was most thoroughly done. In a comparatively short period Dr Nicholson made himself directly acquainted with many kinds of voluntary and statutory activity and with the views of leaders in the work, visiting national voluntary bodies and government departments, county associations for the handicapped, councils of social service and community councils; also hospitals, medical and industrial rehabilitation centres, training colleges, sheltered workshops, residential homes, clubs, fellowships, all over the country. His report†—in general approved by the joint committee which had advised and helped him with their suggestions and criticisms—was fortified by the detailed, first-hand information he had gained with the generous co-operation of so many organisations and individuals, but it revealed the shape of the wood plainly through the trees. There was, he saw, no general answer to the main problem posed by the enquiry—the appropriate place of voluntary service in work for the handicapped. He proposed a number of particular answers on each aspect considered: rehabilitation and training, employment, social welfare, residential care, and schemes of co-operation.

But his main conclusion was the great need for fresh thinking and a new move towards co-operation. The Central Council had made a real effort to create or revive county and town associations which would make it possible to co-ordinate voluntary effort and work closely with local authorities in the schemes for the welfare of the handicapped which they now had new powers and duties to make. But 'looking at the field as a whole, one is driven by the evidence to the conclusion that there is little effective co-ordination apart from a few areas and that, while local authorities must accept their share of the blame for failure to make progress in this direction, the main fault lies at the door of the voluntary

---

* *Report of the Committee of Enquiry on the Rehabilitation of Disabled Persons.* 1956. Cmd. 9883. HMSO.

† *Help for the Handicapped.* 1958. NCSS.

bodies. Until they can hammer out workable schemes of co-operation between themselves, especially in the field, their relations with the authorities are bound to remain anomalous and unsatisfactory'. What was most needed was for each voluntary organisation, large or small, to try to see its work in the wider perspective of the work as a whole; to be ready to give and take, and to distinguish between principle and matters of expediency. Yet, Dr Nicholson concluded, 'the variety of view and practice enriches (if it often hampers) the growth of what should be a common tradition of work and faith. Tensions can be fruitful as well as destructive. It is the task of the statesman, the educator—and the administrator—in a free society to guide the energy they embody into creative channels'. The whole report was indeed a clearing of the field for action; a challenge which, a decade later, has still to be whole-heartedly taken up.

One other full-scale enquiry was launched towards the end of this period: a study of the problems of social development in new communities, which had long been an active interest of the National Council. It was made possible through the co-operation of the Carnegie UK Trust which generously agreed to provide the finance. Dr Nicholson was appointed to direct it, and a joint committee of the two bodies under the chairmanship of Sir John Wolfenden was established to advise him in the conduct of the study. Dr Nicholson set about the task with his customary vigour and clear understanding of the kind of problems involved, and by the end of the first year he had already paid a first visit to each of the New Towns as a preliminary to studying all the types of new communities—housing estates, redeveloped urban areas, and expanded small towns, as well as New Towns; but the subsequent history of the enquiry and his report belong properly to the next decade.

These various types of survey and enquiry gave opportunities for many of the voluntary organisations to put forward their views and experience in different fields of work; but they dealt with only a small part of that aspect of the Council's aim which was to promote the means whereby all the various elements concerned with social welfare could come together and discuss subjects of outstanding contemporary interest. The secretary's proposal in his 1944 memorandum on 'The Future Purpose and Organisation of the NCSS' had been that the full Council should be convened twice a year: once for the transaction of the formal business of the annual general meeting, and once as part of a national conference on social life and work. The British National Conference on Social Work might be said to be partially carrying out this idea; but during the decade a definite move was made to provide a yearly national forum for all the members of the Council, linked with the annual meeting. After the formal business had been disposed of, a subject of current importance to social policy was introduced by one or more speakers, and the meeting was then opened to discussion from the floor. The first of these conferences had as its subject 'The Pioneer Role of Voluntary Organisations'. This was presented in a series of short papers describing half-a-dozen pieces of work which ranged from a boarding-out scheme for the elderly to a short-stay home for backward children. There was something inspiriting here for everyone interested in new enterprises and the conference aroused lively interest. Another year, going outside the customary concern of social work with those in special difficulties, the Council chose the subject of 'Livelihood and Living'—men and women at work and the relation of industry to the community as a whole. On a third occasion the conference was set to consider the impact of a new medium of entertainment and education in 'The Social Implications of Television'.

That so wide a range of subjects was appropriately offered for discussion at these annual meetings can be proved by the extraordinarily wide range of additional organisations which sought membership of the Council during this period. In two years alone new members included, for example, the Coal Industry Social Welfare Organisation and the Association of Child Care Officers; the Royal Alfred Seamen's Society and the National Operatic and Dramatic Association; the British Institute of Management and the Standing Conference of Societies Registered for Adoption; the Church Army and the National Fund for Poliomyelitis Research.

That eminently practical service to voluntary organisations and their staffs, the Social Workers Pension Fund which the National Council had started in 1946, went from strength to strength during these years. The membership of the Fund almost trebled, reaching in 1959 about 2,700 drawn from the staff of over seventy organisations.

Indeed, by the beginning of the next decade the financial position of the Fund was so strong that it was possible for it to become an independent organisation, though maintaining a close connection with the parent body which continued to act as holding trustee of the Fund's assets. As early as 1956, ten years after its inception, these assets totalled nearly £500,000, and by the time that the Fund became independent they had reached over £1½ million and were increasing at the rate of about £25,000 a month.

Early in this period the committee of management, in consultation with the National Council as trustees of the Fund, decided that this rapid growth called for a change in the machinery for handling investments and a well-known firm of investment bankers was appointed to invest the proceeds of contributions month by month, thus relieving the officers of the responsibility of deciding day-to-day questions of finance. At the same time the committee retained full control of policy. They gave constant attention to the maintenance of the flexibility of the scheme so that it was responsive to the special needs of organisations; and they were able to do a good deal towards keeping up the value of pensions despite the continuing fall in the value of money by distributing (after providing for necessary reserves) any surplus, shown at the quinquennial valuations, among members in the form of a bonus addition to their pensions.

Much of the success of this scheme was owed to its first secretary, the assistant secretary of the National Council, Major Eyre Carter, whose pertinacity and loyalty to the concept of the project played a dominating part in its development. This was to be the culmination of twenty-five years of distinguished work with the National Council, during which he had put his wide knowledge, his devotion, and his remarkable versatility at its service in many capacities. When he retired in 1955 he did not sever all connection with it but continued for some time to act as secretary of the Social Workers Pension Fund.

Finance was a most anxious preoccupation of the Council during this decade, especially in the early years when rising costs and government cuts in grant-aid due to the national financial crisis bore hardly on every section of the work. In 1952 the deficit rose to over £7,000 and the small reserves were almost completely exhausted. It was obvious that drastic economies were necessary and, as has been noted in the record of each department and group, considerable staff reductions had to be made to secure the essential ten per cent cut in expenditure. Great care was taken to ensure that the burden of economies was fairly spread over the whole of the Council's services both at headquarters and in the regional offices; and the various committees and associated groups helped manfully in this task. Among other factors the response to appeals for increased contributions from their constituent members was so good that the voluntary income of the Council rose by some £700 to a total of £47,500 in 1953, but there was a drop of over £3,000 in government grants. None the less by a reduction in expenditure of nearly £10,000 the Council contrived to finish the year with a surplus of over £2,000 which went to restore the reserve funds.

It was a triumph for a courageous and prudent financial policy, but at the cost of some weakening of the services and of an increased burden of work on the remaining staff. Only their determined loyalty and the co-operation of all the Council's groups and committees made it possible to maintain high standards of work throughout the struggle.

By the following year these economies and the vigorous efforts to raise more voluntary funds were beginning to show more positive results. Voluntary income was increased by £4,500 to a new total of £52,000; and it was possible to transfer a substantial sum to the reserve fund to build up its depleted resources and to begin to provide for some specific liabilities in connection with staff and premises. Government grants also increased by £1,000 to enable the Council to undertake certain new pieces of work and to maintain services which would otherwise have had to be abandoned.

The improvement in resources now continued year by year, but the demands on the Council's services were such that essential expenditure rose from the £79,000 to which it had been reduced in 1953 to nearly £100,000 in 1956, and was to reach not far short of £150,000 by the end of the decade. The continued support of grants from the Development Commission and the Ministries of Health and Education, and from the Carnegie UK Trust, the Nuffield Foundation, and the King George's Jubilee Trust, were invaluable; and there was a steadily growing number of individual and corporate subscribers.

But more money was needed if the Council was to develop its work as it had the ability and the will to do, and in the mid-fifties a group of leading businessmen under the chairmanship of Lord Heyworth generously took upon themselves to form an appeals committee to approach industry on the Council's behalf. The result was a three-fold increase by the following year in corporate subscriptions (excluding the growing number who supported the Council by using the services of its Benevolent Fund); and, with a continued growth in the number of individual supporters, the ground which the Council had lost at the beginning of the decade was almost recovered towards the end. It was possible to make some improvement in the salary and pension position of the staff, and to strengthen again the financial reserves. Even so the general reserve was only equal to one quarter of the annual expenditure; and by 1959 the full impact of the better salaries and pension rights for the staff and the acquisition of additional premises, made essential by the expansion of the work, had the effect of reducing available reserves. Anxiety about the financial position was by no means over.

There was a steady increase in donations from donors who used the machinery of the Council's Benevolent Fund in these years; and the Fund made considerable progress in its service to charities generally, the amount distributed to charity through this means reaching £650,000 in 1959 as compared with £471,000 in 1952. Much of this success was due to

Katherine Willoughby, the secretary of the Fund for nearly twenty years until her retirement in 1958, whose single-minded devotion to its administration had won the confidence and gratitude of thousands of donors and charities in all parts of the country. With her retirement came some re-organisation involving a change of name to Charities Aid Fund.

The new accommodation which the Council found to increase room at headquarters was a fine William and Mary house at 99 Great Russell Street, a few moments' walk from Bedford Square. In addition to a number of smaller offices this provided two much-needed conference rooms for the many meetings of committees and groups which are the chief method of carrying out the Council's work of consultation.

The National Council was of course not alone in its financial difficulties. The London Council of Social Service, which had won wide recognition as a focus for co-operation among all kinds of societies and authorities in its vast area and was under constant pressure to extend its services, was increasingly hampered by difficulties in raising voluntary funds. This, it seemed, could only be remedied by even closer working with the National Council and sharing its resources. So the London Council, while remaining responsible for policies and activities in London as in the past, became in 1957 an associated group of the National Council, with the assurance of an increased security for its work which was to result in an extension of its influence and enterprises.

As in earlier times the National Council owed its salvation in the economic crisis mainly to a few financial experts who were convinced supporters of its purposes and were ready to serve it with all their skill, ingenuity, and devotion. Sir Edward Peacock continued to guide the finance and general purposes committee as its chairman until he accepted the presidency of the Council in 1954; and, keeping his keen interest in its finances as well as in every other aspect, he became one of the group of leading business men who later undertook to approach industry on the Council's behalf. He was succeeded as chairman by Sir Christopher Chancellor, the honorary treasurer, who brought a wealth of experience and quiet wisdom to the task; and he had the help of Owen Smith, formerly Accountant-General and Under-Secretary of the Ministry of National Insurance, until his sudden death in 1957 bereft the Council of his unique knowledge of financial affairs. The special industrial appeals committee had as its honorary secretary Trevor Powell who had retired early from a distinguished career in industry; and in the few years before his untimely death at the end of the decade he had devised many ways, not only on the financial side, of furthering the Council's work in which he took a lively pleasure and believed in so wholeheartedly.

The fifties saw a succession of distinguished presidents of the National Council: Sir Malcolm Stewart; the Earl of Halifax; Sir Edward Peacock; and finally Lord Heyworth who happily still continues in office. Of the vice-presidents whose loss was mourned during these years two must have special mention: first, Margaret Bondfield who, when she withdrew from active political leadership, had made the National Council one of her principal interests and had strengthened many branches of the work by her remarkable gifts and rare personality, not least the work of the Women's Group on Public Welfare of which she was founder-chairman until 1948. Her death was followed three years later by that of Sir Wyndham Deedes, the much beloved and inspiring leader whose selfless service had been a valuable asset to the National and London Councils, and to many other bodies, for nearly thirty years.

Following the long reign of 'the Warden' as chairman of the National Council, his distinguished successor, Dr Keith A. H. Murray,* Rector of Lincoln College, Oxford, held this key post for three years and the Council greatly benefited from his wisdom and leadership during that time. He resigned on his appointment as chairman of the University Grants Committee in 1953. The period of office of Mr J. F. Wolfenden (later Sir John), Vice-Chancellor of the University of Reading, who succeeded him and continued in it till 1960, covered the major part of this difficult but rewarding decade, and the development of the Council's role in the new society owed much to his dynamic leadership. He had already had a long association with many sides of the work, and his appreciation of its purposes and potentialities and his insight into the nature of current social problems combined to make him a stimulating leader in these days of change. His alert appraisal of the movement of contemporary society and of the direction in which the Council and its associated organisations should be moving in order to keep in step, or one step ahead, may be illustrated by a few sentences from his speech introducing the conference on one aspect of that many-sided movement, 'Livelihood and Living': 'It must be manifest to everyone that we are entering a period of great change in the industrial field. . . . But none of these changes will have gone unaccompanied by social consequences. Will the transformation be for the best? Will the changes carry with them in industry and in the community an enhancement of personal life? . . . Will the changes that go on in personal and social attitudes in community organisation promote or hinder the best evolution of industrial methods? These are questions which cannot be resolved by industry alone—they demand the best attention of

---

* now Lord Murray of Newhaven.

leaders and workers both inside and outside of the factory. That necessary co-operation will not take place unless we begin now to build the bridges for discussion.'

The human aspects of the new industrial developments—here was a single sample of the territories on the moving frontiers of the welfare state which could be made part of a true welfare society only with the help of voluntary enterprise and voluntary partnership.

Lord Murray

Sir John Wolfenden

CHAPTER NINE

The Moving Frontiers

THE roads to lead across the moving frontiers of the welfare state; the bridges between the different clans of frontiersmen: something more than vision and goodwill were needed to build these. The National Council was concerned with the tools for the work as well as with the great design.

The first and most important of these tools was the Charities Act, 1960, which came fully into force, though not all at once into operation, at the beginning of 1961. This measure which the charities themselves, mainly through the medium of the National Council, had done so much to influence is basic to the effective use of both money and service in the field of social work: a new charter for voluntary effort.

The first purpose of the Act was to reconstitute the Charity Commission, extending their purview to all charities and providing the machinery for relating the activities of each charity to other charities and to the statutory services in the same field of welfare. Christopher Hill, who had been in charge of the measure at the Home Office when it was being hammered out, became the Chief Charity Commissioner; and he made a corner-stone of his policy the co-operation with the NCSS which he had found so valuable during those years.

The Council's help was therefore immediately sought with the first stage of the Charity Commission's new work: the collection of basic details about the number, type and distribution of charities by means of registration with the Commission in order to give the public, including social workers and potential beneficiaries or benefactors, full information about charities that might be of use or interest to them; and to provide authoritative means of determining whether an organisation is charitable in law. The Charity Commission publicised widely the requirement for all charities to register, by stages; but the most effective means of making this known and understood was through the conferences which the National Council arranged all over the country, in co-operation with the local authorities, where the Charity Commissioners and members of their staff were able to explain the purpose and methods of registration and the intentions of the Act to national and local charities. These conferences threw a great deal of organising work on the Council's regional officers, the rural community councils and urban councils of social service, and the legal department; and the registration involved the legal department in a considerable increase in its advisory work, since it revealed that many organisations had unsuitable constitutions, or none at all, and needed expert help in drawing up constitutions proper to their particular requirements which would ensure their charitable status.

Besides the central register of charities to be thus compiled, local authorities were given powers, if they so wished, to maintain a local index of charities in their own areas. For voluntary organisations this was of particular importance, not only because it would give them useful information but because the local authority could employ such a body to maintain the index for them. Here again, in several counties the machinery of the county css is used by the authority.

The next step, for which the Act had made provision but which could not be taken till the middle of the decade when the distribution of local indexes was completed, involved the National Council's associated bodies in the country even more closely. This was the inauguration by the local authorities in some places of reviews of local charities with similar objects, as part of the systematic effort to help charities to increase their effectiveness. Virtually every local index had shown that the most numerous class of registered charity consisted of parochial charities of small or moderate means intended to provide aid to the poor in cash or kind: objects now taken over by the state health, social security, and welfare services. Though the trustees of some of these charities had been able to work out methods of co-operation with the local services, many were experiencing difficulty and frustration in finding proper uses for their income. A local review was not intended to relieve trustees of their responsibilities or to interfere with their work but to help them to make better use of their resources and to encourage co-operation between charities with similar objects and with the statutory services. The difficulty would be to persuade the trustees that such a review would not be a move by the local authority to take them over. The answer to this difficulty appeared to the Charity Commission, and to an increasing number of local authorities, to be that a voluntary organisation should be used to carry out the review, when it was requested or agreed to by the charities concerned, in order to make it plain that no threat to independence was intended nor any intrusion of a political element; and in counties and towns in many parts of the country the RCC or css has been welcomed as the obviously appropriate agent, employing usually a special officer to organise the work and to explain personally to the trustees of each charity the purposes of the exercise.

In connection with these reviews the Charity Commission, in cooperation with the National Council, suggested to local authorities that it would be useful to establish a permanent central point of reference with full information about local charities, and that the council of social service, community council, citizens' advice bureau, or family advice centre might well be able to serve this purpose in some areas.

The Charities Act was concerned with the resources of voluntary organisations both in money and in services. There were other measures and proposals during this decade which affected one or the other of these and which the National Council was on constant alert to remark and, if necessary, to oppose or seek to modify.

To take finance first: in October 1964 the government's draft proposals for a corporation tax suggested uncertainty about the future of seven-year deeds of covenant executed by companies. The National Council, with the backing of all the major national voluntary bodies, immediately drew the attention of the Chancellor of the Exchequer and the Board of Inland Revenue to the serious effects on the finances and plans of charitable bodies if such deeds of covenant were to be inadmissable for tax relief under the new legislation. The point was well taken and the ensuing Finance Bill made it clear that this important source of income for charities would be safeguarded.

The following year the Land Commission Bill threatened a considerable resource of some charities by imposing a betterment levy on any development value realised by a transaction in land. Though charities were to be exempt from the payment of the levy when they developed or disposed of permanent endowment land or functional land (that is, land used mainly or wholly for the purposes of the charity for at least twelve months) they would have to pay the levy not only in respect of any investment land but also of functional land not in general use for their purposes. The NCSS took a small deputation to discuss the question with the Minister concerned and the measure as eventually passed went some slight way towards meeting the Council's representations.

Even more important for the position of the whole voluntary movement were the Chancellor's budget proposals in 1966 for a selective employment tax which, when first announced, did not exclude charities from a levy that would have severely curtailed the activities of both national and local voluntary organisations.

The issue was partly a question of finance: research undertaken by the NCSS soon showed that the total cost to charities might be in the region of

£2½ million a year. The underlying principle at stake was even more important, because the proposal challenged the unique position of charities in this country, never before subject to direct taxation, and whose historic rôle had been reaffirmed by all parties in the debates during the passage of the 1960 Charities Act.

As a result of the immediate initiative of the National Council in convening a small representative group of major societies, and subsequently a meeting of some 300, together with its research into the likely costs involved, a strong case was presented to the Chancellor which resulted in his decision to relieve registered charities by the refund of the tax paid. This was widely welcomed and may, in the long run, serve to strengthen the position which appeared to be temporarily challenged in some quarters.

One final example may be given of the concerted action among the voluntary organisations in defence of their financial resources and privileges which the National Council during these years was able to marshall and lead. Towards the end of 1965 a question arose about their liability to pay tax on the profits derived from the publication and sale of Christmas cards, which had become a major source of income for more than 150 charities selling between them several million cards. The NCSS at once called a series of meetings of those principally concerned and sought counsel's opinion on the interpretation of the Income Tax Act, 1952, under which the question arose. When this was received, and it was confirmed that there was a clear liability to tax under the existing provisions, a deputation led by Lord Heyworth, the president of the National Council, called upon the chairman of the Board of Inland Revenue to explain the importance to charities of this source of income and to plead their case. The outcome of this representation was an amendment to the law which had the effect of allowing a charity to establish and control a company to market Christmas cards, and for the company to covenant to pay the net trading profits to the charity without rendering itself liable to tax on these payments. Many voluntary organisations have been able by this means to maintain a growing source of addition to their funds.

It was a useful concession, justifying once again the methods of active co-operation between the voluntary bodies which the National Council has built up over the years, and demonstrating the value of these methods in reinforcing the government's confidence in the strength and importance of the voluntary movement. But perhaps even more useful was the way in which Sir George Haynes,* at the last annual meeting of the NCSS

---

* The director was knighted in 1962.

Sir George Haynes

before he retired as director, put the matter into the long perspective of the history of charities in this country and their future standing. He reminded his audience once again that, for 350 years and more, one of the many privileges which charities had enjoyed, giving them a special place in the community, was that of never having been subject to direct taxation. The device by which tax on the sale of their Christmas cards could now be avoided was perfectly legal and respectable; but it might be wise to treat it with care and restraint for, if advantage were taken of it to trade more widely in other directions, voluntary organisations might end by altering altogether the image of charity and thereby weaken its place in the community and its appeal to the public, to industry and to commerce.

It was partly a concern about this kind of danger aroused by complaints received from various sources on the fund-raising activities of some charities, which led the Charity Commission to suggest to the NCSS that a working party might be set up to consider a code of conduct for charitable fund-raising. After consultation with a number of voluntary organisations the National Council in consequence formed, in 1967, a representative group, under the chairmanship of Robert Egerton, a practising solicitor who was a former vice-chairman of the National Citizens' Advice Bureaux Council, to examine all aspects of the subject and to make recommendations on a code of behaviour for charities in regard to fund-raising and other activities connected with it, such as marketing, advertising, and public relations.

One of the chief aims of the Charities Act, 1960 is, in the words of the first circular about it which the Charity Commission sent to local authorities, to provide a statutory foundation for 'harmonious future development of voluntary and statutory services in partnership'.

Two major government reports published about this time made a significant contribution to that conception of partnership, which must be one of the main instruments of voluntary organisations in developing their work for the community. These were the Report of the Working Party on Social Workers in the Local Authority Health and Welfare Services (HMSO, 1959), under the chairmanship of Miss (later Dame) Eileen Younghusband and the Report of the Committee on the Youth Service in England and Wales (Comnd. 929, HMSO, 1960) presided over by Lady Albemarle. Both were directed towards the statutory services, but both recognised the prime importance of voluntary work in its relationship with these services; and their respective recommendations were of as much concern to voluntary organisations as to central and local government.

Both reports put recruitment and training of the people to staff these services as the first priority—youth leaders, both professional and voluntary, and social workers of many different types and grades in the health and welfare services. These were matters in which the NCSS had always taken an active interest that increased with the increasing opportunities to use both professional and voluntary workers in a large variety of tasks, and the need to ensure that their standards of work matched the rising standards of the statutory services with which they were more and more closely associated.

In the 'thirties the Council had convened a representative standing conference to discuss the subject, and in 1937 this conference set up an advisory committee which, after eighteen months' careful study, produced a report on recruitment and training for social work with far-reaching recommendations that would have been considered by the constituent organisations of the conference in the summer of 1939 if the war had not intervened.

Towards the end of the war the Council decided that these proposals would have to be considered afresh when the longer-term post-war developments could be more clearly foreseen, and that meanwhile it was important to have discussions with voluntary organisations and the Joint University Council for Social Studies on the existing situation. These resulted in the formation of a joint committee on training for social work to advise on emergency questions of preparation for social service. The aim was to provide a clearing house of information on courses suitable for various types of student, to help individual enquirers, and to assist in the planning of courses to meet needs for which provision had not already been made. The National Council made a special appointment to help with the work of the committee and to deal with the many enquirers who were already getting into touch with the Council about social work careers; and two experimental short courses were organised at Morley College to help young people released from various forms of war work who were interested in the possibilities of doing social work either as professional or as voluntary workers. The Council's committee under the chairmanship of Professor (later Lord) Simey, which has already been mentioned, was at the same time studying and making recommendations on the pay and conditions of service of social workers; and many councils of social service were expanding the work they had been doing since the early 'thirties in arranging sessions of practical training for social work students.

As the scope and recognition of voluntary organisations widened in the post-war period their views and experience on the training required by professional workers in their fields of interest developed and began to carry increasing weight. The Younghusband Report, for instance, warmly commended the training courses of various kinds for paid officers, whether statutory or voluntary, which bodies such as the National Old People's Welfare Council and the National Association for Mental Health were already providing, and based on them the final recommendations for in-service training for welfare assistants and residential staffs of local authority homes. Following the Albemarle Report, the Standing Conference of National Voluntary Youth Organisations was not merely asked to submit evidence but was given representation on the joint negotiating committee for full-time youth leaders and on the Ministry of Education's working party to study the training of part-time leaders and assistants. The Council for Training in Social Work which the government set up as a result of the Younghusband Report specifically stated as its first function the promotion of training in social work not only for the local authority health and welfare services but for similar services provided by voluntary organisations; and more than one of the approved courses leading to the Certificate in Social Work subsequently introduced were directed by social workers whose experience had been mainly in the voluntary field. The National Institute for Social Work Training, created in 1961 with the help of the Nuffield Foundation and the Joseph Rowntree Memorial Trust and inspired also by the Younghusband Committee, from the beginning worked closely with the voluntary bodies as with central and local government and the universities. The NCSS publishes some of the institute's teaching material; and in 1966 the Council's information officer was visiting lecturer on social policy and administration to the one-year social work certificate course.

The problem of the shortage of social workers, as well as questions of training, was greatly increased by the development of the education, health, and welfare services, each of which was competing for the limited labour available. The National Council saw that a general examination of the total needs was an essential step to a better appraisal of the situation and to sounder planning. Early in the decade a study was undertaken, in co-operation with members of the staff of the London School of Economics and with grant-aid from the Nuffield Foundation, into existing staffing needs in particular sectors of the social services as they might be expected to develop in response to current trends and policies.

There was no necessity to wait for a general assessment, however, in order to recognise one area where needs were obvious and yet inclined to be overlooked: residential care. In spite of the increasing emphasis which was being given to care in the community, in preference to institutional care, the demand for many kinds of hostel, home, residential school, or sheltered housing scheme—for the old, the deprived child, the handicapped, the delinquent, the mentally unstable, the ex-prisoner—was growing, for a variety of reasons connected with changing social conditions and social policies. The importance of the specialist staff concerned was recognised: teachers in an approved school, child care officers, social workers counselling ex-mental hospital patients, and so on. The importance of the house-mothers or fathers, the wardens, matrons, heads, or whatever they might be called, who actually run the establishments, was on the whole much under-rated. With a substantial grant from the Calouste Gulbenkian Foundation, the National Council therefore launched in 1962 a major survey of the position by an expert committee under the chairmanship of Professor Lady Williams. The aim was to ascertain the numbers and types of staff likely to be needed in this developing field, the existing qualifications and conditions of service and the changed requirements for the future, and in the light of this assessment to devise courses of training for residential service students which would make plain that residential care should be a career with a content and status, and a chance of varied opportunities for advancement which should put it on comparable terms with other types of social work and attract many more recruits to this essential service. The study, extending over four years, was done with great thoroughness and skill; and the report*, published in the summer of 1967, roused the most lively interest in both the statutory and the voluntary spheres and, it is hoped, will lead to important developments in recruitment and training for this work.

Many of these residential institutions are children's homes and nowhere perhaps have the matrons and house-mothers and fathers felt themselves more isolated from others working in the same broad field of care as here. But in child care there are questions of communication between staff at every level that are much more complicated and important than the separateness of institutional and other kinds of work. For a number of years leaders in services for children had felt the need to improve the lines of communication between the multiplicity of services involved and the different professional disciplines; and at the end of the 'fifties they asked the National Council to consider how to meet the need and to sponsor further discussions. Following a conference which the Council called in 1960, a steering committee representative of all the interests concerned,

---

* *Caring for People.* Allen and Unwin, 1967.

from medical officers of health and university research workers to house-mothers and approved school masters, was set up under the chairmanship of Sir John Wolfenden. In two years of hard study and discussion they worked out a plan for a National Bureau for Co-operation in Child Care, with support from a number of major trust funds in the first instance and the prospect, since happily fulfilled, of establishing itself as a permanent and independent institution of great practical value to workers in the field and considerable importance as a centre of information and research. Here was yet another new organisation, having from its inception a life of its own independent of the NCSS but brought into being by the Council's experienced midwifery.

Another new organisation concerned with professional social work—the Social Work Advisory Service—owes much to the experience of the NCSS. As early as the beginning of the 'fifties the information department had recorded that the largest recent increase in enquiries from the general public had been about careers in social work. They came from many different types of people: the young and the mature; the well or less well educated; trained or untrained; some knowing what they wanted to do, some only having a vague idea of 'welfare work'. 'They show,' said the Council's annual report for 1951–52, 'what an acute need exists for an adequate advisory service, in the interests of the profession of social work as much as of the individual.' The need continued to grow. A decade later the information department received 1,324 enquiries on recruitment and training in one year, and many other social work organisations reported the same kind of increase on a smaller scale. Throughout these years the Council had issued a brief careers guide, as well as giving personal answers to enquirers so far as very limited staff and time allowed; and in 1963 the NCSS joined with the Women's Employment Federation, which had long produced some excellent notes on training, in a more comprehensive booklet,* at first duplicated and later printed and kept up to date, which has a wide and constant sale.

Meanwhile the Council did not lose sight of the prime need. It engaged in a series of discussions, sponsored by the Standing Conference of Organisations of Social Workers and the National Institute for Social Work Training, on the possibilities of setting up a centre to provide information and advice about all kinds of professional social work at this critical time, when recruitment for the social services runs far short of demand while interest in such careers is growing. Eventually, with the help of a generous grant from the Calouste Gulbenkian Foundation for an

---

* *Training and Employment in Social Work.* NCSS and WEF.

initial period, the Social Work Advisory Service was established at the beginning of 1967. The NCSS is represented on the council of management, and David Hobman, a former information officer of the council, is its director.

The Social Work Advisory Service is not concerned with voluntary work and the openings for volunteers or the qualifications required of them. But the wish to give service and the very varied new opportunities for it are growing fast. Moreover, voluntary workers are becoming increasingly identified with services provided by professional trained social workers, whether in a statutory or a voluntary setting; and their selection, training, and deployment is therefore of increasing importance and complexity. If this new form of partnership on a personal level is to function effectively volunteers must recognise their limitations as well as their potentialities; and professional social workers must recognise that voluntary service can enhance the work for which they are responsible, not only through the help of additional 'hands' but also through the contribution of different personalities and talents.

This is a field where the National Council, so long adept at fostering the 'amateur' and supporting the professional, and promoting partnership between all those concerned with the social services, has a very special interest. In 1966 it welcomed warmly the opportunity to join with the National Institute for Social Work Training in sponsoring a major enquiry into the rôle, relationships, and preparation of volunteers, made possible by the generosity of the Joseph Rowntree Memorial Trust and the Phyllis Trust. A committee representative of administrators, practitioners, and teachers in a number of spheres was set up under the chairmanship of Geraldine Aves, formerly chief welfare officer to the Ministry of Health. As a first step information was collected from a selected group of councils of social service, old people's welfare committees, youth organisations, and citizens' advice bureaux, about the number of volunteers, the amount of time they are able to give, the scope of their work, the way in which they are used, and any schemes of preparation or training for them.

Before studying how all the departments and groups of the NCSS are using voluntary workers in their different fields, it may be as well to look at those moving frontiers of the welfare state along which they are deployed.

The concept of community care is the key sector in the advance, not only in itself but because it requires the support of that other concept which is basic to the National Council's ideas and practice: community organisation. The term community care is elastic. It may imply care *in* the community, care *by* the community, or care *of* the community for itself. It can mean the help which members of the community give to their less fortunate neighbours, suffering from some physical or mental disability, to enable them to lead a happy, independent life. It may go beyond treating 'ill-fare' and try actively to promote 'welfare' for all citizens, young or old, normal or handicapped. It is recognised by central and local government as essential if the manifold provisions of the welfare state are to be made to work; as much because authority can only act effectively with the interest and support of the citizens as because it has not enough resources in man-power and money to act without them. Community care is more and more clearly recognised as part of the responsibility of citizenship; a participation of the citizens of the welfare state in its workings which alone can transmute it into a living welfare society.

From the beginning of the decade the National Council created opportunities for the national voluntary bodies to think together about this subject. Community care was the theme of the annual general meeting in 1961 when several speakers outlined imaginative schemes for helping some of those in special situations: easing the transition from hospital to home; supporting social casualties; helping young people to take their due part in the life of the neighbourhood.

In 1962 the Council, together with several national voluntary bodies, had detailed consultations with the Ministry of Health on the guidance* the Minister wished to give to hospitals and local authorities on the use of voluntary help in the health and welfare services. The following year the Minister's ten-year plan,† based on the submissions of regional hospital boards and local health and welfare authorities concerning their future requirements and programmes, showed not only the scope for this kind of help but the need for machinery to co-ordinate what was already being given and to provide a springboard for future action. Here was one of the links of community care with community organisation: the pattern of the National Council's method of working and particularly of its local counterparts—the rural community councils, councils of social service, and

---

* *Development of Local Authority Health and Welfare Services: Co-operation with Voluntary Organisations.* Ministry of Health Circular 7/62. *National Health Service: Voluntary Help in Hospitals.* Ministry of Health Circular HM (62)29.

† *A Hospital Plan for England and Wales.* Cmnd. 1604. HMSO. *Health and Welfare— The Development of Community Care.* Cmnd. 1973. HMSO.

the more specialised old people's welfare committees.

The resilience of this springboard for future action is demonstrated in every sector. The welfare of old people began increasingly to be seen not only as an affair of easing the conditions of existence but of enhancing the quality of life: of encouraging schemes which the more active could run themselves, helping the elderly to prepare for a happy retirement, the frail to maintain some independence, the lonely to find companionship.

The malign influence of loneliness on the young and the middle-aged as well as the old began to be understood more fully and handled more imaginatively. A kind of loneliness is an ingredient in mental ill-health, and non-specialist voluntary bodies ventured out to help in that difficult field through clubs and hostels for out-patients and ex-psychiatric hospital patients to bring them back into the community, as well as continuing their customary work of mental hospital visiting and support of families.

They identified other, very varied groups also on the borders of society who could do with the help of the community as neighbours, as well as representatives of official welfare services: the 'unattached' young; Commonwealth immigrants strange to this country; pre-delinquents; ex-prisoners; drug-takers; social misfits; and moved out to them.

They realised that the stresses and the opportunities alike of modern life produce new or aggravated problems even for ordinary people well integrated into society: relations between the affluent, independent young and their families; relations between the sexes, before and after marriage; the rights of the consumer of the bewildering variety and quality of goods, and their comparative values and treatment.

But all these personal problems and chances are influenced more and more by their setting: urban or rural; new town, new estate, old slum; small local authority area with restricted means but close-knit interest, large region with generous resources and impersonal authority. Voluntary organisations must take account of these, the literally moving frontiers, as much as the statutory bodies, if they are to maintain their partnership—a partnership not merely in coping with individual and group difficulties but in the 'creative living' which the amateur, in the true sense, is so peculiarly well fitted to serve: through self-help schemes and leisure-time programme planning; arts associations, and new ideas in music making or drama production; debates and group viewing; special interest holidays and exchange visits abroad; but above all by helping to make a neighbourhood where none need feel themselves strangers.

In the contemporary concept of voluntary organisations not only as pioneers or gap-fillers but as media through which people can make a unique contribution to social life at different levels, the range of their workers, paid or unpaid, full-time or part-time, has widened remarkably.

Some of the latest recruits are the 'good neighbours' whose friendly help has always been readily given but little taken into account until recently in planning organised services. Also drawn into the team more and more often are people with some special skill or experience—catering on a tight budget; craft-work; music teaching of sub-normal children. A very ordinary business man with an interest in people may prove the right person to help an ex-prisoner to find his feet again. A lonely widow may find pleasure as well as usefulness in regularly visiting a housebound invalid. As different kinds of advisory services develop an increasingly wide variety of people of appropriate experience and personality are needed—for ever-broadening citizens' advice bureau work; for marriage guidance; for family counselling.

These are all linked up more readily now with the expert caseworkers on the one hand and the experienced group workers on the other. So the gamut of workers in voluntary organisations runs from 'the people next door' to the highly skilled and trained social worker. To make a framework for all these people and projects demands skilled organisation which brings into play the third main type of work—community organisation, as well as casework and group work—and a type of worker whose rôle is only beginning in recent years to be understood.

Since this last is basic to all National Council work it is proper to consider it first. Naturally it is the Standing Conference of Councils of Social Service which has taken the lead in developing this form of social work. Early in the decade they organised two nine-day seminars for two groups of local css secretaries under the direction of university lecturers, which gave a pioneer opportunity to relate the theory of their organising work to everyday practice. Eventually a trilogy of reports on the subject was published which aroused widespread interest among both voluntary and statutory bodies and in educational institutions. This helped to bring home to all concerned the lack of specific training for a fundamentally important type of social work; and in 1966 a grant from the Calouste Gulbenkian Foundation enabled the NCSS to initiate experimentally a broadly-based six-months' course, planned by a css advisory committee and including among its twenty students not only css secretaries but old people's welfare committee organisers, settlement workers, community association wardens, youth officers, and officers of local authority health and welfare departments. In 1967 the biennial meeting of the standing conference took as its subject 'New Approaches to Community Work', and the published report of the discussions is in great demand. Since then a staff training programme has been launched; and in July 1968 the NCSS published

Community Work by R. A. B. Leaper, senior lecturer in social administration at University College of Swansea and, since September 1967, chairman of the Standing Conference of Councils of Social Service.

Meanwhile, other NCSS groups concerned with community work were making progress in their own types of training. The National Federation of Community Associations worked out, with Westhill College, Birmingham, and the Birmingham Institute of Education, a two-years' course for professional community centre wardens, which was eventually fully approved and grant-aided by the Ministry of Education, and set a pattern for future courses. The six-months' in-service training schemes financed at first by the Carnegie UK Trust provided good experience for similar courses for students who could find financial aid from other sources when the first experiments ended. Later in this period a special seven-weeks' course for wardens of at least two years' experience but without the five years' experience necessary for qualified status gave substantial help to this category, since most of the local education authorities employing them were prepared to second them for training and to pay their fees. So far as training for voluntary leadership is concerned, a grant from the Carnegie UK Trust enabled a number of courses to be arranged, consisting of once-weekly sessions over a period of eight weeks and a residential week-end. But, in general, lack of funds hampered progress here, though much was done by area committees and increasingly by local education authorities.

The growing interest and help of these authorities in the training of workers in voluntary organisations was an encouraging factor in its development in several fields of the National Council's work. By the middle of the decade, for example, the King George VI Social Service Scheme had reached the end of its first phase; the part of the fund available for aiding individual training courses and area schemes had all been applied, so local old people's welfare committees had to look to local sources for support. Many local education authorities began to accept responsibility for such courses and award grants to committees for the purpose. In some counties a contribution from the education committee helped with the appointment of a part-time organising tutor for an experimental period. Thanks to a grant from the Sembal Trust it was possible in 1966 to appoint temporarily a national field officer with special responsibility for promoting co-operation in training plans; to make grants for pioneering schemes; and to offer bursaries to enable welfare workers and newly appointed secretaries to attend national training courses, some of which could still be financed from the King George VI Scheme funds.

These courses covered many aspects of work for the elderly, ranging from committee work to the full use of volunteers, from the organisation of daily clubs to the content and method of 'training the trainers'; and in many places they had the co-operation of the extra-mural department of a university, of a college of further education, or of a branch of the Workers' Educational Association, in addition to or instead of the local education authority. During 1966–67 there were 140 courses attended by some 3,500 people, arranged or sponsored by the NOPWC or by old people's welfare committees; and the Council goes on developing its advice, literature, and national courses to encourage training at all levels.

Training for wardens and matrons continues to be equally important; and when the support given by the King George VI Scheme for so many years came to an end, the National Corporation for the Care of Old People, which originally supported the project, again offered help for a three-year period. This enabled the fourteen-week courses to continue, and new courses with a special slant to be tried out: for experienced matrons and wardens, for example.

The Albemarle Report on the youth service had recommended that the number of full-time youth leaders should be doubled. Early in the decade the Standing Conference of National Voluntary Youth Organisations made some contribution to this aim by providing a special three-months' course, supported by the Ministry of Education, for forty-eight leaders with varying experience who needed to attend such a course to qualify. At the same time the conference was pressing on with the equally important training of the part-time and voluntary leaders on whom so much of the service depends. The Bessey Report* published in 1962, reinforced the view of SCNVYO that there was a basic common element of training appropriate for all leaders, paid or voluntary, in local authority clubs or voluntary organisations; and the conference assembled a working party to consider how best to encourage co-operation between voluntary and statutory agencies in running local training courses.

Local standing conferences are a useful factor in these efforts at co-operation, and towards the end of the period a survey carried out at the request of the Department of Education and Science to find out the progress so far made on these courses produced a fairly encouraging picture. The problem of adequately training the trainers responsible for the courses is proving more difficult. A conference working party was set up in 1963 to study this; but in 1967 a survey of advanced leader training courses and tutor training courses already carried out regionally showed a not wholly satisfactory position, due to continuing doubts as to what the content of

---

* Report of the Working Party on the Training of Part-time Youth Leaders and Assistants. HMSO. 1962.

such courses should be, their length and sponsorship; and the conference is making the solution of this problem one of its priorities.

Like all the National Council's associated groups and departments, SCNVYO has not limited its interest to work and' workers of the well-established types. Work among young people who do not belong to any youth organisation has been a matter of concern for some time. The key figure must be the youth worker acting without a base, seeking out young people instead of waiting for them to come to him. The conference organised two study conferences, in 1966 and 1967, to discuss the varying views and experience of members about his objective, the sort of person he should be, and the type of training needed. That the voluntary youth organisations were not yet playing an active enough part in this 'detached' work away from the conventional youth group base was one of the opinions generally expressed; and the conference is making fresh efforts to encourage its members to press forward here. Other examples of encouragement and help for youth workers a little outside the usual field are a survey recently made of the youth work carried out by undergraduates at English universities, and plans to help a number of those whose experience may be limited by making available the knowledge and experience of those who have been particularly successful in this field.

The importance of relations with the training of young people in industry is another factor increasingly recognised by the voluntary youth organisations. The major youth club bodies, among recent proposals for joint work in the field of training, have also suggested the need for co-operation with the industrial training boards.

There is one National Council group which continues to depend entirely on voluntary leaders for its local work: the National Association of Women's Clubs. It went on using all the methods it could devise to give them suitable help and training; and the difficulties were eased a little in the first year of the decade by the opportunity to appoint an additional part-time paid organiser in the north, though voluntary officers and members continue to do a very great deal of promotional and advisory work everywhere. The association set up a new sub-committee at that time to deal with education. As well as the usual week-end and mid-week schools, training schemes have been gradually expanded to include such projects as a two-day course in London to give intensive training in administration and management; regional schools in the north and the home counties to demonstrate new techniques in such subjects as club management and public speaking, as well as homecrafts, music, art, and a dozen other interests; and training courses for officers and members are now regularly organised by all the local associations of women's clubs.

Citizens' advice bureaux had always welcomed almost as many kinds of people to answer the questions as to ask them, and had steadily widened and deepened their training. Now, as the frontiers of the welfare state were pushed continually forward, their responsibilities grew more exacting and the need for guidance greater. To take one example: the new attitude to mental health calls for co-operation on extremely difficult problems between not only the medical services and local authorities but the voluntary organisations and the community as a whole. Against this background bureau workers must find their place, not as specialists but as the 'first line of defence', where sympathetic and knowledgeable help may prevent a relatively simple dilemma from becoming a serious social problem. Consumer advice work provides another example. Bureaux had for years dealt with many complaints and queries from consumers, and when the government decided in 1963, following the recommendations of the Molony Committee,* to make provision for consumer advice and information as a new social service, it invited bureaux to play a large part in the new programme, with the help of a grant from the Board of Trade. This involved the bureau workers in acquiring a great deal of specialist knowledge about consumer legislation; trade associations; manufacturing processes and standards; and methods of dealing with complaints, which added to the subjects in their training syllabus. But it also required the much more difficult study of the practical application of CAB principles of impartiality, independence, and fair balance of interests to a comparatively new field of advice.

More and more during this decade bureau workers have become aware of this need to consider the proper relationship of CAB aims and methods to the growing and changing problems they are called upon to handle; and the need to keep abreast of social thinking and to arrive at a deeper understanding of the people they try to help and of their own attitudes. Here the appointment of more advisory officers, made possible by the Board of Trade grant, is proving of real value. In the words of a National Citizens' Advice Bureaux Council report: 'The advisory officers must seek to bring about in all of them (new bureau workers) the right approach to the work, an increase of sympathy . . ., a tolerance with their own limitations; and on the technical side, the ability to become more imaginatively exploratory and constructive in their approach to the problems they will receive.'

Basic CAB training, however, is applicable to many other kinds of voluntary social work; and a number of councils of social service run

---

* *Final Report of the Committee on Consumer Protection.* Cmnd. 1781. HMSO.

courses for volunteers on similar lines, often in co-operation with such bodies as the British Red Cross Society, National Association for Mental Health, or Soldiers', Sailors' and Airmen's Families Association, which see these courses as a useful method of introducing to the social services, and to the different types of voluntary work, people whom they may later recruit as volunteers for their own specialised work.

But increasingly jobs are being found for, or by, volunteers who would never do specialised work: volunteers for what has now come to be known as 'good neighbour service'. Many such people are recruited and 'prepared' for their work by bodies like old people's welfare committees, women's clubs, standing conferences of women's organisations, and by other organisations outside the National Council grouping. But, above all, the interest of the Central Churches Group of the NCSS in this kind of social service has had the direct effect of bringing in a large number of volunteers from their own church members, and of encouraging appropriate training and the development of a wide variety of schemes.

Early in the decade the Group convened a conference to discuss the preparation of voluntary helpers in 'good neighbour' projects; and two leaflets were produced on the subject, later embodied in a booklet.* Examples of the kind of work they envisaged as practical and useful are 'sitting in' for mothers obliged to go to hospital or to visit someone, or for those who have the continuous care of the old or disabled; shopping, gardening, or just a chat for the homebound; helping families to settle into new homes; providing transport for the infirm or the handicapped. Elements which they see as essential to any systematic preparation of good neighbours are 'attitude to the work', as a piece of human service, not just another job; a sympathetic understanding of people and their quirks of behaviour; and a fair knowledge of existing welfare services and a readiness to co-operate with them.

To assess the progress in a movement which they felt to be of real value to both parties, the Churches Group later made a survey of schemes undertaken, with the co-operation of local councils of social service, citizens' advice bureaux, and the British Council of Churches. The 'People Next Door' campaign, organised by the British Council of Churches in the spring of 1967, attracted their interest, and they supported it by giving information, to those responsible for its follow-up, on agencies through which offers of help or enquiries about social service could be channelled. So the conception of the 'good neighbour' as a part of the team which the community itself mans for the common good grows and prospers.

---

* *The Caring Community*. Revised 1968. NCSS.

Of all the volunteers in this decade the most interesting and inspiriting must surely be the young. Voluntary service by young people is no new thing. Either formulated or implied in the aims of every youth organisation has always been the attempt to foster a spirit of service, and some organisations plan their whole programme of activities to give their members opportunities to help others. There is an equally long tradition of social service in many schools. The new things in this decade are the 'whole new categories of volunteers', and the speed with which these are multiplying. A third element, which has developed steadily, is the imaginative discovery by the organisers—often the young people themselves—of new jobs which the young can do; and the readier understanding by those responsible for welfare, in the broadest sense, of the special quality of help which the young can give.

This growth of community service by young people, outside as well as inside the framework of the traditional youth movements, has an important bearing on the work of many of the National Council's departments. Early in the decade the Standing Conference of National Voluntary Youth Organisations held two meetings between representatives of voluntary bodies and the Ministry of Education to consider what practical steps could be taken to co-ordinate experiments and agencies concerned with service by youth, and to fit this pioneering work into the scheme of existing social provisions. Already some councils of social service were setting up junior councils where young people could plan and organise their own work; and many more were recruiting young volunteeers as an integral part of their schemes for staffing services. At the same time the National Old People's Welfare Council produced a pamphlet, *Youth Helps Age*, on the ways young people were finding to help the old; and later they held a conference on the subject.

By 1964 it was obvious to the NCSS that their member bodies would welcome a chance to look at 'the magnificent work now being done by young people and to discuss how more of their contemporaries can be given the same opportunity to enrich the life of the nation'; and 'Young People and Voluntary Service' was taken as the theme of an open conference on the occasion of the annual general meeting. Over 700 people, representative of voluntary organisations, local authorities, government departments, and the young themselves, heard a panel of young volunteers describe their approach and response to some of the social challenges they had faced in this country and overseas; and a lively discussion followed which confirmed that, in spite of some difficulties and prejudices, service by young people can be remarkably effective when it is sensitively applied and properly prepared and sustained.

Young people and voluntary service

Report of the 1964 conference

It was evident that, even where the jobs being done by young volunteers were mostly simple, manual tasks, such as repairing a youth hostel, decorating a room for a pensioner, gardening for the infirm, or 'sitting-in' with children, the element of human relationships between the young helper and the helped was coming to be an important factor. There was, too, an extension of the kind of service concerned primarily with those relationships: helping at a centre for mentally handicapped children, regularly visiting the housebound as much to relieve loneliness as to help with the chores; planning an expedition for boys at an approved school. All this was seen to be important for both the young people and the services they helped to man. It gave them the chance to take their place as a real part of the community, and it revitalised the services through the special qualities of enthusiastic and sensitive youth. The problems were to direct this contribution without spoiling the spontaneity and vigour; and at the same time to make new outlets for it by demonstrating to professional social workers, statutory and voluntary, that young volunteers can indeed help them, and by exploring new patterns of service in every social field.

Following the conference the NCSS was responsible for numerous developments both at the centre and in the field. More local councils of social service, in co-operation with their local authorities, started projects for young volunteers, as an integral part of their work of developing co-operation between statutory and voluntary bodies, and seeking out and helping to meet new needs and opportunities. Working closely with SCNVYO, these ventures were encouraged by grants from a fund which the King George's Jubilee Trust provided for the purpose. From the experience so gained it became increasingly clear that some positive planning was needed if the energy and initiative of young volunteers was not to be dissipated, since in many areas their numbers tended to outstrip suitable tasks open to them; and in 1967 those councils which have been able to employ them to good advantage had a first informal conference to discuss the best ways of meeting this challenging situation.

Meanwhile, soon after the 1964 conference, a special sub-committee of the government's Youth Service Development Council was set up, after discussion between the Department of Education and Science and the NCSS, to consider a possible scheme for the co-ordination of community service by young people. Forty voluntary youth organisations and two government departments gave evidence to the committee, and its report[*] was published at the end of 1965; but there was much critical discussion

---

[*] *Service by Youth*. HMSO, 1965.

of its proposals and it was not until two years later that the government's plan for the Young Volunteer Force Foundation was launched—an initiative welcomed by the National Council in principle, subject to the fullest consultation with voluntary organisations at national and local level about specific projects in areas to which the foundation's special teams might be invited.

There are other sectors of the moving frontiers, besides the staffing area, where nearly all the departments and groups of the NCSS have been working during these years.

The first is literally a moving frontier—the growth of new towns, expanded old towns, city redevelopment areas, new housing estates. As has already been shown, the Council had from the beginnings of these projects grasped the importance and complexity of the problems of social development in the new communities; and, with the co-operation of the Carnegie UK Trust, a full-scale study had been launched, towards the end of the 'fifties, under the direction of Dr J. H. Nicholson. His final report,* published in 1960, set out findings and recommendations which were basic to the thought and practice of the Council in this field, and a blueprint for the future, no less for the statutory authorities concerned than for the voluntary bodies.

His main conclusion was that the essential aim should be a balanced community, with the optimum degree of self-containment; the elements of this being a balanced age-composition; a varied pattern of employment and of class structure; and a physical lay-out providing for a proper relationship between the town centre with its main public buildings and the residential neighbourhoods with their schools, shops, churches, social centres, or with sites for these reserved from the start, to stimulate community life.

But important as these physical factors are in nurturing social development, equally vital is the intangible process by which new relations are formed and new groupings arise. While new communities should in the long run depend on much the same agencies and spontaneous groupings as are at work in established communities, in the early days the impetus must largely come from efforts to help newcomers to help themselves. There should be a partnership between the statutory and voluntary bodies in giving a lead in the formation of social groups, in advising voluntary

---

* *New Communities in Britain: Achievements and Problems.* NCSS. [Out of print.]

leaders among the new residents, and not least in providing suitable meeting places, so that the new community may have the chance and the encouragement to plan and enjoy its own new social life.

This put into perspective all the work which the National Council and its groups had been trying to do with new communities, and provided a stimulus to further action. The National Federation of Community Associations, which for long had been emphasising what the Ministry of Housing and Local Government report for this same year officially recognised, that 'community activity is soon stifled and frustrated if there are no suitable buildings or other facilities to enable it to function on an adequate scale', at once set up a working party to examine the practical applications of Dr Nicholson's recommendations. Later it had the opportunity to give the Ministry the benefit of its experience on the social aspects of large-scale housing for two further government studies of the subject, as well as actively helping a good many projects in new towns and housing estates.

A unique opportunity for studying social needs in this sort of contemporary setting, and the community organisation required to cope with them, was provided at the very beginning of the decade for the Standing Conference of Councils of Social Service when the Nuffield Foundation gave a grant, to be used over a four-year period, to start a council of social service and family centre in the new town of Stevenage. It was a method of bringing together, under statutory and voluntary auspices, a group of services concerned with the welfare of the family which seemed particularly appropriate in a new town with so many families trying to adjust themselves to a new way of life in strange surroundings. A series of regular meetings between css officers in the new towns was arranged and, among other matters of common interest, the play needs of young children were discussed and the provision of hostels for apprentices and students working away from home. After close consultation with the other departments of the ncss most concerned, the chairman of the Standing Conference of Councils of Social Service, Sir John Wrigley, prepared a paper on 'Social Development in New Towns' for the Ministry of Housing; and officers of the standing conference had discussions later with members of the Commission for the New Towns.

Information and advice for the inhabitants of these strange lands was of course an obvious need, and citizens' advice bureaux were being set up as soon as possible in convenient places.

The importance of a balanced age-composition of the population in new and expanded towns was an aspect on which the National Old People's Welfare Council had plenty of practical experience and advice to offer. In evidence to the Central Housing Committee of the Ministry, and to the

South-East and East Anglia Planning Boards in 1967, the Council drew attention to the danger of too high a proportion of younger age-groups, not only because the old are left behind in unaccustomed loneliness while the young families often miss their help and support, but also because an unbalanced population structure would produce its own problems in the years to come.

In the meantime, the National Association of Women's Clubs was finding that many young wives in new housing areas, lonely and disorientated, were as eager as their mothers in the old industrial areas had ever been for the chance to meet and do things together. In one year 100 clubs started, many of them among these new, unformed communities, and some launched by individual housewives who wrote to the association for advice and help. By 1967 there were 880 clubs in all, with 27,500 members.

It is not only on the urban sector that the frontiers of society are moving fast. The NCSS from its very beginning has geared its rural work to the changes taking place in the countryside, from the aftermath of industrialisation, through the years of slump, the upheavals of the war, the mechanisation of agriculture, the movement of young people to the towns; and by means of the rural community councils, which bring together all the social resources of the country areas, the National Council has tried to anticipate new problems and opportunities and to devise ways of meeting them.

Early in the decade, the Rural Life Conference, oldest established of the Council's annual gatherings, devoted itself to looking forward twenty-five years, to problems of human settlement, the growth and distribution of the population, the likely influence of industrial and technological developments, the shape of rural educational and cultural developments, and the future form and content of village communities. Two years later, the report* of the Development Commissioners—the supporters and partners of the Council in its rural work—confirmed many of the forecasts and conclusions reached there. The traditional distinctions between town and country, urban and rural, they said, no longer hold so strongly, and the problems of population distribution which arise have far too often

---

* *Aspects of Rural Development.* Thirty-second Report of the Development Commissioners for the three years ended 31st March, 1965. House of Commons Paper 100, session 1966/67. HMSO.

been looked at solely from the point of view of the great cities and con-urbations. The countryside should be regarded as a great national asset for the future, which requires not only the restoration of an active rural life and a viable rural economy, but the cultivation of an agreeable and well-kept countryside to satisfy the growing demand of townspeople to find in it an area for mental and physical relaxation.

Both these aspects of the situation are examined in depth in the report* which an expert group, under the chairmanship of the director of the National Council and with the chief rural officer as secretary, produced as one of the documents for the second 'Countryside in 1970' conference—a conference sponsored jointly by the Nature Conservancy and the Royal Society of Arts. Among the things which this report stresses are the urgent need for a strategy of research into the developing situation of the countryside, and for a new focussing of thought and practice in the planning of smaller rural settlements, in the preservation and development of older villages, and their relation to larger centres of population.

The necessity, which these reports and discussions imply, for urban and rural work to proceed hand in hand is felt increasingly throughout the National Council's interests. It is being found, for instance, that the idea of a council of social service is no longer limited to large towns and cities. Even some small rural districts show keen interest in having a modified form of this kind of organisation. Where the wider area of a county is concerned, there is a further movement towards the aim outlined in the director's 1944 paper on the Council's future purpose and organisation: a council of social service for each county combining both rural and urban interests. So the css and rural departments are drawn into working more and more closely together; and in 1968 their annual meetings were a joint conference on the theme 'Town and Country'. Another and earlier small example of this trend: the five-year experiment, financed by the Carnegie UK Trust, in bringing advice services to the country areas showed the citizens' advice bureaux and rural community councils that, among other things, people in small places prefer to go to a bureau in a town where they can more easily remain anonymous. Various experimental schemes continue to be tried out, the latest being a mobile service by caravan initiated by the Essex Community Council, based on Braintree CAB and manned by some of its trained workers, which makes regular visits to publicised points in six neighbouring small towns.

The moving frontiers of town and country—but there have been even

---

* *Living and Working in the Countryside.* Report of Study Group II. Royal Society of Arts and Nature Conservancy.

wider movements during these years, aimed at giving overall direction to the whole of this advance. To re-organise the complex pattern of local government, to devise long-term plans for regional development: these have been major pre-occupations of government in this decade. Partly this is an exercise in physical and economic planning—the size and area of local authorities; the provision of industrial sites, transport facilities, housing, open spaces, appropriate to a particular region. But, to be effective, planning on this scale must embrace all aspects of development, social and political, as well as physical, economic, and technological.

Here was a whole new territory open to the National Council and its associated organisations: ground that, in co-operation with the authorities, could be mapped and manned, its relation to other types of terrain assessed, its people consulted and helped to take an active part. With only a little prompting the government, central and local, recognised its allies. Since every kind of social question is involved, from the welfare of old people to facilities for sport, every kind of voluntary organisation has a contribution to make to the plans; and a representative body like a council of social service or rural community council, bringing all these together for consultation and action, has a special rôle in giving the authorities a wide view, for example, of the effectiveness of welfare provisions in relation to a changing economic and population distribution, or the need for the expansion and realignment of cultural and physical facilities.

At national level, a Minister concerned with planning stressed, at the 1965 conferences of both the councils of social service and the rural community councils, the importance which the government attached to their co-operation in this work. At regional level, officers of community councils have been appointed to some of the statutory economic planning councils which advise the government on economic and social planning in regions designated for the purpose; and everywhere these councils, and the regional study groups set up in some special areas, have sought information and views from the voluntary bodies. At local level, the commissions responsible for reviews of local government reorganisation have welcomed evidence from community councils on behalf of their member bodies. Special planning teams in some places have asked from the start for the help of the local councils of social service in preparing their draft schemes.

Besides confirming the importance now attached to the statutory and voluntary partnership, not only in working on today's problems but in looking to the future, these exercises have been of value to the National Council from two other points of view. First, the reviews of the government's regional and local structure have offered the opportunity, and the need, to reconsider the Council's own framework of services and administration, and to discuss the whole subject with a number of national voluntary organisations which are also concerned with their pattern of work and its relationship to the statutory structure. And on the local level also, for example, the reorganisation of the Greater London government area, where the CSS coverage had always been uneven and incomplete, gave the opportunity to the London Council of Social Service to help the voluntary organisations to make a fresh start in co-operation and to begin the task of forming a CSS for each borough—the lead in many places being taken by an existing CSS—in order to have a voluntary scheme to complement the statutory pattern. This experiment, in the first area where local government reorganisation was completed, has provided some useful experience for community councils in other parts of the country.

The second point of special interest to the NCSS in this planning work is the unusually good opportunity it gives to forward one of the Council's basic aims: the encouragement of people to play a conscious and satisfying part in planning the setting of their own lives. The rapid growth in recent years of self-help societies concerned with welfare (for example the Association for the Improvement of Maternity Services, the Pre-School Play-groups Association, the Disablement Income Group), or with leisure and environment (arts groups, amenity societies, and the like) show that 'people have a real hunger to see things go right and to become themselves involved'. In social planning on a wide scale, concerned with every aspect of life and where the development of every town and village and of every service must be related to the future needs and resources of its areas, voluntary organisations can help to marshal a much broader range of citizen enthusiasm and understanding for ends which all sorts of people can see to be worthwhile.

These are moving frontiers of the welfare state reaching out towards a welfare society. But there remains the question posed by the late Penelope Hall at the end of the *Guide to Studies* which she prepared for the British National Conference on Social Welfare held in 1967: may not the welfare society of the future have to be a world society, and will any particular welfare state survive except in the context of such a society?

From its earliest days the NCSS has looked beyond the bounds of this country; has helped to build up an international forum for social work, to exchange ideas, experience, and workers with other countries, to welcome foreign visitors and plan multi-national programmes and seminars. But the 'sixties have seen a great expansion and development of all this work, by no means limited to the international department though strikingly illustrated there.

The theme of the Council's first annual meeting in the decade was social service overseas: an apt theme for a year which saw the establishment of a Department of Technical Co-operation to centralise the provision for overseas countries of technical assistance in the fields of economic development, administration, and social services; the beginnings of the American Peace Corps of young people to work in the underdeveloped countries; and above all an enthusiastic increase here in voluntary work to help new and old nations of the Commonwealth which need assistance. The discussions at this conference served to highlight the urgency of providing this help and guidance now, especially for the many Commonwealth countries reaching independence, and of ensuring its effectiveness by close co-operation between the voluntary bodies involved.

Consequently, early in 1962, a Standing Conference of Voluntary Organisations Co-operating in Overseas Social Service (VOCOSS) was formed—for which the National Council undertook to provide the secretariat—not to initiate or direct projects, which remain the independent responsibility of agencies in membership, but to encourage general planning of effort, exchange of ideas and information about needs overseas among the fifty-three bodies concerned, and to clarify methods of co-operation with overseas authorities and organisations.

Closely associated with this is another undertaking concerned with overseas service, first known as the Lockwood Committee from the name of its original chairman, Sir John Lockwood, and later as the British Volunteer Programme. This was initiated by the government in collaboration with a small group of voluntary organisations concerned, and is again serviced by the NCSS, to co-ordinate schemes for overseas social service of a more specialised group of young volunteers: graduates and others with equivalent training. In 1963, over 250 of these qualified volunteers (in addition to a roughly similar number of school leavers and apprentices in the VOCOSS scheme) were working under the sponsorship of five voluntary organisations in some fifty countries, giving a minimum of one year's service. Three years later the yearly number had risen to about 1,200, going to some seventy countries; and a ceiling of 1,500 was authorised for the 1968 programme. The costs of sending them are partly met by government funds (the proportion having increased from about fifty per cent at first to seventy-five per cent by 1966), partly from funds raised by the voluntary organisations concerned. The majority of these young volunteers teach in secondary schools. Others work in agricultural and health projects, and in community development schemes, co-operating with the people of the country and helping them to discover ways of helping themselves. The demand for them, and the variety of tasks they are asked to tackle, grow each year; and efforts are increasingly being made to find more technically qualified but non-graduate volunteers to fill the many technical jobs.

In 1964 the Council for Volunteers Overseas, under the presidency of the Duke of Edinburgh, was formed to provide a focus for all this overseas voluntary work, with members drawn from leaders in public administration, industry, and the professions, together with a number of returned volunteers; and a secretariat provided by the National Council.

The Council, in servicing these bodies, is therefore the hub of a national movement—new on this scale if not wholly new in character—for the development of social service by young volunteers overseas. To act in this effectively, close contact is kept with the ministries concerned and with a number of national, overseas, and international agencies, as well as with employers and university appointments boards through which many of the volunteers are recruited. General orientation and training courses for them are planned, and schemes discussed for raising the additional funds needed for the rapidly expanding programme. On behalf of the British Volunteer Programme, the secretary has visited South America and the Caribbean area to discuss on the spot with representatives of statutory and voluntary organisations the potential for service by young British volunteers. In 1968 VOCOSS was represented at a conference in Strasbourg when delegates from European industry, co-operatives, trade unions, and voluntary societies met to explore ways of co-operating in overseas aid. VOCOSS early prepared a directory, *Overseas Service and Voluntary Organisations*, which served not only as a source of reference, but to illustrate the diversity of interest and approach of its member organisations; and is compiling a long series of background papers on social services in developing countries, as well as notes on the overseas work of voluntary societies in a number of European countries.

In the meantime the long-established international work of the National Council was continuing and developing, on the many different but convergent lines already mapped out, its rôle in the world scene—symbolised by the appointment of the director, Sir George Haynes, to represent the United Kingdom at the Social Commission of the United Nations.

In 1961 the British National Conference on Social Work changed its title to the British National Conference on Social Welfare in order to represent more adequately the activities of many of its ninety member organisations. Two more national conferences were organised during this decade, on 'Communities and Social Change: Implications for Social Welfare' in 1964, and 'Welfare State and Welfare Society' in 1967. The methods of preparation for them were improved, by such means as seminars in London for leaders of the local study groups in all parts of the country which had been discussing the theme of the conference, so that they could consider special issues raised by the groups and themselves make suggestions for the conference programme. Both conferences roused great interest and attracted some 500 delegates; but the general committee of the British National Conference decided, towards the end of this period, that it was time to revise the organisation of the permanent body and the procedure for the conference. A memorandum recommending a new structure has been prepared and is under consideration.

Already, in its rôle as the British Committee of the International Conference, the BNCSW had prepared proposals for the future organisation and conduct of international conferences, and had been studying a draft of a proposed new constitution which would revise and extend the powers of the international conference. Such a constitution was agreed at the conference in Washington in 1966, and the international body was there converted into an International Council on Social Welfare, with its seat in New York but as an independent body no longer linked with the American National Conference.

Another sector of international work which has come under review in these years is the United Nations European Social Development (formerly Social Welfare) programme. The beginning of the decade saw the completion of the tenth year of its activity, in which the NCSS, through the British Committee for the International Exchange of Social Workers and Administrators, had from the first taken a leading part. The UN headquarters in New York decided to send a team of investigators to the United Kingdom and three other European countries to collect opinions about the value of the scheme with a view to its extension and modification. Since then regular planning conferences have been held in Geneva for representatives of the countries participating in the scheme, with observers from other European countries and from some of the UN specialised agencies. Thus reinforced, 'exchanges', individual visits, group tours, and seminars have flourished. In one year alone the British committee arranged, under this scheme, visits to this country of a group of Polish specialists concerned with the social aspects of housing; Dutch social workers studying problem families; and a group from Yugoslavia interested in family and child welfare. In the same period, British social workers were recruited for study visits to Denmark, Finland, Greece, Israel, Netherlands, Norway, and Poland, and to attend UN seminars and study groups in

Belgium and Italy. A point of interest has been the special study of rural as well as urban development. In 1964 the committee organised a UN seminar in Leicester on the rural work undertaken here, and two years later the Council's chief rural officer and the chairman of the rural committee took part in a similar seminar in Southern Italy which studied the experiments in rural development in that part of Europe. As in earlier years, however, the problems considered at these seminars have at one time or other covered nearly every aspect of modern society. Six regional meetings under this programme have been held in the United Kingdom since 1954, and a seventh on 'Community Care' is being planned for 1969.

The links with the United States also have been strengthened. Attempts have been made to advise British professional social workers interested in employment or study in the USA; and American and Commonwealth social workers wishing to work in the United Kingdom. Memoranda giving practical advice to both these groups have been prepared. The international department has continued to recruit workers for several projects including, for the first time in 1965, the Cleveland (Ohio) international programme for professional and voluntary youth leaders and social workers primarily concerned with young people's problems.

Towards the end of this period the British Committee for the International Exchange of Social Workers and Administrators suffered a sad loss by the death in 1967 of John Ross, who for ten years had been the devoted chairman.

But the international work of the NCSS has never been wholly channelled through one special department, and in the 'sixties every group and department has had a hand in breaching the frontiers between nation and nation; exploring foreign practice and sharing their own experience with that of other peoples.

Each has of course helped the international department to provide information, contacts, and exchange of ideas on its particular interest to the constantly growing number of visitors and students from all over the world.

The Women's Group on Public Welfare, for instance, has taken a special interest in women visitors from the Commonwealth, and has found many ways of helping them to make the best use of their time here. But perhaps the group's most enterprising and important project during these years has been the exchange of visits with women of the Eastern European countries. Beginning in 1960 with an invitation, through the Great Britain-USSR Association and with the collaboration of the National Council of Women, to the Soviet Women's Committee to send a delegation to this country as guests of the women's organisations here, living in the homes of members and seeing something of British social work at first hand, and a return visit to the Soviet Union the following year, this project has been extended year by year, through the enterprise of officers of the Women's Group, to Poland, Hungary, and Czechoslovakia. The visitors have all been women of influence in their own countries—the first Polish guests, for example were a paediatrician, a director of the Institute of Home Economics, the chairman of the trade union concerned with women working in the field of health, and an officer of the Ministry of Agriculture with special responsibility for groups of countrywomen—and there is no doubt that these exchanges are making an important contribution to a better understanding among the leading women of nations with which contacts have hitherto been very limited.

Though the priority necessarily given in this period to the development of the Youth Service in the United Kingdom has meant that the youth department could no longer take full administrative responsibility for some of its international work, several members of the Standing Conference of National Voluntary Youth Organisations maintain an active interest in this, and the department has continued on their behalf to co-operate in exchange schemes between young people and youth leaders with at least one East European country—the Soviet Union—and in several new overseas exchange projects.

The expertise of the National Old People's Welfare Council has been in great demand at international conferences and UN seminars concerned with the care of the elderly, and in devising programmes for visitors and students coming to learn about the work here; and a feature of the overseas contacts lately has been the organisation of tours for superintendents and matrons of homes in this country, and for secretaries and members of old people's welfare committees, to study similar work in some European countries.

The community association is another institution which continues to attract a great deal of interest and many visitors from abroad; but here again it has been by no means a one-way traffic in ideas and experience. A particularly useful chance of seeing some of the same sort of work in the United States, for instance, was the ten-day 'seminar-on-wheels' organised by the American Federation of Settlements and Neighborhood Centers after the international conference in Washington in 1966.

Nor are these exchanges across the frontiers restricted to welfare or administrative techniques. The Standing Conference for Amateur Music started in 1964 a 'Sing for Pleasure' movement for young singers and conductors, in association with the French choral movement A Coeur Joie. Summer schools and week-end courses have attracted growing numbers of young people, and it is hoped to strengthen connections with other European youth choral movements by holding an international course in Great Britain, in association with the European Federation of Youth Choirs, and sending choirs to take part in festivals abroad.

How far the women's clubs have moved beyond the limits of the old industrial areas which nurtured them or even of the new and expanded towns is shown by the formation recently of an international sub-committee of their national association, to establish informal links with club members who have emigrated to Commonwealth countries, and to try to make contacts with the many women's clubs already in existence all over the world. Another overseas activity during the last two or three years has been the organisation of several ten-day courses in Switzerland for club members, combining a holiday with the study of the Swiss way of life, customs, government, and culture.

Councils of social service and citizens' advice bureaux are able to make a special contribution to social work overseas: no less than the exemplar of their whole concept and practice. In the older Commonwealth countries councils of social service, and in some places citizens' advice bureaux, were no new thing; but during this period their numbers have increased quite rapidly. At the beginning of the decade, for instance, a series of visits to Southern Rhodesia by experienced css and CAB workers, sponsored by the Joseph Rowntree Memorial Trust, helped local leaders to set up a css and a multi-racial CAB service in several cities and townships, since they were convinced that, in spite of the great differences in social conditions and background, these patterns of co-operation between statutory and voluntary effort were applicable in Africa—and so they have proved to be. In 1962 Richard Cottam, one of the National Council's regional officers was seconded for eighteen months to the Uganda Council of Voluntary Social Service as special adviser on its development; and in neighbouring Nairobi a CAB was started which had, however, to close for lack of funds. In Ghana, in spite of a visit of the then secretary of the National CAB Council at the invitation of the government (and again aided by the Rowntree Trust) the shortage of voluntary workers meant that the service had to be initiated by the government there, but with the aim of eventually converting into bureaux on the British pattern the 150 advisory centres which it had established. A bureau was early set up in Cape Town, and later in Johannesburg. Others have followed, all over the world from India to Israel, from Guyana to Australia (where many of them develop on a state basis backed by councils of social service). Interest is particularly keen in North America and, as the result of a study here, directed by Alfred J. Kahn of the Columbia School of Social Work, a number of experimental citizens' advice bureaux are likely to be started in the USA.

There are other opportunities reaching out beyond the familiar frontiers, besides exchange visits between social workers, and conferences and projects overseas. More and more Commonwealth immigrants have been coming here in these years, bringing with them different customs and cultures, trying to find a footing as an integral part of their neighbourhood or, at the least, as a group within the host community. From the days of the early arrivals in the 'fifties, councils of social service had recognised their chance to help here as an obvious extension of their community work. At the beginning of the decade they had already sponsored a dozen or more co-ordinating committees for immigrant welfare in areas where coloured workers had congregated; and representatives of these councils were meeting regularly in London to discuss the problems of family welfare, health, education, employment, and leisure which were being faced not only by the West Indian migrants but even more by the Pakistanis, Indians, and Arabs with their very different cultures, religions, and languages. Close contacts were formed with the representatives of the immigrants' respective governments; discussions held with the Ministry of Education about the difficulties of non-English speaking children; conferences organised in different parts of the country to give social workers, teachers, and voluntary helpers a better insight into the very varied backgrounds of these newcomers.

Meanwhile citizens' advice bureaux were trying out ways to make their services known and easily available to immigrants in the neighbourhood; and many standing conferences of women's organisations were taking a special interest in the situation in their own towns and devising schemes to help. SCNVYO member organisations were ready to welcome the rising generation to mixed clubs and activities, as a good way of bringing them into the community; but were often finding resistance, especially from the parents, and the conference was able to give evidence on this angle to the government committee studying young immigrants and youth work.

All this was pioneer work, helpful in itself and of value to the government when it began to take a more active interest in these immigration problems. With controls on the number and type of Commonwealth immigrants, some indication of a growth of racial prejudice, and a greater awareness among immigrants of many disadvantages in their present position and future prospects, the situation has become much more complicated, and the experience of the voluntary organisations at first-hand all the more important. In October 1967, the National Council was invited by the Home Office to join with six other voluntary organisations (including the National Committee for Commonwealth Immigrants and the Kent Council of Social Service Committee for the Welfare of Migrants) in considering the form and method of establishing a combined welfare and advisory service in connection with the proposed new appeals procedure for immigrants refused entry at sea and airports. The agreed report of the representatives of the seven organisations was submitted to the Home Secretary in July 1968.

But the Council's most striking opportunity to bring some of the resources of our welfare society to the service of those all over the world who are bereft not only of the benefits of modern welfare but of any society at all, came when the National Council undertook to re-assume responsibility for the Standing Conference of British Organisations for Aid to Refugees at the close of the World Refugee Year in 1960. When that campaign was planned, the Standing Conference had stood adjourned; but, the year completed, the leading organisations concerned with refugees expressed the need for a continuing co-operative body. It was decided to merge the old Standing Conference with its limited aims into a larger organisation with a general refugee interest; and the Standing Conference of British Organisations for Aid to Refugees, under the chairmanship of the late Lord Astor, became a most active group of the National Council. Twenty-four national organisations became members and more joined later.

The conference at once set about reviewing what had been accomplished by the appeal year, what was left to be done, and how British organisations could help to fill the remaining gaps. But each succeeding year the gaps increased, as in a troubled world more and more people fled or were driven from their homes. Sub-committees were formed to co-ordinate and develop the work which the voluntary organisations were doing in each area, and have had frequently to be consolidated or extended to meet new situations: for the care and re-settlement of refugees in and from many parts of Africa—Algeria, Sudan, Congo, Mozambique; from Tibet, in India and Nepal; in and from Vietnam and Laos; in Hong Kong and Macao.

Nor have the problems of refugees and 'persecutees' of longer standing been overlooked in the spate of new distress. The German indemnification sub-committee has continued throughout these years its work for victims of Nazi persecution on grounds of nationality and its representations to the German government on the need to revise the laws governing compensation. The UNRWA Liaison Group (later renamed the Middle East Committee) has been active in forwarding programmes of training and education for Palestine refugees, and in pressing for the extension of the mandate of the Commissioner-General and for an increased contribution to the work from HM Government. This Middle East scheme is an example of the determination throughout the voluntary organisations to work for permanent solutions, (though relief measures continue to be essential in some areas): the training of young Palestine refugees in useful trades; permanent resettlement in agriculture and industry of Tibetan refugees in India; sheltered workshops in Germany for refugees resettled after the closing of the camps; and so on.

By providing a focus for discussion and exchange of information for the wide variety of British organisations concerned with refugees; a means of joint consultation with governments and international agencies where appropriate; and a national centre for such enterprises as the 1966 European Campaign for World Refugees, the standing conference is able to strengthen considerably the whole voluntary effort in this field. An important part of the influence and activity of the conference over the first six years of the decade was owed directly to its chairman, Lord Astor, whose sudden death a few months before the European campaign, when he was whole-heartedly engaged on the preparations for British participation, was a very serious loss to the refugee movement. It was indeed fortunate that Lord Lothian was able to take over the chairmanship at this critical time.

There is one vast area, spanning all the frontiers of the welfare state, where every section of the NCSS has been advancing steadily in these years: the area of 'communication' in its broadest sense.

In this sense 'communication' ranges from research, through studies, surveys, and presentation of evidence, to distribution of information, publications, and publicity: all of them different methods of connecting one kind of activity, one discipline, one group of people with another, making them better known to each other and to the world they serve, so that the best use can be made of ideas and resources.

In 1963 the government set up a committee, with Lord Heyworth (President of the NCSS) as chairman, to look into the question of research into the social sciences. In its evidence to this committee the National Council was able to draw attention to the fact that it had sponsored, or engaged in, seven major projects in the past six years, for which it had secured financial aid of more than £60,000; but that, nevertheless, general lack of resources had limited this work. The Council made a reasoned plea for the establishment of a central advisory body on social research; and these views were in keeping with the main recommendation of the committee, at once accepted by the government, that a Social Science Research Council should be set up, 'to provide support for research, to keep under review the supply of trained research workers, to disseminate information, and to give advice on research in the social sciences and its application'.

In the meantime the Women's Group on Public Welfare had published a report* on the education of girls, the result of a two-year study by a committee of experts, undertaken in the light of widespread public concern about the place of women in society today and the kinds of education needed to fit them for it. The Council's enquiry into the subject of residential care, already noted here, was proceeding steadily, to be concluded at the end of 1966. The study of the rôle and preparation of volunteers, still in progress, was launched at that time. These are broad subjects, of basic and continuing relevance to social policy. Two other questions with which the Council has concerned itself during these years reflect changing attitudes and behaviour. The first was one aspect of the prevention of crime and treatment of offenders which has taken a place among the most urgently debated social problems: a brief survey conducted by a group presided over by Lord Pakenham (now Lord Longford) of the position relating to the employment and welfare of ex-prisoners. This is a field where there is now seen to be wide scope for voluntary help, both by individuals befriending ex-prisoners and their families, and by voluntary bodies running hostels, clubs, and so on; and several of the Council's associated groups are interesting themselves in it.

The second current problem which the Council is studying is that of drug dependence: a problem that may be comparatively small in size but is of rapid recent growth, especially among the young, and has serious social repercussions. No formal study of the subject is being made but information has been collected through NCSS channels, conferences held and consultations with government departments. Already by the middle of the decade the Women's Group on Public Welfare and many of its local standing conferences had become much concerned about the danger of drug dependence among young people. A great deal of work was done locally and nationally to forward legislation for the registration and supervision of coffee bars where drugs are often available to the young; and as a result of a delegation to the Home Office on this subject, where it was evident that the main preoccupation was with the situation in London, the

---

* *Education and Training of Girls.* NCSS, 1962. [Out of print.]

standing conferences were asked to carry out a detailed survey in their own localities, covering evidence on drug-taking in schools and among young people generally, on drug-pushing, and on provision for counselling and treatment. The report on the large volume of evidence received was sent to all the ministries concerned and aroused much interest. Several councils of social service have been co-operating in educational and experimental rehabilitation schemes; and member organisations of SCNVYO are active in briefing youth leaders on ways of helping with the problem.

In addition to such studies and surveys, there are more and more frequent opportunities to submit evidence—based on the general experience of the Council or, in appropriate instances, on that of individual departments or associated groups—on a wide variety of subjects to government committees or similar bodies. In the last two or three years, to take a few examples, these have ranged from the Fulton Committee on the Civil Service to the National Insurance Advisory Committee reviewing the earnings limit for retirement pensioners; from the Seebohm Committee on the Personal Social Services of Local Authorities to the Archbishops' Commission on Church and State; from the Milsom Committee on the Youth Service and the Adult Community to the Lord Chancellor's Committee on the Age of Majority.

On an increasing number of such problems the National Citizens' Advice Bureaux Council is one of the groups which is specifically invited to give evidence. It is now widely recognised that, though the CAB service is not a research organisation, the main function of the bureau workers—to listen to all comers and give advice or information concerning any question which is put to them—gives to the evidence they can collect some special values. It relates to all kinds of problems and difficulties which ordinary people face; it is spontaneous, not obtained by carefully framed questions; and it includes the experience of the inarticulate person for whom there is no other channel available through which he can make his views known.

To make the best use of all these resources of information, ideas, and methods from all the groups requires, however, not only co-ordination and orderly presentation at the centre but a constant exchange between the centre and the localities and between one area and type of activity and another. The National Council has always recognised this, but it has grown rapidly during the decade. Several departments have their own information service, and publish their own specialised bulletins to give their local groups the latest material relating to their work and to tell them what other groups are doing: the CSS *Matters Arising*, for example; the Women's Group *News Letter*; the NOPWC's *Quarterly Bulletin*; the Women's

Clubs' *Discussion and Action Sheets*, and so on. Field officers of several different departments tour their areas, advising, briefing, arranging courses and conferences.

Beyond all this, there has been increasing recognition, both in the Council itself and in the voluntary movement generally, of the importance of effective public relations: relations not limited to communication between different types of social workers and of social work, or between them and the government or other policy-making bodies, but with society as a whole, so that there may be better appreciation of what is being done in social welfare and a stimulation of new approaches. As the result of a number of requests for guidance on this aspect of their work from other voluntary agencies, the Council's information department set up in 1963 a representative group of people connected with information, public relations, and publishing for voluntary societies to consider common problems. A series of local meetings were organised in co-operation with the Institute of Public Relations, which itself formed a voluntary movement group. Following the success of these meetings, a seminar on 'Communication in Social Welfare' was held in the mid 'sixties, when twenty experienced public relations and information officers from a wide range of voluntary organisations took part in a week of discussions with some leaders in their field on this aspect of social administration; and further local courses have subsequently been organised jointly with regional and county councils of social service.

A great deal of effort has been put into developing the Council's good and friendly relations with the press and radio, as two of the best means of drawing the attention of all kinds of people—from the 'common reader' or listener to the serious student—to the work of the NCSS and its member bodies, and enlarging people's interest and knowledge. There has been close co-operation with a number of producers on sound and television in London and in the regions on feature and current affairs programmes; appeals; and in the developing field of further education, most notably in the 'Social Workers' series on BBC 2, linked with an experimental correspondence course by the National Extension College at Cambridge, in the organisation of which members of several NCSS departments assisted.

More opportunities have been found for mounting exhibitions to illustrate the work of the Council or one of its specialist groups: a display of NCSS publications in the House of Commons library; an exhibition 'In the Service of the Community' at Congress House, generously lent by the Trades Union Congress, when the main feature was a model CAB, as a part of the silver jubilee celebrations of the service; an exhibition of National Council work in the library of the London Borough of Camden.

Together with these developments the information department has continued to work on its customary lines, though these stretch more and more widely year by year. In addition to its basic task of supplying factual information to other departments of the Council and to voluntary organisations generally on developments in social legislation and administration and in voluntary work, and of answering enquiries from individuals and outside bodies of all kinds, there has been a notable increase in the amount of advice or guidance asked for: by senior administrators from overseas, for example, who want to discuss in the light of our experience, their own evolving policies; by donors of charitable funds needing guidance through the maze of good causes they might help; by government agencies or educational institutions enquiring about recent survey work on some social problem; by young people seeking help about a career in social work—though since the establishment of the Social Work Advisory Service it has been possible to pass on some of these last enquiries.

The bi-monthly *Nacoss News*, which attempted to bring into relation with one another the major developments and trends observed in the welter of statutory and voluntary activity, continued until near the end of the decade; and a series of *Occasional Papers* on subjects of special interest was introduced. *Citizens' Advice Notes* have gone on growing, both in comprehensiveness of contents and in number of subscribers which has now reached over 5,000.

Thanks to the growing interest in British social work and in the NCSS contribution to it both at home and abroad; the desire of all the departments and groups to communicate their experience more widely; and the rather better financial position of the Council during the 'sixties, the publications department has been extending its scope with increasing vigour and effect. Around 100 separate orders are placed with printers each year, from publicity leaflets to full-length books. In seven years the number of publications (other than periodicals and leaflets) sold annually rose from some 26,000 to over 45,000. The range of subject and of treatment broadens in concert with this growth—from the UK report to the International Council on Social Welfare on *Social Aspects of Urban Development* to a booklet on *How to Read a Coat of Arms*; from *People in the Countryside: studies in rural social development* to *Social Welfare Directories and How to Prepare Them*; from pamphlets such as *Health Hints for the Over-Sixties* to a substantial survey of adventure playground schemes. Or, to put it in another way—from full reports of national conferences and meetings to pamphlets on specialised departmental interests; from surveys or text-books published on behalf of another voluntary organisation or trust to NCSS reference books and periodicals.

The range of audience also broadens. Something like seventy per cent of all sales are now through ordinary bookshops. Publications receive informed reviews in journals as different as the *Municipal Review* and the *Daily Mirror*, *The Times*, and the *Nursing Times*. A campaign to increase the subscription list of *Social Service Quarterly* has been meeting good success, and in one recent quarter some 140 new subscribers were added. 15,000 copies of *Interviewing in the Social Services* were supplied for the use of one government department; and 6,000 copies have been ordered by other countries. Another government department bought 4,600 copies of *Young People Today* to send overseas. Increasingly training and examining bodies are including NCSS titles in their lists of text-books; while the man-in-the-street finds invaluable hints in the CAB booklets on *Buying a House or Flat* or *Every-Day Insurance*, and the voluntary organisation trying to augment its funds in the pamphlet on *The Law Relating to Lotteries and Gaming*. A carefully considered policy becomes all the more necessary with this growth, and a director's advisory group on publications is now meeting regularly; and as a further encouragement to voluntary organisations to use the services of the department, the group endorsed a proposal to make use of a special imprint—The Bedford Square Press of the National Council of Social Service.

A review of policy and structure has indeed been a feature of the work of most departments and associated groups of the NCSS in this decade.

The rural department has the opportunity, and the need, to make a review at least every five years when the Development Commissioners consider their grant-aid policy for the general work of rural community councils during the next quinquennium. At the beginning of the decade the commissioners decided to renew their grants from April 1961, which enabled the work to go forward with the same confidence and vigour as before. In 1966, after consideration of a detailed report from the rural committee on this work, they announced a new policy of increased grant-aid amounting over a period of five years to approximately eighty per cent over the existing figure, in order to encourage expansion and the development of new activities. This is welcome evidence of confidence in the community councils and, since the requirement remains that there should also be increasing local money found, it provides a reinforcement from the centre for the tripartite partnership characteristic of National Council work. The rural department is giving much thought to the criteria on which grants should be provided so that the best use may be made of them to strengthen the increasingly wide services needed in the countryside.

One of these services, with which the NCSS has been closely associated for very many years, is now being reorganised. By the middle of the decade the rural department was already giving detailed consideration, in consultation with the Development Commission and the Rural Industries Bureau, to the future shape of the field force for the development of rural industries and to the work of Rural Industries Loan Fund Ltd. Subsequently, the Development Commission, after close examination of the situation, decided that this fund, grown out of a war-time service pioneered by the NCSS for rural craftsmen and now recognised by the commissioners as one of the main instruments of their rural policy, needed to have its capital resources expanded and its administration strengthened to deal with growing responsibilities; and that the other two parts of the rural industries service—the Rural Industries Bureau and the field force—ought to be brought together with it under a single executive authority so that they might form a more cohesive force for the development of rural industries all over the country. The expansion of Rural Industries Loan Fund, still vital in this new development as providing the financial inducement for rural economic growth, meant that the accommodation and other facilities which the NCSS had provided since the inception twenty-six years ago would no longer be adequate. In 1966 it was therefore rehoused in its own premises with an independent administration; and Nora Newton retired from the post of chief administrator which she had held from the beginning, taking with her gratitude and admiration from all who had seen the devoted skill with which she built up this outstanding enterprise—not least from the craftsmen in all parts of the country whom the fund had helped through her in a way at once competent and sympathetic.

Meetings to consider the integration of the three branches of the rural industries service in a new Council for Small Industries in Rural Areas went on throughout the later years of the decade; and the re-organisation, involving the integration of the field force which very closely concerns the rural community councils, is expected to be completed in this jubilee year. The National Council's long connection with the work is maintained at the centre by the new director's participation as vice chairman of the COSIRA, and the chief rural officer's membership of the Loans Committees of the Credit Services Division (previously Rural Industries Loan Fund Ltd., of which the former director had so long been chairman).

During most of this period the NCSS Rural Committee had the devoted leadership as chairman of John Cripps, chairman of the Rural District Councils Association, who succeeded Sir John (later Lord) Fulton, then

273

principal of the University College of Sussex, in 1962.

A working party to undertake an objective review of the aims and work of the Standing Conference of Drama Associations was set up early in this period, and recommended that there was much work it could usefully do but that its membership should be widened and its administrative resources strengthened. As a result, representatives of university drama departments, extra-mural departments, training colleges with lecturers in drama, and local education authorities were invited to become members. The financial support of the Carnegie UK Trust, which has helped to make the work of the standing conference possible since its foundation in 1946, is continuing for the quinquennium 1966–70, both for experimental work and for the work of affiliated county committees. As one result of this support, a policy has been agreed to organise regional conferences and to set up a group of 'stimulators'—experts in their particular fields of drama—to examine the needs of the amateur theatre movement and to suggest projects which the conference might sponsor and services which it might provide. The first enterprise of the panel of experts was an examination of the needs of the amateur theatre movement throughout England and Wales. Their conclusion is that the present pattern of dramatic activity is fragmentary and that those able to provide opportunities for drama for school children, young people, and adults are working in isolation from each other. Here is obviously a field where the conference can help towards a more integrated plan of action. At the same time the conference has been thinking about the future position of county drama committees in view of the possible development of arts associations at regional, county and local level, where the emphasis is on the arts as a whole rather than on the promotion of each separately. A report has been issued, giving details about existing arts centres in England and Wales, which has been in great demand from government departments, libraries, and museums, local education authorities, architectural students, organisers of county youth services, and others. Meanwhile, new activities have not been neglected. A successful experiment was a course on décor under a lighting expert; and attention is being directed for the future to other special functions which are outside the responsibility of other drama bodies.

The Standing Conference for Amateur Music has also spent some time on reviewing its policy in order to establish a list of priorities and an orderly programme for submission to the Carnegie UK Trust when the Trustees consider their support for the conference at the beginning of each quinquennium. So far as structure is concerned, the conference has evolved a method of working largely through specialist committees whose expert members deal with the many different aspects of the vast subject.

The programme has indeed been remarkably large and varied during this decade, ranging from the compilation of a list of recommended contemporary orchestral music for adult amateurs to a pamphlet for local education authorities on a policy for the purchase and maintenance of pianos; from courses for youth leaders and senior members of youth clubs to specialist reports on such subjects as 'Music Centres and the Training of Specially Talented Children' and 'Music and the Newsom Report'. But perhaps the most outstanding projects are the 'Sing for Pleasure' movement already described; and the development during the last ten years of work based on the belief that music has a special contribution to make to the education and the life of the handicapped. After consultations with experts on the best form of training for teachers in this field, the Conference organised a series of exploratory courses for teachers of educationally subnormal and of physically handicapped children. As a result of the experience thus gained, the Conference has now planned with Dartington College of Arts a three-year research and development project, to be financed by a grant from the Carnegie UK Trust. It is hoped that this scheme will lead towards the goal of making Dartington College a permanent centre for the training of teachers of music for the handicapped; but as the Standing

Music for the handicapped

Conference will administer the grant, they will have a continuing responsibility for some years for the work which they have pioneered.

Efforts to involve local history committees more closely in the work of the Standing Conference for Local History, and consideration of a possible alteration in the constitution to allow individual local history groups to affiliate, have marked the Conference's determination still further to improve its contacts and the coverage of its services. More and more national bodies are coming to appreciate these, and new members in recent years range from the Society for Folk Life Studies to the Wesley History Society; the Monumental Brass Society to the Catholic Record Society.

Convinced that one of the most effective ways in which it can encourage the study of local history is through publications for the guidance of amateur historians, the Conference early in the decade reviewed its policy in this field and speeded up the revision of earlier booklets and the preparation of new titles. Pamphlets published in the space of one year included *A Directory of Authorities and Organisations*; *Crafts, Trades and Industries*; *A Book List for Local Historians*; *The Historian's Guide to Ordnance Survey Maps*; and *Some Types of Common Field Parish*. The conference also assumed responsibility for the publication of the quarterly journal *The Amateur Historian* (a title later changed to *The Local Historian*) whose circulation thereafter rose in two years from 300 to 1,500.

The Standing Conference of Councils of Social Service has always had to keep its policy and work under constant review, not only to find ways of working out adequate coverage of the country and a proper relation between urban and rural needs but also to activate the continual struggle to raise more money for the councils' basic consultative and planning services, which have so little immediate appeal. The 'sixties were no exception. In the first year the Standing Conference devoted a one-day meeting to considering in detail how in fact local councils do raise their funds and discussing further possible methods. In preparation for this an analysis was made of the incomes of twenty-five councils, from which emerged very varied patterns of statutory grant-aid, contributions from voluntary bodies and from trusts, and money raised by special efforts.

The Conference recognised that more public understanding of the character of the work was the best hope for increasing support, and worked hard towards that end—not least the chairman for nearly a decade, Sir John Wrigley, who devoted his wisdom and wide experience untiringly to the Conference throughout most of this period. The success of these efforts can be gauged from the fact that the number of new councils of social service grew progressively each year, and in many different types of place. In 1967, for instance, fourteen new councils were formed: two in county boroughs, three in new London boroughs, four in non-county boroughs, two in urban districts, one in a rural district, and two in new towns. A county committee in Cheshire, administered by the Cheshire Community Council and formed at the request of local councils of social service, indicates the growing awareness of the need for closer ties between urban and rural groups; as also in Staffordshire where, following the reorganisation of local government in the West Midlands, the main work of the South Staffordshire css has been taken over by councils of social service formed in four county boroughs in the area, and the Staffordshire RCC has become the Community Council of Staffordshire so that it may undertake the remainder of the urban work within its predominantly rural context.

The silver jubilee of the citizens' advice bureaux in 1964, and a number of developments since that date, marking definitively their acceptance as an integral part of the social services by both the public and the government, have led the National Citizens' Advice Bureaux Council to make a fundamental review of policies, functions, and structure during the latter half of the decade. Though the principles which the founders had written into the movement from the start, first set out in a pamphlet* published soon after the war giving the guide lines for a service of information and advice midway between the officials and the professionals on the one hand and the man in the street on the other, remain basically unchanged, the growth in quality and quantity of the bureaux, their relationship with local authorities increasingly interested in information services, and the intricate nature, in new social situations, of this service by 'extraordinary ordinary people' (as a Minister once described CAB workers), seemed to call for a survey both of the standards of organisation and work, and of the structure.

As a first step a registration committee was set up, to review for the sixth time since the inception of the service the conditions of registration of bureaux—conditions devised to demonstrate the mutual obligations between the individual bureaux and the National CAB Council, and their joint responsibility in maintaining a reasonable standard of service to the public, related to the increased demands made upon it. A year later a constitution committee began to review once again, as in 1955 and 1962, the structure of the movement, in order to improve means of communication with, and participation by, bureaux in the affairs of the service.

---

* *The Citizens' Advice Bureaux Service—Aims and Methods*. Reprinted 1967. NCSS.

Meanwhile the service was expanding rapidly. Partly as a result of the consumer advice work which the government had asked bureaux to undertake, supported by a grant from the Board of Trade first made in 1963–64, requests for new bureaux, mainly from local authorities, flowed in. The enlarged team of regional advisory officers was at first too busy responding to these to have much chance of relating the development to any scheme of priorities. A new plan, however, soon began to be worked out, in consultations between headquarters, the advisory officers, regional committees and county organisations, with a view to bringing the service within reach of as large a proportion of the population of England and Wales as possible. It is influenced by such considerations as population, communications, the existence of other bureaux in the area, possible changes in local authory boundaries, and the likely development of new or expanded towns; and it is kept flexible so that it can be amended with changing local circumstances. The rate of progress has varied, depending on local conditions and interest; but by 1968 the number of bureaux in the United Kingdom had risen to 489. This included an extension of the service in Northern Ireland, and accelerated development in Scotland and Wales as well as in England.

For six years, since the mid 'fifties, the CAB Council had benefited from the skilful guidance and close personal interest of Leslie Farrer-Brown as its chairman; and it was a loss to CAB work, though a gain to the NCSS as a whole, when he resigned in 1961 shortly after becoming chairman of the National Council. No one, however, could have been better fitted to succeed him at this time as CAB chairman than Sir Harold Banwell, formerly secretary of the Association of Municipal Corporations, with his great experience of the services of local government and his understanding of the human problems in society with which bureaux are more and more deeply concerned. He was the third chairman to have at his right hand as secretary of the National CAB Council Kathleen Oswald who, succeeding the 'founder secretary' Dorothy Keeling when she retired at the end of the war, had been chiefly responsible by her dedicated skill and vision for establishing the movement as an integral part of the social services of the country. Her death in the silver jubilee year of the bureaux was a bitter blow. It was fortunate that her deputy, Joan Pridham, who had worked with her for several years, was able to carry on the work.

For the Women's Group on Public Welfare the decade started with a campaign by national organisations in membership to bring to the notice of their local branches and clubs the value of working together in the partnership of a local standing conference of women's organisations. As a result, twenty-nine enquiries about methods of forming them came to

Leslie Farrer-Brown

headquarters in the space of two months; and within five years the
number of these conferences had risen to 111. Here again a 'coming of age'
year—the women's group attained its majority in 1960—gave a special
opportunity to discuss the effectiveness of co-operation at both local and
national level; and the subject chosen for the 1962 biennial joint conference
with the standing conferences was a 'Re-Statement of Principles'. Following this, presidents and chairmen of the member organisations were invited
to meet and to consider how, within the framework of the report produced, they could achieve the widest possible co-operation, and exactly
what the rôle of the group should be in the future.

An index of resolutions passed by member organisations, which the public questions sub-committee prepared, showed how wide were their interests and how sensitive to the needs of the day: food hygiene, day nurseries, danger from pesticides, maintenance allowances, women prisoners, *au pair* girls, the young chronic sick, home safety, drug dependence, women and work, refuse collection . . . the list is as long and as varied as the number of problems where, it is recognised, this joint concern and action of women working together can influence policy at both national and local level. Each issue of the quarterly *Newsletter* of the standing conferences is now concentrated on one theme so as to give the conferences a broad view of the implications of some important question and a lead for their own work on it. The spring number in Human Rights Year, for example, took 'Human Rights and Responsibilities' as its subject, relating to it adolescent training in personal relationships, gypsies' problems, world hunger, preservation of the countryside, drug-taking, women's use of the vote and, above all, the right to a home—the aspect of Human Rights Year with which the women's group has concerned itself most actively.

' Ever since 1948 when Margaret Bondfield retired the women's group had had the good fortune to retain the wise leadership of Dame May Curwen as its chairman; and it was with deep regret that the announcement of her retirement was received in the first year of the decade. Lady Brunner was welcomed as her successor, and has been the inspiration of many of the achievements of these years, supported by the long experience of the secretary, Dorothy Homer, until her retirement in 1964 after seventeen years of outstanding service to the group.

The National Old People's Welfare Council was another of the NCSS groups whose silver jubilee in the middle of this decade gave occasion to review policy and work. The conclusion was set out in the annual report for that year in this way: the council's purpose is still the same as in 1940, 'to study the needs of old people and to encourage and promote measures for their well-being', and 'there must still be great concern for those older people—fortunately a minority—who have special material needs, whether for cash, housing, hospital or home services, and for whom much still remains to be done. But today more time can be given to the wider aim of work for the majority, and the council is above all concerned to encourage provision of a better quality of life for all the elderly'.

So the council's work of encouraging the formation of local old people's welfare committees, and their schemes for visiting, clubs, domiciliary help, laundry services, and the like; of helping to promote housing projects; of training organisers, voluntary workers, matrons of homes—this has continued and developed. But through it all has run a wider interpretation of 'needs' and a shift of emphasis to 'well-being'.

One of the most striking examples of this trend is the work on preparation for retirement. It was in the mid 'fifties that the NOPWC became acutely aware that much of the distress and loneliness of old age came less from infirmity, isolation, or poverty than from lack of forethought in preparing for a future, after working days are over, which should be a time of opportunity rather than frustration. A study group recommended that some definite action should be taken in co-operation with industry and commerce, the educational services, religious bodies, and voluntary and statutory agencies; and in 1961 the council set up a Preparation for Retirement Committee and, with the help of a grant from the National Corporation for the Care of Old People, a full-time officer was appointed for three years to develop the project. A series of booklets was published on various aspects of preparation for this period of life, from *Living Arrangements and £.s.d.* to *The Years Still Unexplored*, on the philosophy of ageing. Courses in this new kind of adult education were run by voluntary groups, trade associations, industrial firms; and special committees were set up in several cities and towns. By the end of the experimental period it was decided that the work should be taken out of the context of old people's welfare and function as an independent body, associated for a time with the NCSS; and in 1964 the Pre-Retirement Association was established.

The NOPWC, however, having launched this campaign to persuade the middle-aged to prepare themselves for the long leisure ahead when they retired, went on developing the facilities they would want and which their seniors needed now. They invited representatives of interested voluntary organisations, together with an observer from the Ministry of Health, to meetings to consider leisure activities in general and the social facilities provided in clubs; and followed this with a conference attended by a large number of people from adult education organisations, voluntary bodies, and some local committees. Special enquiries are being made into both club facilities and the leisure activities of non-club members, and a series of leisure leaflets prepared.

This concern with the quality of life in the later years, no less than in youth and middle age, is a field where all the different interests of the NCSS can come together, more especially the councils of social service which, through their contacts with their local education authorities and with local employers, can do a good deal to stimulate interest in pre-retirement preparation; and the Central Churches Group and the individual churches and religious groups which have much to offer on the spiritual aspect of these re-adjustments.

Alderman Fred Messer resigned the chairmanship of the NOPWC in 1951, having succeeded Eleanor Rathbone, the first chairman, in 1946. His place was taken by John Moss, who had a special interest and experience in the welfare of elderly people, largely gained during his years as chief officer of the Kent County Council concerned with public assistance (as it was then called). He continued to lead the work of the Council with tireless devotion for sixteen years, until his retirement in 1967, when he was succeeded by Mrs D. Newman who had long been closely associated with the Council.

The substantial and continuing growth of leisure-time was increasing the demand from all kinds of people for more opportunities in recreation and informal education, so that they could pursue interests which gave them personal pleasure whilst at the same time contributing to the well-being of their neighbourhood. This was a challenge to the National Federation of Community Associations which set out to meet just these needs; and at the beginning of the decade the federation decided that it was time to make a new assessment of its impact throughout the country, and a detailed study of its own administrative machinery in the belief that a close analysis might result in a fresh view of policies and their effectiveness.

Following an annual conference devoted to considering internal and administrative matters during 'The Next Seven Years', a plan for the thorough revision of the federation's constitution and terms of reference was made, and a development sub-committee set up as a focus for forward thinking. The first task of this committee was the preparation of *Creative Living* (NCSS, 1964), a publication setting out the views of the federation on matters of concern to local associations in addition to stating the broad policy which should guide developments in the movement. In preparation for this policy document a number of basic questions about relationships had been considered: the role of community associations in the field of education; the place of the paid officer; the Ministry of Education 1946 report on community centres; and answers to a questionnaire to members of the federation had been collated. The trends thus shown—that most associations have a larger individual membership than was previously thought; that the catchment area served was generally more extensive than had originally been planned for a single association; that about one in four centres had a warden, and so on—raised points of both principle and practice which gave the federation useful pointers to future policy.

It was soon recognised that the key point in the development programme was the work of the area committees. These were given a new structure and operational basis so that they could play a fuller part in the movement; and their first meeting under the revised constitution in the spring of 1964 proved how helpful consultation between the community associations themselves could be in establishing a general pattern of activities. No less important was the need for local associations to re-examine their position and impact on the life of their neighbourhoods.

By the date of the federation's twenty-first birthday in 1966 the long process of reorganisation was well advanced. It was clear that the new structure would provide a two-fold benefit in simplifying the day-to-day work of the department while allowing a more constructive contribution to social policy to be made by the federation as a whole. The work already described on such matters as recruitment and training of voluntary and professional workers, planning, or the social aspects of new housing, prove that this is so. The membership of the federation increased during the decade from about 400 to well over 500.

Owing to a variety of circumstances the national federation had four different chairmen in the 'sixties. They were specially fortunate in having for half the decade the leadership of F. J. Symonds who, with his long experience of several sides of NCSS work and his understanding of the aims of the national federation, had just the qualities needed to guide the re-appraisal and replanning which he set in train. Throughout this whole period continuity in the work was well maintained by Frank Milligan's successor as secretary, K. M. Reinold, who came to the federation after five years as community development officer in the new town of Bracknell.

The National Association of Women's Clubs has made no formal review of its organisation and policy during these years, but the very pressure of demand for its help in forming clubs or taking existing groups under its wing has led to some new developments. For instance, in areas where there is no organiser, either paid or voluntary, several more honorary promotional officers have undertaken to do this work; and there has been a considerable increase in the number of area associations of clubs which, by pooling experience and resources, can do a great deal to help with training of leaders and advising on committee work and activities. Over the whole country new clubs have been started at an increasing rate, so that there are now not far short of 900 with something like 40,000 members, ranging from the ordinary groups, often of young housewives, to a club in a hospital for short-stay patients.

The resignation in 1965 of the Central Churches Group's chairman, the Bishop of Colchester, who had been its leader for nearly twenty-four years, was a severe loss. Nonetheless, it served to stimulate the thorough appraisal of the group's rôle in the changing pattern of interdenominational co-operation which had already been recognised as necessary with the increasing interest of clergy and ministers in the problems of the welfare state and the steady development of ecumenical relationships. Early in the decade steps had been taken to strengthen the staff of the group; and through the British Council of Churches wider representation was secured so that its members should include nominees of the Baptist, Congregational, and Methodist churches, the Society of Friends, and the Salvation Army, in addition to the Anglican and Roman Catholic churches and the Jewish community. Later the membership was further extended by representation from several departments of the National Council and by individual co-opted members with special skills and experience. During the interim period between the Bishop of Colchester's resignation and the appointment of the Reverend Lord Sandford as chairman, the group met under the chairmanship of the National Council's director—appropriately, since its work is clearly rooted within the structure of the NCSS itself—and was helped to define anew and positively its functions in modern society.

The question of organisation to which the Standing Conference of National Voluntary Youth Organisations has needed to give special attention during at least the earlier part of this period is the perennial problem of how to strengthen existing local standing conferences and to encourage the formation of new ones. The Ministry of Education's decision that from 1963–64 onwards application for grant-aid for local capital projects must be submitted in a single joint programme made local co-operation even more necessary. A travelling officer was appointed for a limited period to visit existing standing conferences and to promote others; SCNVYO correspondents were tried in some counties or county boroughs; and a booklet was prepared outlining practical work which might be undertaken locally, with advice about the most effective methods of administration.

But the existing structure and policy of the national Standing Conference has proved sound and flexible enough to cope with the radical changes in outlook and methods which the youth service has undergone in recent years. The old limitations are disappearing, and work with youth aims to link up with every other kind of social and educational work, and to share resources and facilities. It was, for example, mainly as a result of discussions at one of SCNVYO's biennial conferences that the Department of Education and Science decided to set up a working party to consider relationships between the youth service and the schools and further education, and another to study how closer understanding and greater co-operation can be achieved between the youth service and the adult community as a whole, for both of which the standing conference was asked to collect evidence.

In this work the conference has been fortunate in having as its chairman Professor Norman Haycocks who, succeeding Dame May Curwen in the early 'fifties, has continued to give invaluable leadership throughout all these years.

The ever broadening spread of work described in this chapter makes ever increasing demands on the financial resources of the National Council, exemplified by the growth of total expenditure from nearly £150,000 annually at the end of the 'fifties to over £340,000 in this jubilee year.

Fortunately, the increase in support from the public, the statutory authorities, voluntary agencies, trusts, and industry has been steadily maintained throughout the decade; and thanks to the care and skill of members of the Finance and General Purposes Committee, led by Lord Heyworth, and the honorary treasurer, C. M. Vignoles and later R. J. Kirton, these resources have been deployed to the best advantage. In so doing the committee have shown intimate understanding of the requirements and responsibilities of the various services and groups, a continuing regard for reasonable conditions of service and remuneration for the staff, and a keen eye for the commitments that lie ahead, which have won them the appreciation of the NCSS, and of all those agencies who collaborate in its work and value their partnership with it. In all this they had for seven years the outstanding service of Major-General C. B. Fairbanks as administrative secretary, and latterly of Colonel R. J. Chaundler who, after two years as appeals secretary, succeeded him on his retirement in 1965.

By the end of this period money from voluntary sources and funds raised by associated groups still exceeded the total of government grants, though these have been increased considerably in recent years. As has been earlier shown, the Development Fund continues to be a source of generous support for the rural work, and later the Board of Trade for CAB development, with a smaller grant from the Ministry of Overseas Development for the British Volunteer Programme. The grants previously provided separately by the Ministries of Education, of Health, and of Housing and Local Government have been consolidated since 1962, for triennial periods, into a single grant for the general purposes of the Council, channelled through the latter Ministry. This procedure has in no way weakened the close relationship and sympathetic co-operation which the NCSS has long had with the Ministries of Education and Health (now the Department of Education and Science and the Department of Health and Social Security) for particular services; and it has facilitated the Council's financial arrangements and assured it of increased government support.

On the voluntary side, contributions from commerce and industry now comprise a substantial part of the annual income; and these contributions include not only welcome additions to the funds but an active interest by many leaders of business life in the work of the Council.

The generosity of some of the large charitable trusts, notably the Carnegie UK Trust, the Nuffield Foundation, and the King George's Jubilee Trust, had for many years, as previous references have demonstrated, enriched the Council's services; and during this decade more recently formed trusts have given discriminating and most welcome aid for special projects—for instance the Joseph Rowntree Memorial Trust to finance a continuing programme of work overseas to develop citizens' advice bureaux, and councils of social service, and enquiries such as the current one on the role of volunteers; the Calouste Gulbenkian Foundation for such schemes as experimental courses in community organisation, and the study of residential staffing needs.

Financial support from numbers of voluntary bodies and groups in the community, some with very limited resources and able to make only small contributions, constitute a significant part of the total income, and are particularly valuable as providing tangible recognition of what the partnership with the National Council means to them.

The Charities Aid Fund, under its new name and with some reorganisation, has made remarkable progress during these years. Its services have come to be increasingly appreciated by donors ranging from large companies with considerable funds earmarked for charity to small charitable organisations with insufficient staff themselves to operate deeds of covenant, and to a host of individuals who value the flexibility and efficiency of the scheme. Since 1924 the total amount paid to charity through the Fund, is in excess of £23,000,000, and now annually amounts to over £2,000,000. This progress owes much to the leadership of A. G. B. Burney who had succeeded to the office of chairman, which George Mitchell had ably filled in the earlier years of the Fund; and not a little to the energy and acumen of its secretary, J. D. Livingston Booth.

Despite the increase in all sources of income, however, the continued tendency towards higher costs, the need to keep staff salaries under constant review and, above all, the importance of being in a position to seize the opportunities for new work which the future will present, make it essential to look for new ways of adding to the Council's resources. In this jubilee year a special appeal, aimed largely at industry, has been launched with the unfailing help and guidance of Lord Heyworth, the president of the Council.

The need to find new ways of adding to the Council's resources is

Lord Heyworth

important. Even more important is the need to judge how these resources should be deployed in a society whose rapid changes are bound to influence the position of the whole voluntary movement in the near future. At the Sixth British National Conference on Social Welfare in 1967 one of the most controversial topics raised was the role of voluntary organisations in today's welfare society, and especially the question of co-operation and co-ordination between them and with public agencies. While believing in the virtues of 'voluntaryism' and individualism, the National Council has always sought—with what success may be in some degree gauged from this record—a partnership between voluntary organisations and public authorities, and a balanced appreciation of the place which each can best take in the social pattern.

J. K. Owens

But relationships alter with the times and patterns form and re-form; and the NCSS decided towards the end of its first five decades that the moment had come to reconsider its future policy and priorities. The executive committee therefore appointed a working party of the Council's honorary officers, with powers of co-option, to review in the light of social, economic, and administrative changes in the local, national, and international scene the work undertaken by the National Council over the past ten years; to consider whether and in what direction present policy and priorities require modification and what new activities should be undertaken; to consider the Council's relationship with the voluntary movement, with statutory authorities and with social organisations in the international field; to examine the over-all structure of the Council and to recommend any necessary modifications.

This was a timely decision, not only because it came at a period when new ideas about modern society were abroad, but also because the year 1967 marked the culmination of an historic era for the Council, when George Haynes retired after more than a quarter of a century of service as its director. What the Council has become and what, in the process, it has accomplished in the stimulation and harnessing of the will to voluntary social service and its harmonious working with statutory service, are in large measure his creation.

But he himself is the first to recognise that, in the words of his last address to the British National Conference on Social Welfare, 'the future is open'. It lies open here to his successor, J. K. Owens, with his different but allied experience, latterly as a highly regarded acting director of education long concerned with the interaction of statutory and voluntary enterprise in the field of education in its broadest sense.

'There *is* tremendous change,' as George Haynes said in another farewell speech. 'The content of much that we do is changed. . . . But what impresses me as I scan the years is the continuity of effort.' Above all stands 'the great value of association and of our continued search for unity in the diversity of social life and action.'

The character of that diversity may change with changing times; but that search for unity has been the lodestar of the National Council from the beginning. Beyond the moving frontiers, the open future, it will still point the way.

The Council and Carnegie rooms (*top*)
Meeting of the executive committee (*bottom*)

Patrons
His Royal Highness the Prince of Wales, later
His Majesty King Edward VIII
His Majesty King George VI
Her Majesty Queen Elizabeth II*

Presidents
The Rt Hon James W. Lowther, PC, MP
The Rt Hon J. H. Whitley, PC, MP
Captain the Rt Hon E. A. Fitzroy, PC, MP
The Rt Hon the Viscount Bledisloe, PC, GCMG, KBE
The Rt Hon the Lord Snell, PC, CBE
Sir P. Malcolm Stewart, Bart., DL
The Rt Hon the Earl of Halifax, PC, KG, OM, GCSI, GCIE
Sir Edward Peacock, GCVO
The Rt Hon the Lord Heyworth.*

Vice-Presidents
The Rt Hon J. H. Whitley, PC, MP
Lord Lindsay of Birker
R. C. Norman
The Rt Hon Margaret Bondfield, CH
Sir Wyndham Deedes, CMG, DSO
Dr W. G. S. Adams, CH
Sir John Hanbury-Williams
The Rt Hon the Lord Murray of Newhaven, KCB*
Sir Christopher Chancellor, CMG*
Sir John Wolfenden, CBE*
Sir David Hughes Parry, QC*

* *Present office holders*

Chairmen
A. V. Simmons, CB (later Sir Aubrey Simmons)
Dr W. G. S. Adams, CH
Dr Keith A. H. Murray (later Lord Murray of Newhaven, KCB)
J. F. Wolfenden, CBE (later Sir John Wolfenden)
L. Farrer-Brown, CBE*

Vice-Chairmen
Dr W. G. S. Adams, CH
Sir Percy Alden
F. G. D'Aeth
Sir Henry Rew, KCB
R. C. Norman
Sir Wyndham Deedes, CMG, DSO
The Rt Hon Margaret Bondfield, PC
Dr Keith A. H. Murray (later Lord Murray of Newhaven, KCB)
A. W. Oyler, OBE
Dame May Curwen*
L. Farrer-Brown, CBE

Honorary Treasurers
Sir Charles Stewart, KBE
Lt Col G. R. Crosfield, CBE, DSO, TD
R. A. Lewis, DCM
J. Gilmour Wylie
Roger Chetwode
David Bell
E. Holland-Martin
D. H. W. Hall, OBE
Sir Christopher Chancellor, CMG
C. M. Vignoles, CBE
R. J. Kirton, CBE*

Index

Abercrombie, Professor Patrick, 52
Adams, Professor W. G. S., 17, 20, 32,
  33, 86, 120, 174
Agriculture and Fisheries Act (1919),
  35
Albemarle Committee, 210
Albemarle Report, 236, 238, 246
Alden, Petcy (Sir), 27, 28, 121
American Federation of Settlements
  and Neighborhood Centers, 263
Anderson, Sir John, 100
Anglo-Egyptian Resettlement Board,
  193
Archbishop Bourne, 11
Archbishop of Canterbury, 11
Archbishops' Commission on Church
  and State, 269
Army Education Corps, 114
Association for Improvement of
  Maternity Services, 258
Association of Child Care Officers,
  224
Association of Municipal Corpora-
  tions, 39
Astor, Lord, 266, 267
Attlee, Clement, 30
Aves, Geraldine, 241

Bank of England, 122
Banwell, Sir Harold, 278
Barker, Professor Sir Ernest, 63, 87,
  121
Barlow Report, 122
Barnardo, Dr, 4

Barnes, Mrs, 20
Barnett, Canon, 6, 33
Bell, Rev. G. K., 33
Bessey Report, 246
Beveridge Committee on Social
  Insurance, 106
Beveridge Report, 134
Beveridge, Lord, 169, 176
Birchall, Edward Vivien, 6, 13, 17, 18,
  36
Birkett, Miss F. M., 165
Birmingham Citizens' Committee,
  15, 29
Birmingham Citizens' Society, 100,
  188
Birmingham City Aid Society, 6, 15,
  119
Birmingham Civic Aid Society, 6
Birmingham Institute of Education,
  245
Bishop of Colchester, 208, 283, 284
Bishop of Derby, 209
Bishop of Ripon, 5
Bishop of Stepney, 9
Board of Education, 20, 29, 35, 40, 84,
  87
Board of Inland Revenue, 178, 234
Board of Trade, 191, 248, 278, 285
Bondfield, Margaret, 98, 117, 121,
  228, 280
Bostock, Sam, 32, 51
Boughton, Rutland, 15
Bourne, Mrs Marjorie, 122
Boy Scouts, 41

293

Representation of the People Act (1947), 136

Rew, Sir Henry, 30, 32

Rice-Jones, Nancy, 217

Richmond, Arthur, 43, 86, 109

Ross, John, 213, 262

Rowntree, Seebohm, 15

Royal Alfred Seamen's Society, 224

Royal Commission on Marriage and Divorce, 192

Royal Commission on Taxation of Profits and Incomes, 177

Royal Institute of British Architects, 51

Royal Society of Arts, 256

Rural community councils, 34–5, 39, 43–6, 48–50, 52, 65–8, 83, 86, 88, 90, 91, 108, 110, 124, 131, 132, 135–6, 138–42, 182, 183, 185–6, 187, 192, 219, 232, 255–7, 272–3
  Bedfordshire, 182
  Cambridgeshire, 43, 48, 49
  Cumberland, 182
  Derbyshire, 43, 209
  Dorset, 52, 65
  Forfarshire, 43
  Gloucestershire, 43, 44, 46
  Hampshire, 65, 182
  Herefordshire, 43, 52
  Hertfordshire, 43, 52, 65
  Kent, 43, 44, 45, 46, 82, 87, 132
  Leicestershire, 43
  Lindsey (Lincs.), 43, 52, 82
  Monmouthshire, 43
  Northumberland, 182, 183
  Nottinghamshire, 43, 44
  Oxfordshire, 33, 34, 43, 44, 49, 96, 141
  Shropshire, 52
  Somerset, 43, 46, 52
  Staffordshire, 182, 277
  Surrey, 182
  West Sussex, 43, 48, 65

Rural Industries (Intelligence) Bureau, 35, 46, 48, 72, 110, 183, 273

Rural Industries Loan Fund, 110, 140, 183, 273

Rural life conferences, 65, 255

Rural work, 45, 48–9, 52, 65, 67, 108, 127, 139, 173, 185–6, 255–6, 262, 273, 285

Rushcliffe, Lord, 93

Rushcliffe Committee, 191

Sack, Leonard Shoeten, 43, 86, 95, 121

Saint, A. B., 6, 16

Salvation Army, 12, 146

Samson, Miss E. D., 107

Samuel, Rt Hon. Herbert (Lord), 11, 170, 171

Sand, Dr René, 161–2

Sandford, Rev. Lord, 284

Schooling, N., 20

Schuller, Erwin, 118

Scott Committee, 112, 128

Scott, Lord Justice, 136

Scottish Home Department, 137

Seebohm Committee, 269

Sembal Trust, 245

Shaftesbury, Lord, 4

Shuttleworth, Ray, 4

Simey, Professor T. S. (Lord), 168, 237

Simmons, Sir Aubrey Vere, 17, 19, 20

Sir Halley Stewart Trust, 121, 173, 202

Small, J. G., 20

Smeal, John, 185–6

Smith, Owen, 227

Snelson, H. S. E., 186

Social Science Research Council, 268

Social Service Bulletin, 55, 128

Social Service Quarterly, 165, 188, 217, 272

Social Service Review, 165

Social Welfare Association (London), 11

Social Work Advisory Service, 240, 241, 271

Social Workers' Pension Fund, 172, 224–5

Illustrations are gratefully acknowledged to the following: Rural Industries Bureau (page 47); *The Times* (page 51); John Gay (page 57); Fox Photos Ltd. (page 77); Radio Times Hulton Picture Library (page 193); James Neill (page 201); Gloucester Newspapers (page 252); John Vickers (page 288); Euan Duff (page 290).